Middle Eastern Women and the Invisible Economy

Middle Eastern Women
and the
Invisible Economy

Edited by Richard A. Lobban, Jr.

Foreword by Elizabeth W. Fernea

University Press of Florida

Gainesville Tallahassee Tampa Boca Raton
Pensacola Orlando Miami Jacksonville

Copyright 1998 by the Board of Regents of the State of Florida
Printed in the United States of America on acid-free paper
All rights reserved

03 02 01 00 99 98 6 5 4 3 2 1

Library of Congress Cataloging-in-Publication Data

Middle Eastern women and the invisible economy / edited by Richard A.
Lobban with a foreword by Elizabeth W. Fernea.
p. cm.
Includes bibliographical references and index.
ISBN 0-8130-1577-4 (alk. paper)
1. Women—Employment—Arab countries. 2. Informal sector (Economics)—
Arab countries. I. Fernea, Elizabeth Warnock.
HD6206.M53 1998
331.4'0917'4927—dc21 98-12588

The University Press of Florida is the scholarly publishing agency for the State
University System of Florida, comprised of Florida A & M University, Florida
Atlantic University, Florida International University, Florida State University,
University of Central Florida, University of Florida, University of North
Florida, University of South Florida, and University of West Florida.

University Press of Florida
15 Northwest 15th Street
Gainesville, FL 32611
http://nersp.nerdc.ufl.edu/~upf

With love and gratitude, to my wife and colleague,
Carolyn Fluehr-Lobban, for our endless conversation
about women in Middle Eastern societies

Contents

Foreword

The invisible economy, the informal economy, the shadow economy, the spontaneous economy: these are relatively new terms in academic writing, coined to describe a phenomenon that does not appear in conventional statistical analysis of economies. This phenomenon is work by women that is unnoticed, uncounted, and unacknowledged. Since such "informal" work is performed daily by thousands of workers but is *not* included in national or global statistics, the overall economic picture is sadly distorted, especially in the developing world. The book that follows, *Middle Eastern Women and the Invisible Economy,* is an important and welcome effort to correct that distorted view.

Twenty years ago, it is unlikely that this book would even have been attempted or, if attempted, accepted for publication, since it deals not only with the idea of an informal economy but also with Middle Eastern women. As late as the 1970s, women were stereotyped by perfectly respectable social scientists as having no role in the economic life of their societies. If they ever had such a role, according to the argument, it lay in the past, when women were part of the agricultural production unit of the extended family. This stereotype of contemporary Middle Eastern women as economic ciphers was unsatisfactory to many anthropologists, particularly women anthropologists, for it did not reflect the realities of everyday life that they observed in both city and country. In 1971 and 1972 our family, for example, saw a different reality in the old city of Marrakech, where we lived while my anthropologist husband, Bob, was doing fieldwork. All around us in our neighborhood was evidence of women at work, both inside and outside the home, work they performed in addition to their daily chores of housekeeping, cooking, and child care.

Our landlady, a widow, owned three houses on the street, collected the rent in person, and negotiated for repairs with local plumbers and carpenters. Among the large family next door, one daughter earned money preparing brides for their wedding days, painting their hands and feet with intricate designs of henna; her sister specialized in facial makeup (glitter on the eyelids!) and hair design. Still another sister told fortunes, for a fee. Two of the family matrons worked as full-time attendants at the women's public bath. In other houses, women did piecework, cutting and sewing housedresses or hand-finishing the elaborate caftans stitched up by men tailors in the souk; they crocheted the braid trim, and they covered the scores of tiny buttons with colored thread to match the silk of the garments. Our full-time maid lived across the street from us. A woman recited the Quran under our window during Ramadan, the month of fasting, and those of us who lived on the street contributed small amounts of money as payment for this service. The hotels in the square of Djemaa el Fna employed women to clean the rooms and make the beds every day. Several women, described as very poor, sold goods such as eggs and bread laid out on squares of cloth near the larger stalls in the market. In the spring, groups of women appeared on the tree-lined streets of Gueliz, the newer section of the city built by the French, to pluck the orange blossoms for perfume and flavoring. An old *dallala,* a woman peddling secondhand clothing, visited the houses on our street from time to time, to buy as well as sell. Why were all these activities ignored in official labor reports?

True, the labor of some of these women was invisible; they worked inside their homes and their efforts were not immediately apparent to the casual observer. But some of the working women were clearly visible—as were the men of Marrakech who performed special services or worked part-time as vendors, entertainers, ordinary laborers, car washers, deliverymen, apprentices, beggars, errand boys. All this labor contributed both to household economies and to the Moroccan national economy. But the definition of work used by statisticians excluded such "informal" labor. That definition had been formulated in the offices of international agencies by economists and demographers and statisticians who worked with theories and abstractions and numbers rather than with people. The definition was also based on a certain vision of the nature of work dating from the European Industrial Revolution and the emergence of state capitalism. Peddlers and ordinary full-time laborers conformed to this definition. But a poor woman who occasionally sang for pennies; a poor man who walked from market stall to market stall, unloading crates of manufactured goods; or a women who sewed at home—they did not fit the image of the regulated and taxed individual, working-class or middle-class. Such workers lay outside the framework of that labor construct, with its advantages (labor laws and benefits) as well as its disadvantages (taxation).

But academic times are changing. Fieldwork is being conducted by scholars who question the old stereotypes, and research reports are being published that critique the old categories, the old images. Some of that exciting new work is assembled here, thanks to the creative energy of Richard Lobban, an anthropologist of note who has himself worked in several Middle Eastern countries. The fourteen impressive essays deal with women's work in Sudan, Egypt, Tunisia, Yemen, and Lebanon, with the activity of entrepreneurs, artisans, rural workers. The old terms surface in the titles of the pieces, terms such as *informal, marginalized,* and *shadow.* But the analyses in the essays themselves suggest that the time has come to discard such words and to develop new terminology that more accurately describes the diversity of women's work patterns, the strategies they have devised to survive and to better the economic position of themselves and their families. The hoped-for next step would be the appearance of comparable studies showing the roles that men, too, play in the unregulated, untaxed parts of national economies. Only then will a more realistic picture emerge of human labor throughout the developing world.

Elizabeth W. Fernea

Preface

As a non–Middle Eastern male, what am I doing writing about Middle Eastern women and their often unrecognized role in the economy? My answer rests chiefly in intellectual curiosity and methodological challenge. True, I have spent a quarter of a century researching and writing about Middle Eastern urbanization in Sudan, Egypt, and Tunisia, as well as traveling in Yemen and Lebanon, but there is more. As an anthropologist, I have always sought to see human society from the grassroots, from the bottom up. I have always been skeptical of the top-down approach, or the analysis of "significant" figures and events that were supposed to reflect what was really happening. Published documents, statistical tables, and detailed census counts seemed to lack a measure of authentic street sense. Common, practical domestic activities never seemed very clear. Most of what people do during a day escapes official record keeping and personal diaries. I knew that I was not getting the full picture.

Writing about the Middle East as a Westerner is always problematic because the quest for balance is difficult to achieve; the approaches of sympathetic interpretation and critical analysis can sometimes result in contradictory positions. As a male writing on gender, I feared additional pitfalls, not to mention examining an "invisible" economy that many think does not exist, an activity that might border on madness. Yet I believe it was these methodological and empirical circumstances that made me curious and kept me vigilant. A heightened consciousness has been required for this unusual work. This comment is certainly not meant as a defense or an apology for weaknesses and failures in my analysis, or integration, for which I am compelled to take responsibility.

Three years of research on urban social networks in the Sudan, during 1970–72, 1975, and 1979–80, proved that even the traditional approach of kinship analysis was not adequate to capture many important social networks and economic relationships and the ways in which they interact and adjust over time.[1]

In 1978 Helen I. Safa organized a very stimulating conference panel in New Delhi. She directed us with notable vigor, urgency, and clarity toward the central issues of labor migration, urban survival mechanisms, small-scale entrepreneurs, and the informal sector. The conference proceedings appeared in Safa's edited volume,[2] and I remain most grateful for the sharper focus she has provided to us all.

Two additional years of directing urban research projects in Egypt (1982–84) at the Urban Development Unit of the Social Research Center at the American University in Cairo only served to underscore how very much activity was missed by standard social research. My first effort to correct this problem was a conference I organized in Cairo on urban research methods, the results of which were published in 1983.[3] Thinking back to those days, it is clear that the discussion among a range of experienced researchers focused most intensely on the informal economy, especially on women's participation. The paper presented by Mahmoud Abdel Fadil[4] remains a frequently cited landmark in the study of the Egyptian informal economy. Yet the topics of women and informal commerce were usually left out of the official picture. This is a serious omission, indeed, when the neglect of policy planners can leave costly developmental programs to stagger and fall. Together, women as a whole and men who are part of the informal economy easily represent the numerical majority of the entire Middle Eastern population, yet their recognition is minimal.

In 1986 in Tutzing, Germany, the informal Middle Eastern economy again took center stage, at a conference organized by Peter Von Sivers and supported by the Social Science Research Center. The conference carefully defined and scrutinized the informal economy and proposed various models. Continuing my interest in 1990, while on sabbatical leave supported by the Rhode Island College Research Fund and the American Institute of Maghreb Studies, I spent the year studying the informal economy of Tunis. My research also took place in libraries at Dartmouth College and at the Center for Urban Research in the Arab World (URBAMA) at the University of Tours. In acknowledging Tours, I am deeply appreciative of the very friendly atmosphere and supportive staff. In particular, Pierre Signoles and Jean-François Troin did much to help me, and our friendship has continued long afterward. However, given my research orientation, it was on the back streets and alleys of Tunis and its environs, as well as in the libraries of the Center for Maghreb Studies in Tunis, that a great deal of my own research was conducted for this book. For their help, I am most grateful to Jeanne Jeffers Mrad and Khalid Mrad.

Thus I have long been intrigued by the informal economy, especially in tackling the difficult methodological problems of measuring and studying what many failed to recognize at all. Another aspect of this challenge is the question of gender in Middle Eastern studies. Until recent decades, the subject had been profoundly neglected. It is not that studies did not mention women, but their presentation was so stereotyped and slanted as to be of little value to empirically based social research. As a young researcher in the Sudan I tried to correct this problem, but I was usually unable to penetrate the various layers and barriers erected in societies where gender segregation is notable. I began to overcome my limitations through the presence of the three significant others in my life, my wife Carolyn Fluehr-Lobban, also a full-time professional anthropologist of the Middle East, and my two "assistants," daughters Josina and Nichola.

The profound influence of changing my status to that of a male researcher accompanied by two daughters and a wife made all the difference. Their company not only gave me wider acceptance but also assured me continually that this topic was well worth investigation. Among the growing published literature on the importance of gender and the status of anthropological researchers are the edited works of Joan Cassell, Tony Whitehead and Mary Ellen Conaway, and Ilva Ariens and Ruud Strijp.[5]

In recent years, research on gender in the Middle East has become a huge enterprise. A wide variety of books have penetrated the universal and particular aspects of the political economy of women and the roots of their global exploitation. Some researchers have probed the nature of Islam to explore some of the ideological roots of gender segregation and subjugation. However, this book does not intend to treat these significant topics in depth, focusing instead on creating a foundation of empirical data from which comparative, theoretical, and methodological judgments may be made.

In 1993 Middle Eastern urban poverty was the topic of a group that Michael Bonine brought together in Tucson, Arizona, where my contribution was a general survey of the Tunisian informal economy. That meeting convinced me to advance the study in a comparative, multiauthor work that would look only at Middle Eastern women in their often "invisible" economy. (The collected works of this conference have been published by the University Press of Florida.)[6]

The complexities of putting together a multiauthor work are well known in the academic world, but when the authors must transcend sev-

eral languages, continents, and spans of years—not to mention two genders—the task becomes formidable at times. The proof of these challenges
now rests in accumulated boxes and files of chapter drafts, letters, e-mail,
and faxes. Most supportive of this aspect have been the mail and telephone
services of Rhode Island College, for which I am grateful. The gestation of
this project has been long, and I express my gratitude to Richard Weiner,
dean of Arts and Sciences, who awarded me sabbatical leave for 1997,
when many parts of this book were coming to closure. The time away from
teaching schedules was of critical assistance, and I deeply thank him for
making it possible.

Probably there are some who would have abandoned the project as too
frustrating or too difficult. Nevertheless, all of the contributors have maintained a sense of confidence and mutual purpose that always supported our
collective effort. I personally appreciate the unique opportunity to write for
and edit a book about Middle Eastern women that is otherwise written
wholly by women. Being an unabashed feminist, I can only trust that I am
capable of editing this collection. Although I believe that male researchers
can and should investigate the subject as well (the potential contributors
included men), I have confidence that the women writing here have made
probing studies because their gender allowed them greater access and flexibility. I am also very grateful to Elizabeth ("BJ") Fernea for her willingness
to write the illuminating foreword, which highlights some of the context
and goals of this work. So, very many thanks to you all for your understanding and for your immense patience.

Thanks are also due to Walda Metcalf, formerly of the University Press
of Florida, for her support and encouragement, and to the successive edi-
tors at the Press, especially Gillian Hillis and Alexandra Leader, who have
watched this work materialize. Their understanding of the importance of
this book was always supportive and professional. Michael Senecal, formerly of the Press, very effectively continued the work begun by Walda,
and I appreciate his support.

Acknowledgment and thanks are due to Ablex Publishers for permission
to allow reprinting of some portions of the work of Barbara Larson first
published in "Women's Work and Status in Rural Egypt," *NWSA Journal*
3, no. 1 (Winter 1991). Similarly, I am grateful to Marcia Inhorn for granting permission, as the copyright holder, to reprint parts of a chapter from
her *Quest for Conception: Gender, Infertility, and Egyptian Medical Traditions* (University of Pennsylvania Press, 1994). The permission granted by
the Prints Department of the Boston Public Library to reprint some photo-

graphs from their collection of nineteenth-century prints is also very gratefully acknowledged.

Finally I wish to express my gratitude to Ghislaine Geloin of the Modern
Language Department of Rhode Island College for assisting with translations, supported by the Faculty Research Fund. I would also like to express
my thanks to Kharyssa Rhodes for checking references and assisting in the
creation of the statistical appendixes.

A note on translation and transliteration is also required, since there is
often some academic controversy about the "correct" format of transliter-
ated Arabic texts. On one side are the Arabists, orientalists, and many
historians who work with texts often written in classical or modern standard Arabic. Among this community of scholars, the accepted universal
style is Latinized letters with diacritical marks, for purposes of precision
and uniformity of understanding. (Sometimes this approach is termed Islamic studies from the top down.) On the other hand, anthropologists,
who are among the majority of writers in this book, see society, especially
gendered and sometimes illiterate society, from the bottom up. Local and
national colloquial forms of Arabic are what is in fact spoken, not the
classical forms of the language. Thus, for this work I have chosen authen-
ticity of speech over standard transliteration. For those familiar with the
colloquial forms of Arabic in specific nations, this will be the most under-
standable form, and English translations will guide the informed reader of
Arabic to the corresponding formal word. No doubt this approach will be
welcomed by anthropologists and frowned upon by others.

Richard A. Lobban, Jr.

Notes

1. My published research of this period includes Richard A. Lobban, Jr., "Alienation, Urbanization and Social Networks in the Urban Sudan," *Journal of Modern
African Studies* 12, no. 2 (1975): 491–500; "Class and Kin in the Urban Sudan,"
Africa 52, no. 2 (1982): 51–76; "Sudanese Class Formation and Urban Migration,"
in Helen I. Safa, ed., *Toward a Political Economy of Third World Urbanization*
(New Delhi: Oxford University Press, 1982); "A Genealogical and Historical Study
of the Mahas of the 'Three Towns,' Sudan," *International Journal of African Historical Studies* 16, no. 2 (1983): 231–58.

2. Helen Safa, ed., *Toward a Political Economy of Third World Urbanization*
(New Delhi: Oxford University Press, 1982).

3. Richard A. Lobban, ed., "Urban Research Strategies for Egypt," *Cairo Papers in Social Science* 6, no. 2 (1983).

4. Mahmoud Abdel Fadil, "Informal Sector Employment in Egypt," *Cairo Papers in Social Science* 6, no. 2 (1983): 55–89.

5. Joan Cassell, ed., *Children in the Field: Anthropological Experiences* (Philadelphia: Temple University Press, 1987), 237–55; Tony Whitehead and Mary Ellen Conaway, eds., *Self, Sex, and Gender in Cross Cultural Fieldwork* (Urbana: University of Illinois Press, 1986), 182–95; Ilva Ariens and Ruud Strijp, eds., "Anthropological Couples," *Focaal* (Universiteit Nijmegen) no. 10 (1989): 45–53.

6. Michael E. Bonine, ed., *Population, Poverty, and Politics in Middle East Cities* (Gainesville: University Press of Florida, 1996).

Introduction

Richard A. Lobban, Jr.

Our book seeks to document the economic achievements made by Middle Eastern women, while identifying gaps still unfilled. Here the focus is on women in the "invisible economy," in which their role in economic production and control of wealth has usually escaped attention. Most often studies of Middle Eastern women find a direct correlation between women as active members of the labor force and indicators of their economic well-being, such as control of fertility, heightened educational achievement, reduced mortality, and political participation. Thus, the recognition of their roles in economic production can contribute toward their empowerment, or toward overcoming the barriers still ahead.

This exploratory work is guided by the conviction that an informed and empowered population of men and women freely making personal and mutual choices is a healthy path to individual and national development. Equality by gender is not a zero-sum game but is ultimately indispensable for the mutual advancement of both men and women. Nawal El Saadawi[1] described the situation quite succinctly by saying that no oppressed group can hope to advance unless three conditions are met: (1) consciousness of the true reasons of oppression, (2) political organization, and (3) the ability to organize economically.

This book focuses on documentation and analysis in line with these three conditions. Insofar as Middle Eastern women are poorly represented in the formal labor force or are marginalized in the informal or "invisible" economy, they are deprived of economic and political equity and justice. Sharp gender segregation and social alienation from the workplace must be transcended if progress is to be made. El Saadawi advocates a personal jihad by, and for, women, for the purpose of reflection and growth in knowledge that will lead to this needed transformation in status.

The study of Middle Eastern women has oscillated from envisaging the romantic, exotic harem life to portraying the oppressed, veiled, obedient second-class spouse. Commentary has ranged from apologias to paternalism and from indifferent relativism to extreme Western feminism. Much research on the Middle East utterly neglects women, while other scholars see women as liberators, pioneers, and exalted heroines. Where is the reality?

From my personal and scholarly experience in the Middle East, and as the reward for preparing this book, I can say that we have now evolved to look at women on their own terms, in their own nations. The time for simplistic stereotypes and generalizations is happily over. The time for mature, honest, empirical research is at hand.

Certainly there are important common features observed here, but one of the most significant observations is that Middle Eastern women are not marching in lockstep. The religion of Islam is as much a dependent variable as it is a universal for this region. The contributors to this book show substantial differences in the levels of development, education, and status of women within the Middle East. This region is far from homogeneous, despite the icons and individuals that suggest it is such, or those who wish it to be such.

For some Middle Eastern women, achievements and protections exceed those in the "West." We have also discovered that the ill-defined "West" need not be the measure of such qualities of life in the first place. The universality of gender in the division of labor and power suggests that people from all lands may benefit from reflecting on new information. On the other hand, it is apparent that many women of the Middle East region are suffering multiple hardships in health, work, political empowerment, and social status. Time after time, the heaviest burden for women is a low degree of literacy, which confines them to unproductive or unrewarded labor. As their education advances, the position of women shifts markedly; this process is taking place at an astonishing pace, but it has a great distance yet to cover.

The statistical data on women of this region are notoriously poor in quality; the study of women's employment must be undertaken carefully. For example, the low wages of women in exported factory work may be only a new means of exploitation rather than their liberation in the cash economy. It is not to be assumed absolutely that informal work has an inherent low status, nor is such work necessarily unremunerative. Some women become centrally involved in decision making and in control of informal economic activities that contribute to their economic health and vitality. Certainly each circumstance has meaning only when judged in its context, as a 1984 UNESCO work has illustrated so well.[2]

Definitions

Since so many Middle Eastern women appear to be marginal to the main arena of the formal economy, our research task is to investigate women in the invisible, or informal, economy.

The study of the informal sector is often dated to the 1973 work of Hart,[3] who was drawn to this murky area when country after country showed a gap between the actual numbers of workers and the formal labor statistics that sought to represent them. Even as early as 1978, the growth of informal-sector studies resulted in a comprehensive, innovative, but quickly outdated bibliography on the subject by Stuart Sinclair.[4] More recently Gilbert and Gugler have provided a handy guide to evolution of this literature.[5] The literature has varied in its picture of the informal economy, from a trap for the poor to an imaginative pathway to wealth,[6] sometimes worthy of governmental support, sometimes seriously in need of further restraint. The invisible economy has also been known by other names, such as the *nonstructured sector,* the *informal sector,* and the *spontaneous economy,* but such terms result in much methodological confusion in practical field study. The nature of "invisible" economic activities and their public locations show predictable, regular patterns—quite contrary to what one might expect from terms such as *informal* and *nonstructured.* Although they may be small-scale economic activities, in many cases they are certainly socially and economically structured.

Confusion also exists in the related area of informal-sector housing, often known as *squatter housing.* Such housing, too, follows regular patterns of evolution, design, and construction that accommodate varying degrees of municipal services and authority. In informal housing, it is the scale and financing of the structure, rather than its basic nature, that sets it apart. Thus we cannot be content with the term *informal* for housing, either, as it leads to the dualist consciousness that is not sustained by empirical work. With such potential pitfalls in mind, a view of the range and classification of the field data will at least help to identify the subject of this study.

The informal sector appears to operate outside conventional administrative structures, especially the marginal or illegal parts of the informal sector, for which there are few records. Social and economic transactions are deliberately ephemeral and obscure. The nations in which the informal sector is the largest typically have a crisis in rural production. Decades ago, while studying Cairo, Abu-Lughod[7] noted the "ruralization" of its population, which falls heavily in the informal sector. Even formal-sector employment may be at such low levels that the term "underemployment" is more apt, and many formal-sector workers may have income supplements in the informal sector. For sure, the investigation of the informal sector is filled with contradictions and difficulties in measurement.

Refinement in studies of the informal sector must include work on: (1) definitions that aim toward cross-cultural comparison; (2) structural issues, such as the dualistic or unitary nature of the urban economy; and (3) microlevel empirical field studies that give a concrete expression of taxonomic, structural, and functional dimensions of the informal sector.

The urban informal commercial sector exists within both capitalist and state-planned economies. It functions as a survival mechanism that articulates and serves the economic interests of poor and low-income merchants and consumers. These functions are often maintained by small-scale investment and inventory and low prices. Service functions of the informal sector are especially difficult to observe and describe, but they form a large part of informal economic activities. This is especially true in ephemeral construction and transport labor.

The commercial portions of the informal sector are located largely in public space and at transportation nodes having high-density pedestrian traffic. Service portions are usually hidden from public view, especially those in the marginal, illegal, and female-based portions of the informal sector, in which gender dimensions have generally been underestimated and unappreciated. If regulated by police, licensing, and administrative supervision, the informal sector, given a lack of realistic alternatives, may be incorporated into or tolerated by the larger urban economy; when this is not the case, there can be active state repression and regulation. The informal sector is thus better defined as a special economic niche within a unitary but structurally diverse economic system, rather than as one of a set of parallel or dual systems.

The informal sector has notable diversity and heterogeneity in terms of services and commodities offered, scale of activity, official recognition, labor resources, and location. Direct participants in the informal sector follow a pattern of internal organization and regulation; the economic activity is not spontaneous or unstructured, despite terminology suggesting the opposite. Historical studies of the urban Middle East suggest that the informal-sector economy is not a new phenomenon, although it is probably expanding in the context of rapid urbanization and rural-to-urban migration.

Nineteenth-century
Egyptian woman date seller.
Photo: Tupper Scrapbook.
Courtesy of Boston Public
Library, Print Department.

Looking at the volume and diversity of newly manufactured products available in the informal sector, one can again see that the dualist model of formal-informal sector analysis cannot be sustained. That is, the sale of such products is simply another means of retailing for those who are not private shop owners. The greatest degree of state intervention in the informal sector occurs in the locations where private merchants are present. In other locations, such as the weekly markets, there is a police presence but no intervention or disruption. The unitary model of the informal economy appears to reflect that reality with far more utility and precision.

That the informal sector is a survival mechanism for many urban poor is without question. With a few important exceptions, the largest number of both merchants and clients are the poor. Operating at relatively low costs of merchandise and overhead, the informal-sector merchants can both make some additional income and serve others.

To describe the informal economy as unstructured or spontaneous is clearly far from the mark. Quite the contrary; the participants in the informal economy have regular locations, or regular days, on which they sell an established range of goods and services. The activity is highly organized and structured by internal and external forces. It is closely connected to the wider global economy and follows its economic logic, perhaps on a smaller scale. Even the idea that the informal sector is small in scale is refuted by the fact that central wholesalers can use the informal sector for the break-in-bulk of manufactured products and agricultural goods. The global transport and commercial network underlying the disposition of an immense volume of used clothing is anything but small-scale or simple. In order to maximize profit, sophisticated judgments are required about the degree of density and the frequency of markets and clients.

The Nature of the Problem

Another difficulty in defining the informal economy is the lack of agreement among disciplines about the focus and methods to be used. For example, geographers seek to situate the informal economy in terms of spatial or morphological dimensions. Statisticians and demographers seek quantified expressions of the size, characteristics, and distribution of the informal economy. Some planners see the recent rapid process of Third World urbanization as creating a context for the expansion of the informal economy.

Meanwhile, sociologists have found the role of the informal economy intriguing as it relates to processes of class formation and social stratification. In an earlier edited work,[8] I examine the linkages among the general processes of urbanization, migration, and class formation, particularly in Africa and the other parts of the Third World. I note that the contradictory nature of women's urban experience can be explained largely on class lines: some middle- and upper-class women may intensify their degree of segregation, while poorer women, facing survival needs, venture out into the wider population in greater degrees than before.[9] On the other hand, upper-class women are exposed to wider economic choices and greater social mobility, which can militate against increased seclusion or gender differentiation. Poorer women may have to adopt conservative clothing or veiling in order to enter the public commercial or employment sphere.

For their part, historians might turn to the roots of the informal economy in guilds, crafts, and artisan groups, thereby discovering that the informal economy is not really new at all and that distinctions are to be found under precolonial, colonial, and independence regimes. Political scientists might study the political administration and legitimization of informal activities, at the periphery, as they affect state relations at the core. Economists may study the developmental potential of shadow economies that divert tax revenues. More radical economists insist upon placing the informal economy in a "world systems theory" of marginalization and superexploitation of the Third World labor force.

Feminists naturally turn to the role of women in the informal sector, and they reveal the remarkable level of exclusion or peripheralization of women in the process. Others see sexism, gender-based fragmentation, and wage differentials of the labor market as main factors in maintaining this situation. Anthropologists have explored the "culture of poverty," using grass-roots and neighborhood-level case studies to demonstrate the ways and means by which the informal economy actually functions. Clearly the informal economy is a formidable topic, and as Charmes[10] has noted, it cannot be limited to a single definition or held to a single discipline; it is only a general field of study.

The question of the role of women in the informal economy is further complicated by its cultural and religious context. "Western" frameworks make a sharp distinction between religion and culture, while the prevailing "Eastern" model seeks unity of the sociocultural order within religious traditions including Islam, Christianity, and Judaism. This leads to methodological confusion in seeing religion alternatively as a cause, effect, barrier, and provider in gender relations. In fact, the position of women in Islamic nations may be a function of the general level of education and the economic and political development of the region even more than it is an effect of religion. After all, there is a wide range of women's statuses in Islamic nations, a clear indicator that religion may be more of a contextual setting for political struggle than a cause of it. Indeed, religion may simply be a correlative function of multiple forms of traditional patriarchy, irrespective of which faith is followed. The practice of religion may outweigh static interpretations of scriptures. No doubt this debate about female status and Islam will long continue.

The study of women in the informal economy is also frustrated by notable unevenness of regional statistics in the quality of data collection. Such factors as the discipline and gender of the fieldworker and the nature of the inquiry have profound impacts on the quality of data collection. For example, research that is academic or scholarly may lead to quite different conclusions than will state-sponsored research having policy, administrative, fiduciary, or census objectives. Government support or intervention has been one motivation for expanded research on the informal sector, while other efforts have focused on expanding the labor force, with hopes of increased production.

Toward a General Model

Given these complexities, it is apparent that any study must be integrative and interdisciplinary if any advance is to be made. Consequently, a unitary model of the economy, which incorporates the informal economy, is proposed in Table 1.[11]

Social research on Middle Eastern women has expanded greatly in the past twenty years. The first step in the evolution of these studies of Middle Eastern women was to confront the simplistic stereotypes of orientalist scholars, which often saw women as background decoration in the harems of the elite, or as passive victims of Middle Eastern gender segregation. The context at the time was the increased prominence of feminist studies in the Western world in general, especially the growing numbers of women in the social sciences. In the Middle East there was a parallel increase in women researchers native to this region. The nationalist and secular movements in a number of Middle Eastern nations added further to the momentum.

The recent work of Leila Ahmed[12] has been especially effective in presenting a comprehensive view of the historical evolution of the position of Middle Eastern women. She states that, until recently, gender had not been a major part of historical studies. In fact, the seclusion of Middle Eastern women created special economic niches in which women could attend to their social segregation. Positions for women as bath attendants, servants, tutors, teachers, midwives, physicians, business operators, and specialists in clothing and food production all emerged in this context. They served to intensify female bonding and gave internal diversity to women's roles. Often the diversity provided a sharp contrast between public bourgeois ideals and the practical realties faced by women. Ahmed takes a detailed look at the varied statuses, ethnic origins, and occupational variations even of the several wives of the prophet Mohammad. As much as one can find a strong basis for inequality of the sexes in Islam, Ahmed reminds us of egalitarian roots and reforms. Even the provision for plural wives (with the parallel injunction that they should be treated equally) has often been interpreted as meaning that monogamy is preferred. Indeed, monogamy is the most common practice.

Ahmed notes that the practice of veiling is debated among scholars at great length and intensity as a means of enforcing male control of female sexuality in public spaces and also as an instrument of female protection from other men. One can even conclude that public space in the Middle East was, and is, "male space," in which women are "trespassers." Male control of women is also seen in the forms of unilateral divorce, male guardians,

Table 1. A Unitary Model of the Economy

I. *Primary Capital*
Foreign and domestic capital; state bank and financial institutions

↓

II. *Primary Production*
Regional agricultural produce
(Role of women in farming, weeding, and harvesting)
Mining and petroleum resources

↓

III. *Secondary Production*
International manufacture
Domestic manufacture and processing
(Household production of food and clothing)

↓

IV. *Primary National Distribution*
Bulk importers and transporters
Wholesalers
Large-scale retailers

↓

V. *National Secondary Distribution and Services*
(Informal Sector)
Small-scale retailers of food and clothing
Weekly markets and street sales
Household and domestic sales and services
Informal or illegal sexual services
Loan pools and cooperatives
The survival economy

---

concubinage, eunuchs, *idda* (abstinence after divorce), polygyny, infant betrothal, intraconfessional marriage for women, unequal inheritance, and male negotiation for *mahr* (bridewealth).

The opposition to veiling, female seclusion, and "veiled" economies emerged from colonialist values, sometimes as a patronizing justification and legitimization of the colonialists' culture and of the need to suppress the "culturally backward" Orient. In resistance to this ethnocentrism, Ahmed points out, veiling often increased as a cultural and political icon of Middle Eastern cultural self-expression, autonomy, and revival. On the other hand, the rise of female education and literacy and the expansion of women in the labor force in manufacturing, industry, clerical work, and the professions—including ministerial appointments—in the modern Middle East has certainly been associated with an erosion of female seclusion. That the position of women is homogeneous or static is not sustained in empirical study.

Ahmed concludes her monograph:

> The study of anthropology "should not merely tell us how others live their lives: it should rather tell us how we may live our lives better," and ideally it should be grounded in the affirmation "that every culture needs others as critics so that the best in it may be highlighted and held out as being cross-culturally desireable." Perhaps feminism could formulate some such set of criteria for exploring issues of women in other cultures, including Islamic societies—criteria that would undercut even inadvertent complicity in serving Western interests but that, at the same time, would neither set limits on the freedom to question and explore nor in any way compromise feminism's passionate commitment to the realization of societies that enable women to pursue without impediment the full development of their capacities and to contribute to their societies in all domains.[13]

In the second stage of the evolution of social research on Middle Eastern women, two schools of thought emerged, both of which projected women as heroic history makers in their own right. Documentation focused on the movement for women's rights, antiveiling campaigns, the role of women in nationalist movements, the advances of women in education, and women's health. The excellent edited work by Tucker[14] is a bountiful source on the "Old Boundaries, and New Frontiers" of the historical, cultural, and political evolution and the gender discourses of Arab women. However, Tucker's contributors do not give much attention to the modern informal economy, except for some work of Evelyn Early,[15] which is also represented in the book in hand.

Fluehr-Lobban[16] has advanced a theoretical expression of these gendered interests. She sees Arab-Islamic society and sexual segregation as a modified form of patriarchy that may differ in degree in specific cases but does not differ in general expressions of gender relations across the globe. She adds that female solidarity resulting from seclusion also has positive

Nineteenth-century Egyptian woman poultry seller. Photo: Tupper Scrapbook. Courtesy of Boston Public Library, Print Department.

aspects and that it must be viewed in the context of anticolonialism and nationalism. Whether Middle Eastern women opt for conservative or secular forms of self-expression, both may be viewed as movements from the private or domestic sphere into the main public arena of political mobilization.

The diversity in the experience of Middle Eastern women also led to a radical critique of their economic and social subjugation, as well as special problems such as veiling, legal exclusion from public spheres, female circumcision, and religious restraints to women in society. These sometimes contradictory trends are still central features of much of feminist scholarship. Even the articles in this book can be taken to illustrate both the marginalization of the economic role of Middle Eastern women and their creativity, independence, and female bonding, which has given them a sense of solidarity and strength. The study by Early of *baladi* women in Cairo, for example, provides an important reminder that even within the low-status domestic domain, women are empowered by their daily care-giving skills, food preparation, seamstress skills, and sophisticated manipulation of kinship and neighborhood ties. Such foundations may actually be a form of preadaptation for wider mobility into the public domains of food, clothing, and textiles production and sales, where women are found in great numbers.

The general and persistent economic crisis of Middle Eastern societies has witnessed a massive male emigration to nations offering higher wages. The absence of husbands and brothers working abroad has positioned or required women to exercise greater domestic and local autonomy and initiative in street sales of food and clothing and in household daily services. Women with direct links to rural production have also been able to engage in relatively rewarding sales of livestock and agricultural surplus, which can subsequently be transformed into pushcart food trade. Such products—noodles, sandwiches, cheese, fruits, ghee, and sweets—require low capitalization and can easily generate income through bulk purchases from wholesalers. Similarly, women may own seamstress shops or sell tea, groceries, and cigarettes as a collaborative or individual effort.

The contradictory evidence and perspectives are a function of the diverse experience of Middle Eastern women in each nation, especially given that the nations range from radical secular to conservative feudal in their political administration. In graphic form, the evolution and context of this scholarship is illustrated in Table 2.

Many agree that the new age of the study of Middle Eastern women was pioneered by the Moroccan social scientist Fatima Mernissi.[17] Her influential *Beyond the Veil* is, appropriately, often revisited. It sets much of the agenda of feminist research. First Mernissi, like Fluehr-Lobban, stresses caution in looking at Middle Eastern women through a paternalistic or Western lens, and she makes the point that religious and cultural values that support male supremacy are effectively universal. Mernissi also asks her readers to recognize that the formal expression of Middle Eastern and Islamic values differs greatly from their actual practice.

It is the area of economics and political freedom that Mernissi targets as her main subject of investigation. She proclaims that an intense struggle is currently underway in the Middle East between male power over women and the assertion, by women, of women's power. Sometimes the struggle emerges as open conflict between traditionalist revival and modernist secularism and economic liberation. In areas where legal restrictions on women's human rights and roles are in place, the intensity of Mernissi's focus grows.

Mernissi shows that this struggle emerged in the context of anticolonialism, in which radical nationalism liberated the conflicting tendencies of reinforcing tradition; gender equality was a way to confront the colonial

Table 2. Themes of Feminist Research in the Middle East

Colonial Western Values (women as objects of sex in the harem; women as victims)	vs.	*Anticolonial Eastern Values* (women as objects of love: mothers, wives, and daughter; women as the protected gender)
Secular Modernist Values (women as the reserve force of change and national empowerment; women as liberators)	vs.	*Sacred Traditionalist Values* (women as the guardians of family, religious, and social values at a time of crisis; women as heroines)
Sexual Desegregation (women in equal economic production and social service)	vs.	*Sexual Resegregation* (women as economic and social rivals of men)

Economic and Political Tension and Crisis

Increased role of women in formal-industrial-public production and service	vs.	Increased role of women in informal-domestic-private production and service
Large-scale industrial and public sector of services and production.	vs.	Small-scale subsistence and household production and domestic services.

New Gender Order in Middle Eastern Societies?

culture effectively. The Middle East postcolonial crises of military dictator-ships, monarchical succession, violence, regional ethnic revival, lack of democracy, and religious extremism have only served to redirect the de-bates over the rights of women. In this new context, Mernissi emphasizes that much of what is taking place in Islamic nations is not so much about religion itself as about the use of religion as a weapon in the struggle be-tween conservative and progressive forces in general, and specifically in the heated combat over who will control women and to what degree. The debate about modernization and Westernization that was popular in de-cades gone by is shown to be peripheral, the West being simply another pole around which the Middle Eastern conflicts can revolve.

One aspect of Mernissi's[18] work is especially relevant to the study of the presence or absence of women in the informal economy. Her perceptions about the gendered nature of space in the Arab world are built upon the notions of the *hudud* (boundaries), the *harim* (prohibited space reserved for or confined to women), and *fitna* (temptation, which is ascribed to women and which must be controlled). Men's lust, their susceptibility to temptation, is projected as being so strong that it cannot be controlled except by the liberal allowance for polygyny, concubinage, and easy divorce. This double standard seeks to regulate the sexual tensions and desires between men and women by relegating public space to men and private or domestic space to women. When women are present in male space, the special solution of veiling emerges as a "logical" response. It follows from this sociosexual thinking that women without a veil are essentially *arean* (nude) and that women entering a male domain are virtual *ta'addiyeen* (trespassers). At conflict with these concepts are the exigencies of economic development, which often require gender desegregation, expanded education, and labor mobilization. Mernissi warns that modernization is not simple and that radical Arab nationalism or ethnocentrism must be considered if such changes are to be accommodated within an authentic national character.

Probably much of the current strife over Islamic fundamentalism is *not* about religion or women at all but instead a male struggle for political turf, for leadership in the coming phases of economic and political change. The current intensity of this battle should be contextualized, suggests Mernissi, by seeing the contradiction between traditionalist and modernist paradigms. Women's issues and roles become a battleground for male politicians seeking to demonstrate their power over women. Women themselves seek to redress their own grievances, protect their group self-interest, and carve a path toward a new economic future. Thus, women in the public sphere cannot be considered only a neutral empirical fact, but must be seen as an economic, political, and finally religious statement, in ways that Westerners cannot easily comprehend without Middle Eastern socialization.

In the personal ethnographic-biographical account of *Street Life in Marrakech* by Elizabeth Fernea,[19] we learn a good deal about what really takes place, rather than what some top-down or orientalist perspective imagines to be the case. Fernea presents rich firsthand anthropological data about women who work long hours as water carriers (p. 45), who suffer hardships as beggars (409–10), or who find modest employment as *shuwafa* fortune tellers (84, 215) or *mateeyalum,* folk remedy healers (304). We also learn of women who gain a small income from applying henna dye to the hands in decorative designs and embroidering fabric at home for sale outside (120–21). Nevertheless they are subject to endless aggressive behavior by males in the public domain (53), and women's employment is relegated to the category of chores, while men do "work." Similarly, women are given few resources but are expected to supply tea and other hospitality for guests at the home; in the main, it is only for weddings and funerals that women are adequately provided with finances for expenses. Significantly, Fernea also documents that rural women are much less veiled than urban women (173) and that their role in production of crops and livestock is essential, not marginal. However, when these goods are sold at market, the control of the cash falls largely to men.

Writing on Tunisia in the Maghreb, the research collective known as the El Amouri Institute[20] has made parallel observations. Among its recommendations is support for domestic production and manufacture as a formal part of national and regional development plans. Adequate attention to credit, water supply, and fuel would enhance, to collective advantage, the domestic production of carpets (kilims, *mergoums*), pottery (*kanouns,* jars, and lamps), and traditional clothing (*chechia, kabous,* and burnouses). Marketing of home crafts and seasonal agricultural produce could be structured in a way that would assist women and increase cash return on their labor. Naturally such notions need not conflict with the aim of increasing the numbers of women in formal-sector areas such as manufacture; instead they seek to address women's presence in local initiatives. If the informal sector is viewed as a competitor to state planning of the market economy, it will certainly become just that, and the positive features of increased production will be lost, while the negative features of an imposed state bureaucracy will become ever more burdensome.

In a comparative study of gender and change throughout the Middle East, Valentine Moghadam[21] has offered her perspectives on the general relationship of gender, development, domestic production, and the state. Together, she says, they create a "cultural construct that is itself constituted by social structure." Any means to perpetuate the inequalities may be used to preserve this cultural system, which embodies power and economic relations. She thus reminds us that the issue of gender must be viewed in the context of stratification and state ideology. Her perceptive recommendations are accepted here to help make sense of the presence, evolution, and nature of the informal economy in general and the presence or absence of women in this sector.

Beyond the findings that apply to women in general in the informal economy of Middle Eastern nations, the status of women differs among selected nations of the area.

Egypt

The vast historical and religious complexities of Egypt make one reluctant to write any brief generalizations. Known widely as "the mother of the world," Egypt has long been dominant in regional politics and events. The postcolonial Egyptian economy is relatively diversified and has relied on tourism, Suez canal revenues, oil production, agriculture, foreign aid, domestic commerce, and major labor exports to keep itself afloat. Oil production and revenues have not been consistent for various reasons, and in the 1990s tourism has been affected by attacks from religious extremists.

The economic and military aid of the United States to Egypt has become essential, but it has added to Egypt's domestic political vulnerability. The agricultural backbone of Egypt can no longer provide self-sufficiency in food production of meat or wheat, and remittances from overseas Egyptian workers have taken a downturn. As a result of these economic disruptions, privatization, and marked class stratification, the "benevolent authoritarian" regime of Egypt has faced a persistent crisis situation. At the same time, Egypt has made huge advances in public transportation and education and has embarked on an ambitious program of urbanization.

Within this wider context are several salient features that affect women and their informal economy. The demography of Egypt includes high fertility and large-scale rural-to-urban migration. As educational achievements have increased for Egyptian women, there has generally been a decrease in fertility, but the many rural-to-urban migrants have brought rural fertility patterns to the city.

The levels of literacy for Egyptian women have increased, but at about half the rate for men. From 1960 to 1976 the portion of illiterate Egyptian women has fallen from 84 to 71 percent, but in absolute terms the number of illiterate women has increased.[22] Female illiteracy in Egypt stays quite high for a nation so urbanized and industrialized.

In these circumstances, the position of women has found both advancement and severe challenge. Certainly the issue of women's liberation in Egypt is nothing new, the nation having had such stalwart feminist leaders as Huda Sharawi, Saiza Nabarawi, and later Fatma Nimat Rashid, Duriyya Shafiq, Inji Aflatu, and Latifa Zayyat—all pioneers in the struggle. But it is the boldness of Nawal El Saadawi that has really shaped the feministic dialogue in Egypt. For those with education and connections, there is unprecedented socioeconomic mobility; for those without, there is an alarming sense of frustration and hardship.

Embodying these contradictions, Egyptian women include members of Parliament as well as the traditional villager still carrying water in jugs to her home. Dress patterns in Cairo vary from the most Western types, seen on women in expensive cars, to the heavy veils of the *muhaggabat,* who reflect an important trend in Islamic values, especially among lower-middle-class urban women. A fascinating study by Arlene MacLeod has put the topic of "the new veiling" into sharp focus as a mechanism for "accommodating protest" amidst rapid economic change in an ambivalent social setting.[23] The inevitable conflict between gender, on the one hand, and economic options and public space, on the other, is temporarily "re-solved" by use of the veil. In this way, Egyptian women gain access and mobility in the public sphere while reproducing the gender inequalities that exist in law and practice.

Relative to the role of women in the informal sector, MacLeod says that they "participate in the gathering of economic resources in ways that cross boundaries of standard definitions of employment, working in informal service jobs somewhere between household and workplace."[24]

The probing work of Heba Handoussa and Gillian Potter[25] has con-firmed the fallacy of dualism by showing that the informal sector has become an essential part of the Egyptian economy. Since the start of the *Infitah* (open-door) economic policy of 1974, the public sector has been unable to provide sufficient formal employment opportunities. Handoussa and Potter state that the informal economy is growing at 2.8 percent per year, particularly household subsistence enterprises and neighborhood mi-croenterprises that may have viable growth potential.

They note the heterogeneous nature of informal economic activities, which vary from a "response to temporary recessionary conditions" all the way to activities that justify "support and promotion in any long term development strategy." In some instances they are "successful enough to become an engine of growth" that makes little demand on infrastructure and spurs competition and efficiency.

The heterogeneous nature of Egyptian women's economic roles is a function not only of the varied experiences in the twentieth century but also of pronounced class stratification and notable rural-urban differences. Rural life, for example, is tied to agricultural cycles, and the involvement of women in traditional agriculture is declining because of urban migration, mechanization of farming, and attractive industrial work.[26] On the other hand, urban life is confining for some and liberating for others. Domestic textile or carpet production keeps some urban women at home, while others are engaged in industrial textile manufacture.

Legal Advances of Egyptian Women

In 1917 the Ottoman rulers initiated a family code that sought to modernize Turco-Egyptian society. While some restrictions were placed on polygyny, progress was slow, and legislation that opposed aspects of Islamic law was resisted.[27] Even so, Egyptian women were considered in the vanguard of the feminist movement in the Middle East. One often hears of the 1923 action against veiling as a symbol of this early fervor in Egypt. In 1933 legal reforms provided for additional possibilities for women to hold and inherit wealth, to gain political rights, and to improve their personal status.[28]

After the 1952 revolution, more progress was made for women in equal pay, job training, and free education. The 1956 constitution allowed women to vote and to be elected to the People's Assembly, while the young, male, nationalist officers simultaneously sought to restrict the independence of women's political organizations. Law 91 of 1959 officially ended employment discrimination by sex. By 1979 thirty seats in the assembly were set aside for women; this provision, however, was a restraint by quota.[29]

Nawal El Saadawi, who graduated from Cairo University only a few years after the Nasser revolution, has taken special note of article 40 of the Egyptian Constitution of 1971, which appears to be broadly supportive of equal rights on the basis of gender, race, language, and so forth. A deeper reading reveals that these rights obtain only in the public domain. Elsewhere, the same constitution grants rights to women as long as they do not violate the laws of Islamic Sharia.[30] As a result, El Saadawi determines that Egyptian women live in a context of legal schizophrenia, in which public and private rules differ and women are formally free but limited by the Quran.

The ambiguities in women's status are more apparent when they become the battleground for the wider political struggles of men. An example is the Islamist movement's effort to drop the more liberal Personal Status Law no. 44 of 1979 and replace it with law no. 100 in 1985. The 1985 law had more conservative provisions for women in divorce, polygyny, and child custody.[31] After an intense struggle by women, most of the provisions of law 44 were restored a few months later. The observations of El Saadawi confirm that Egyptian women advanced at times of national revolution and reform, but their position deteriorated when conservative forces were

Nineteenth-century Egyptian women bread sellers. Photo: Tupper Scrapbook. Courtesy of Boston Public Library, Print Department.

in the ascendancy. A fuller history of the nineteenth- and twentieth-century history of the Egyptian women's struggle is recorded by Badran.[32]

A significant legal development for Egyptian women in recent years has been the curtailment of legal gains that were won under the influence of Jihan Sadat. The Mubarak administration, apprehensive about offending Islamist sentiments, has restrained legal progress on the feminist agenda and has sought to limit the activity of El Saadawi, and her Arab Women's Solidarity Association.

Women in the Labor Force

In the wake of the Nasser years, women now find roles in all sectors of the economy. Their share of the overall formal labor force ranges from 7 percent to perhaps 14 percent.[33] Women account for about 20 percent of those considered "economically active." However, of these only 38 percent are salaried, according to International Labor Organization data analyzed by Moghadam.[34] By type of work, 41.3 percent of Egyptian working women are in agricultural pursuits, 17.6 percent in professional and technical fields, and 12.9 percent in clerical jobs. Yet the official statistics of Egypt's CAPMAS office[35] fail to account for large numbers of working women.

Nineteenth-century Egyptian women mandarin sellers. Photo: Tupper Scrapbooks. Courtesy of Boston Public Library, Print Department.

The pioneering study on this topic was launched by Mahmoud Abdel Fadil,[36] in part because of the unexplained gaps between known populations and workforce estimates. The state is one of the greatest employers of women, but the numbers of good government jobs and wages in Egypt are notoriously low. The weak economy and large-scale return migration from the Persian Gulf has caused unemployment to become a substantial social issue, which may attract some to Islamist movements.

Based on a survey of the changing patterns of female employment in Egypt by Sullivan and Korayem, they concluded:

The employment of women in the monetized sectors of the economy has increased in both absolute and relative terms during the past two decades. The typical female worker now lives in an urban rather than a rural area. Furthermore, while 51% of working females were under 20 years of age in 1961, only 24.6% were under 20 in 1976. Now, roughly two-thirds of Egypt's working women are between the ages of 20 and 49 and over one-third are between 20 and 30. The most notable change to occur in the last two decades, however, may been seen by considering that two-thirds of the female work force is at least literate and most have gone through preparatory education or more.[37]

Sullivan and Korayem remark, "In the Egyptian context, the mere fact that education and employment take women outside the home, unsupervised by 'their' men for a good part of the day, is significant as a *de facto* challenge to the social limits placed on the public behavior of women. For at least part of the day, these women have a private life in the public world, separate from the role of daughter, wife, or household manager."[38]

Microstudies of Egyptian Women

As the articles in this book indicate, many Egyptian women are engaged in varied informal income-generating projects and activities, which include domestic production of foods and clothing and street vending of agricultural goods either bought wholesale or provided by their links to agricultural networks. The research in this book has broadly followed the micro-level model established by Barbara Ibrahim.[39] In the words of Mostafa Kharoufi, "the 'micro' level studies are more informative and relevant. They allow us to identify those characteristics of the informal sector which do not appear in the major statistical surveys carried out at the national level."[40]

Aside from the research reported here, studies of informal sector fruit and vegetable sellers, small-scale aluminum workshops, and trash recyclers are underway, but they do not focus specifically on the question of women.[41] The study by Sarah F. Loza has advanced the concern for women in the informal economy, seeing their substantial role as food vendors on urban streets.[42] Nicholas Hopkins, in discussing household production by women, differentiates among socially obligatory work, voluntary work, and "real" (income-producing) work for women. He reminds us how very much women are already contributing to the invisible economy. He concludes with a skepticism of statistics and definitions but says there is common agreement that the developmental process is underway, that there are structural and unitary linkages in the entire economy, and that the informal economy functions as a "survival strategy package."[43]

Anne Jennings's work in chapter 1 of this book illustrates Egypt's cultural diversity by viewing Nubian women in the shadow economy. Jennings's detailed microethnography shows how Nubian women not only generate income but also dispose of it in their household and public activities. As do the other contributors, Jennings defines the informal economy as suited to her research on Nubian women, and she notes that most studies on the "shadow" economy have concentrated on men or have taken no special note of women at all. Her reflections on the discussion of public/ private domain in Islamic societies are rich in historical, ethnographic, and contemporary detail.

Barbara Larson views the rural side of the Egyptian informal economy, where women are even more often neglected in social research (see chap. 7). Larson's work is of value not only for comparative study but also to help fill a gap in the literature. She does not stop with a view of rural women but carefully considers their articulated connections to urban life and economy. Her valuable descriptive data on agriculture and crafts production from Beni Suef are then linked to the weekly markets that we see in other places in this volume. Finally, she analyzes their value in the informal economy in terms of policy, development, theory, and the relative advantages for women so employed.

Marie Butler's study of rural women in Kalyubia and of home-based microenterprises shows that women are much undercounted, while being very significant contributors (see chap. 8). They are involved in domestic and farm production and they are increasingly involved in rural-area production of goods and services that are marketed in the cities. This is possible because of improvements in technical and financial assistance and systems of agricultural credit. Women who stay in rural areas can find steady employment in modernized chicken farms. Once again, past measures of the wider economy are rendered questionable at least, if not obsolete. Butler's statistical and ethnographic data emerge from within the homes and lives of the women workers.

Marcia C. Inhorn probes the health delivery system of the informal economy (see chap. 5). This fascinating and sensitive study in Alexandria discovers informal health services, not otherwise provided, that meet women's needs. Many women find remunerative employment in providing the services of folk healers and midwives. Like the wider informal economy, the domain of informal health care is connected to a formal system and has arisen because of inadequacies in access, poor communication, and recurrent marginality of women to the larger system. Inhorn shows clearly that Egyptian women consider their health care system unitary but syncretic. It has different parts and practitioners, just as there are specialist departments in the West for medical or health care. The history of these two interacting systems going back to ancient Greek and Islamic health beliefs and practices is a strong feature of Inhorn's work.

Evelyn A. Early deepens the connection between rural women and the urban informal economy with her study of *baladi* (rural) women in Cairo as migrants and as permanent residents (chap. 6). Early's research moves the focus from countryside women to those of the Cairo neighborhood of Bulaq Abu 'Ala. They mobilize social and economic resources in this poor, industrial neighborhood. Partly from necessity, women find work as domestic servants and as street food sellers; gradually their social and monetary capital has accumulated. The long history of women in both household and industrial employment shows that the informal sector may not be new at all, though it has grown. Whether selling Egyptian bean sandwiches and cheese, providing domestic or family services, or drawing on gold resources from marriage or work, women are shown to be most resourceful and creative in meeting the difficulties of life in Cairo. Early's four qualitative case studies of baladi women are so authentic, lively, and engaging that they verge on the territory of the popular novelist Naguib Mafouz. Just as the informal economy has been kept in the shadows, it is the women described by Early who find notable freedom of movement in the same shadows.

Keeping the focus on urban life in Cairo, Homa Hoodfar examines the question of why poor working women utilize the informal economy so heavily (chap. 13). Her investigation uncovers the macro-micro linkages that are a central feature of Egyptian studies. Step by step, Hoodfar poses a subset of questions that relate to the general topic. To what extent is the Islamic religion a variable, or to what extent is it a patriarchal social system that keeps women in a marginal position? Her data reveal that both may be factors, but the primary cause of economic marginality rests in the rigid, male-dominated structure of the formal labor market. Since the formal economy is not really rewarding, it becomes reasonable for women to seek the flexibility of the shadow economy, allowing maximum freedom for family support. Given the few alternatives, the relatively low levels of monetary rewards are acceptable.

Other facets of the position of women, such as domestic and household work or the issue of veiling, all become reasonable in this context. But they are effects, not causes, of women's positions. The field data collected by Hoodfar from three low-income neighborhoods in Cairo document the position of women vis-à-vis the larger labor force and give solid confirmation of her thesis.

Another researcher in Cairo, Diane Singerman, looks at the topic of women, work, and politics, finding high rates of labor force participation among some women in the low-income communities, alongside extensive involvement in the informal economy (chap. 14). Singerman discovers that even though earnings in the informal economy might be low, the flexibility and diversity of employment opportunities still make it attractive. Women fill various niches in the labor hierarchy in the informal economy, where they can organize vital rotating credit associations for the basic needs of business capital, marriage, and housing.

Beyond the income-generating aspect, participation in the informal economy enables women to be deeply involved in politics, especially at the local, informal level. In relatively authoritarian Egyptian politics, the state seeks formal intervention and regulation of most economic and political activities. The informal economy allows women to escape some of these restraints, and they have begun to transform their economic participation into a little-recognized political force.

The Sudan

Sudanese women have probably the greatest ethnic diversity represented in this book. In ancient Kush, Sudanese women were sovereign rulers, and dimensions of matrilineality kept women in positions of notable influence. There is also great variation in their experience with Islam, ranging from strong folk or popular traditions to very orthodox practices and beliefs. Even the term *informal economy* has little relevance to a society based on subsistence production. Likewise, the regimes in postcolonial Sudan have varied from radical secular to fundamentalist. Urban and rural differences in the Sudan are also marked. The Sudan itself is an unstable state—barely a state at all. Any generalizations about the Sudan easily risk contradiction.

It should not be surprising that some of the most secular models of development and of women's status are found in the Sudan, a nation that has had the largest Communist Party membership in the Middle East and a fine tradition of university education. Its nationalist struggle was celebrated as one of the first in Africa to apply to women the right to vote; it did so, in principle, in 1953.[44] Sadly, the Sudan has failed to resolve the conflict between north and south, which is complicated by factors of race, religion, ethnicity, language, and economic development.

The complex position of Sudanese women has produced significant women leaders, professors, ministers, and parliamentarians on one side, while other women and their entire families have been so savagely exploited that term *ethnic cleansing* and, amazingly, renewed practices of domestic and export slavery are now known. The Sudan has been under sharp criticism for the widespread practice of female circumcision as an extreme control of fitna, or sexual temptation, that cannot be excused by cultural relativism.[45] Gender-based ailments such as obesity, depression from social oppression, and related psychoneuroses may also need attention.[46] Other forms of gender inequities also appear in household segregation, polygyny, veiling, and early arranged marriage.

Under the initial period of the Nimieri regime (1969–85), the Sudan took huge steps in addressing such inequities; it appointed women at the ministerial level and eliminated *bayt ata'a,* the legal practice that forced a woman, against her will, back to her husband. Women became Islamic court judges, where Islamic (Sharia) law was as much tradition as it was religion. Many of the forward-looking positions in the Sudan were chipped away in the late 1970s and early 1980s. By 1983 the Nimieri government, desperate for new political allies, did an about-face and introduced a wide range of very conservatively interpreted Sharia laws, including capital punishment for apostasy, crucifixion, stoning, and amputation. Shortly afterward, in 1985, the Nimieri regime was toppled, for a complex mix of political and economic reasons, and the present military government of Omer Beshir took power in 1989.

This government is essentially guided by Hassan Al-Turabi of the National Islamic Front, which has curtailed advances in the status of women and has tried to apply Sharia law everywhere. In fact, the multiconfessional, culturally plural nation has been deeply rent by this effort. Opposition comes from the one-third or more of the people who are not Muslim and by Muslims who see Islam as a guide to personal behavior and not as an overarching national law.[47]

The Sudan is one of the world's poorest countries. Its wealth has come from agricultural exports. Industry and manufacturing in the Sudan are only slightly developed. The substantial reserves of oil in the southern Sudan are not accessible during the civil war; production is suspended. Worsening the situation are the labor exodus and brain drain, exacerbated by political instability, ecological vulnerability, and economic misery. The nation's ability to repay its foreign debts has collapsed, and were it not for the backing of oil-rich regimes such as Iran, Iraq, and Libya, the Sudan might collapse utterly. It has become an economic basket case rather than the breadbasket of the Arab world, as once optimistically predicted.

The percentage of women in formal, wage-earning production has varied within a very low range, from 5 to 7 percent. In manufacturing the proportion is somewhat higher, about 15 percent in fairly dated statistics, largely in the textile factories around the capital city. In clerical, civil service, and professional positions, additional women find salaried employment. The vast majority are not officially listed as economically active but are hard at work in agricultural tasks of harvesting, livestock management, or domestic production. Some urban poor have survived by means of prostitution or illegal sales of fermented beverages, which have been aggressively curtailed, as have been the huge amount of informal-sector housing, often destroyed by bulldozer blades.

Other general measures of the status of women in the Sudan include very little knowledge or use of contraceptives, resulting in high fertility rates. Infant and maternal mortality rates have declined somewhat but are still very high. Life expectancy statistics are quite dubious in the context of civil war and famine, and there is no reliable recent census. The very low male and female literacy rates did show some signs of improvement but are half as much for females as for males; as the level of education advances, the proportion of educated women declines even further.

Nada Mustafa Ali in chapter 4 describes survival strategies for women from the Sudanese railroad town of Atbara.[48] This work seeks to address the widely unacknowledged position of Sudanese women. It reveals their creative means to survive in the Sudan during the crisis of food shortages, high prices, and growing impoverishment. Ali believes that much of the problem rests upon the neopatriarchal nature of northern Sudanese society. Four of the women in her study are small market traders and one is a housewife. They cleverly purchase wholesale for their retail sales, and they create a system of rotating credit of goods and services, including the traditional practice of psychotherapy known as the *zar*. These Sudanese women may be developing a new sense of consciousness and identity.

Despite rapid urbanization for reasons of ecological, political, and military security, the Sudan is still vastly rural. Barbara J. Michael in chapter 2 studies rural Baggara women as informal market strategists. The Baggara are one of the largest populations of the western Sudan. Their cattle-based economy is one of pastoral nomadism and urban marketing for domestic consumption or export. Michael reflects upon the sometimes stereotyped image of nomadic people, and she sees that the apparent dichotomy between rural and urban is, in fact, much connected in economic reality. In the case of women herders and marketers among the (Hawazma) Baggara, she finds intimate links between the rural production of milk, yogurt, butter, and cheese and the women's shrewd and informed market strategies, which allow them to control more of the economy than one might expect in traditional Arab society. Numerous government policy implications may be drawn from her important study, which shows that rural women, although socially and economically oppressed in many cases, are much involved in key decision making in other cases. The income of Baggara women goes directly toward family food purchases and general self-reliance.

Lebanon

In decades gone by, Lebanon was often called the Switzerland of the Middle East. It had lulled itself into believing that the ethnic, religious, and military conflicts of the region would never upset its peaceful commerce and apparently harmonious intercommunal relations. Balanced in numbers, the practitioners of both major faiths, Christianity and Islam, have significant internal differences, divided by almost a score of sects and families. Unity among these heterogeneous groups has been an elusive constitutional objective of this "minimalist" state.[49]

Lebanon is small-scale, heavily urbanized, and cosmopolitan by Middle Eastern standards. It has seen the crushing poverty of Palestinian refugee camps as well as marvelous opulence and luxury. This land of contrasts, with few natural resources except its strategic position on the eastern Mediterranean, has long served as a commercial marketplace for European products entering the Arab world. Like their Phoenician ancestors, modern Lebanese have relied on their diasporic kin groups as a foundation for their commerce.

Destabilized by hundreds of thousands of Palestinian refugees after the 1948 partition of their land, Lebanon fell into its own civil war and became a regional battleground for neighboring powers. When the militias and proxy forces were not fighting the larger enemies, they fought one another to rewrite the national balance of power. The nation's struggles have also been between secularism and fundamentalism. The wounds inflicted by the bloodbath in Lebanon starting in the mid-1970s have started to heal, but with major social and demographic change.

Much less well known is the important role of Lebanon in silk production for European textile industries. Buried still deeper is the fact that Lebanese women in rural and mountainous regions have been chiefly responsible for the collection and care of silk for this export market. In production of high-cost carpets and textiles, the low cost of women's labor was considered necessary to make the goods competitive overseas. The clear link between the social devaluation of women and low labor costs is instantly apparent in the Lebanese case, which may be one reason it is often relegated to the shadow economy. The expansion of the Lebanese merchant class since independence in 1943, and the weak central state that backed it, only served to maintain these gender relations in suspended animation.

Pronounced male migration from Lebanon is a pattern that has kept women involved in domestic activities. Only limited numbers of Lebanese women have engaged in supplemental income generation, through either factory work or informal economic measures, to the degree experienced in some other Arab nations. The early and extensive exposure of Lebanese to international cultures and economics has resulted in a position of Lebanese women that is not easy to categorize.

Family matters and personal status are subordinated to Christian or Muslim patriarchy, based upon their respective sectarian and religious codes. This domain is excluded from state authority and results in a high level of national fragmentation. Any effort to impose state authority toward reform in these areas would risk throwing the entire precarious system out of order. In this context, Lebanese women, who earned the right to vote in 1957, are still virtually absent from elected and appointed governmental bodies. Some few may have been engaged in the recent military conflicts.

The majority of rural women in the labor force are still engaged in agriculture. In urban areas they are found in domestic services, education, clerical services, and in industry they are found in textiles. The political participation of Lebanese women has a long path ahead, yet advances have been made in reducing fertility as well as infant and maternal mortality in recent years. The level of female literacy and overall primary education (at least in the main urban areas) is probably as high in Lebanon as anywhere in the entire Middle East. Not surprisingly, the use of modern contraception is also quite widespread.

The Lebanese case in this book is represented by Suad Joseph's bioethnography of Marcel, who sought a survival strategy between the formal and informal portions of the Lebanese economy (chap. 12). It was not possible to conduct fieldwork during the long war, so Joseph's work refers to an early period in the 1970s, before war was heavily underway. Probably little has changed in the major pattern of gender relations or the structure of the economy since the war's end.

The Camp Trad site is a cross-section of Lebanon's diversity and socio-religious complexity. It represents the virtual dynastic nature of Lebanon's political economy. Marcel, the independent-minded working woman, proves the point that the informal economy is not of a dualistic nature but is a part of the wider unitary, capitalist system represented in the Levant. One of the chief insights of the Joseph paper is that women like Marcel must link the two domains by a *wasta* (broker) to preserve and maximize their economic and political options. Her ambiguous identity as a worker speaks of her flexibility and mobility within the complex economic circumstances in which she operated.

Tunisia

The position of women in Tunisia is relatively homogeneous as measured by religious and linguistic practice; virtually all profess their general allegiance to Islam and essentially all speak Arabic. However, Tunisia is quite different from the other nations in this work because of the postcolonial secularism introduced by the Bourguiba government in the 1950s and maintained by the successor Ben Ali administration. In Tunisia the status of *jihadat* (strugglers for self-improvement and against ignorance) took a special meaning unlike that of the mujahideen (or militant, armed strugglers) elsewhere in the Arab world.

A notable feature of Tunisia's secular path is that it is guided by comprehensive civil law that is highly adapted from Islamic Sharia law. In most other Arab nations, the personal status code is mainly built upon Sharia. Tunisia has outlawed polygyny and unilateral male divorce, similar to the positions taken in South Yemen, but the Tunisian case appears to be more deeply rooted. It has also signed the 1979 United Nations conventions seeking the elimination of all forms of discrimination against women. Tunisia has provided the right to vote for women since 1956 and has managed to have a number of women judges appointed. A few women have been elected to parliamentary seats in support of the ruling party, in addition to those activists in the National Union of Tunisian Women. The Tunisian Personal Status Law of 1956 (especially articles 12 and 18) paved the way for more progressive reform in 1968 (greater gender equality in divorce) and in 1981 (improved child custody provisions).[50]

Since 1960 women in the formal sector have a twelve-week pregnancy leave before and after birth. State-sector workers even have a child-care leave policy. Wage-earning cooperative workers also have a social security system in place. Public education and literacy programs, while not completely equal by gender, have made very considerable advances in Tunisia. Such liberal policies and programs are still to be achieved in some Western nations. Women may not legally marry if younger than seventeen years (men must be twenty), and the average age of marriage for females has already risen to twenty-four years, according to United Nations data. Tunisian women must attend their marriage ceremonies and must freely give their consent. The use of contraception in Tunisia is widespread, and fertility has decreased. Maternal and infant mortality among Tunisian women is generally declining, as is the overall rate of population growth. Given the many conservative traditions in gender relations in the Arab world, one must conclude that Tunisia has been a pioneer.

The Tunisian economy has long rested upon a history of labor export to France and southern Europe. This has left women in positions of relative importance in Tunisia. Recently Tunisia has shown such remarkable development that it may lose its "Third World" identity. Despite high levels of unemployment among youths, it can be characterized as a middle-income country; oil reserves are declining, and there is a heavy reliance on recreational and archaeological tourism.

Tunisia maintains a "benevolent authoritarian regime" that has accepted "structural adjustment" imposed by the International Monetary Fund. The Ben Ali government has endorsed privatization, partly in hopes of attracting sufficient capital to offset its foreign debt payments. This strategy has resulted in Tunisian manufactured goods accounting for 42 percent of its exports.[51] According to one source, there has been steady growth in the female labor force, which now exceeds that of men.[52] Forty percent of women in the labor force are in industry, largely the mass production of clothing, which makes heavy use of lower-cost female labor. The portion of females in the Tunisian labor force ranges from about one-fifth to one-quarter of all production workers and well over one-half of all manufacturing employees, while only about 15 percent of the salaried positions are occupied by women. A fifth to a quarter of economically active Tunisian women are engaged in agriculture, where their control of earnings is weak.

The downside of extensive female employment is that, even at low wages, they may experience industrial layoffs. Layoffs can expose them to unemployment and vulnerability to a degree not known when their activities were mainly at the household level. To absorb the shocks of marginal employment or unemployment, Tunisian women have created their own informal social security system based on visiting networks, which provide daily aid to friends and neighbors in economic need and a form of insurance against life crises. A rotating assistance union can be drawn upon as needs require.[53] This is not to say that such informal aid systems are fully adequate to meet all economic needs or to accommodate even temporary unemployment. The distribution of women workers in the Tunisian economy is more balanced by sector than in other nations represented in this book.

The relatively well educated, highly urbanized population of Tunisia has produced a number of leaders of the Tunisian expression of Islamic fundamentalism. This movement is based particularly among urban, middle-class, marginally employed youth, including some females. Unlike the leadership of Algeria or the Sudan, the Tunisian government has managed to deal with this complex issue with relative justice and relative respect for human rights, although some opposition groups, such as En-Nahda, would probably disagree. In Tunisia, the path to separation of religion and state, especially for women, has been traveled far enough that there is a broad base of opposition to religious extremism.

While Tunisia can be presented as a stable state, the civil war in neighboring Algeria is an alarming case of religious-political strife out of control. It keeps the Tunisian authorities in a condition of anxiety. At the same time, the difficult economic times just past and those lying immediately ahead act as grievances for a frustrated Islamicist group, En-Nahda. The existence of such revitalistic movements in Tunisia is proof of a society in transformation. This is particularly true for Tunisian women, who are defining their new social and economic position. In a study of mental disorders among Tunisian women, Mouinne Chelhi states:

> It is women—the greatest losers in traditional society—who wholeheartedly support the modern ideology, once they have truly discovered it, because it allows them to fight for their own desires, desires which the new norms have put on an equal footing with those of men. But it is women who also most threaten the authority of the father. . . . women pose the greatest threat to the patriarchal system, the greatest pressure is brought to bear upon them, to prevent them from acceding to that power of achieving their own ends. Our hypothesis is that the greatest stress to which Tunisian women are currently subjected stems from their exposure to two contradictory ideologies [i.e., one modern and one traditional].[54]

Such complaints are not easily vented in a state that is virtually ruled by one party. The effort by Tunisian women to earn a place in formal wage labor, and to survive in the informal economy, is an important indicator of the nature of the political and socioeconomic structure of modern Tunisia. Tunisian women in the invisible economy are deeply involved in crafts and small industries, which rely heavily on young women and low wages to sustain them. The largest portion of money earned does not usually stay with the women workers but is given back to meet family needs and is under family control. Even when work is performed in the formal sector, the returns can quickly be channeled into the informal or domestic economy.

Often women's object of employment is to earn enough money for marriage costs, and working is not considered as permanent or career-oriented. If not for economic exigencies, the young women might not be working at all; their wage work also diverts or delays them from continuing their formal education. There is also evidence in Tunisia of historical depth for women working out of the household.

The intensive research of Isabelle Berry-Chikhaoui on the informal economy inside the medina (old city core) of Tunis is instructive (see chap. 11).[55] She shows that rural-urban contrasts of the roles of Tunisian women are not great, especially in agricultural and textile work. The diverse, lively informal sector is essential in the commercial and service needs of the urban poor. The jobs available to women are strongly gender-stereotyped in food and clothing production throughout the entire region. Berry-Chikhaoui gives a great deal of attention to definitional and typological matters, which will assist other students doing comparative work. Her ethnographic detail on a street-by-street basis re-creates an authentic atmosphere of the exciting informal markets in Tunis.

Like Berry-Chikhaoui's, the work of Richard A. Lobban examines the informal economy in the suburbs (see chap. 10). Being constrained by male gender in the area of in-depth household interviews, Lobban's work uses an extensive methodology to give complementary views of working women in Tunisia.[56] The study finds women present in the "visible" public economy but in relatively low numbers. Tunisian women enter the formal economy based on their strengths in the domestic economy, that is, in the areas of food and clothing. In the instances of their greatest numbers in the weekly suburban markets (rather than daily street markets), women are often seen selling poultry, animals, and agricultural products, sales that reveal their important role in rural agriculture.

Lobban's study did not investigate the illegal economy to a great extent, nor did it view the area of domestic service, where women are found in great numbers. On the other hand, these weak areas are well covered in other works on Tunisian women, which neglect the role of women in public commerce. Thus, male researchers can add another perspective to this inquiry; both genders have unique contributions to make.

In Sophie Ferchiou's study of informal-sector work, domestic work, and the condition of Tunisian women, we learn of the cultural, socioeconomic, and religious context in which Tunisian women find themselves (see chap. 9).[57] This leads her to focus on sexual hierarchy, patriarchy, and gender dichotomy in Tunisia. Although Ferchiou considers that Tunisia has made notable progress in addressing these concerns, she stresses that Tunisian women still experience a degree of marginality and entrapment between modern development and their traditional identity. As do other contributions in this book, Ferchiou examines the dynamic, sometimes contradictory roles of females between salaried and domestic work, especially in the period since independence.

The rapid growth of jobs in textiles, tourism, administration, professions, and agriculture has certainly changed the position of Tunisian women, but gender barriers and discrimination remain. Ferchiou considers that this paradoxical situation can be resolved with an understanding of the "hybrid" process of modernization in which women are found: filling traditional and domestic roles while also being engaged in the formal sector to varying degrees, enhanced by increased levels of education. Her study helps to bridge the rural/urban, agricultural/industrial dichotomy by seeing an overall division of labor by gender, or "feminization" of "invisible" labor irrespective of location.

Yemen

Before 1963 the women of Yemen had barely any public role in urban life, and in rural society they were free insofar as their roles were performed mainly in agricultural tasks.[58] Although the mountains of northern Yemen are famed for their productivity, especially in coffee, it is young, mainly female labor that makes the land valuable. For centuries, the interior parts of Yemen were among the most isolated populated regions on earth. The vast majority of women were illiterate and thereby restrained from full participation in Yemeni society.

After the middle 1960s, Yemeni women began two very different sociopolitical experiences: one in the south, one in the north. After five years of armed struggle, the National Liberation Front (NLF) of (Southern) Yemen finally expelled the British from their strategic position in 1967, while British forces were otherwise occupied with Middle Eastern conflicts and the closure of the Suez Canal. A few women in the NLF became true national heroes in the war as messengers, spies, and even unit commanders. Instances of the mobilization of women were also found in the armed struggle in neighboring Oman at the same time.

A year after independence, the People's Democratic Republic of Yemen

(PDRY), or Southern Yemen, created the General Union of Yemeni Women (GUYW) in February 1968. The PDRY was launched on a startling new path unlike anything seen before in the Middle East. It quickly became known as the "Cuba of the Middle East," having the objective of building a new Arab society based on scientific socialism. Castelike social relations, feudal values, and a fragmented nation were all to be left behind in building a socialist and centralized state. If this revolution were to be successful, the position of women had to be transformed fundamentally—not only to create new allies for the revolutionary government but also to undermine the traditional power bases. Thus the PDRY attempted to create a Marxist-Leninist regime with the attendant objectives of radical liberation by gender and the elimination of traditional classes.

Clashes in 1968 and 1969 left the more militant wing of the NLF in power. By 1970 this led to nationalizations, the formation of cooperatives, and land reform laws designed to eliminate feudal land ownership. These laws immediately precipitated the 1970–72 peasant "uprisings" against rural landlords throughout the country, and conflict briefly erupted between both Yemens. Several provisions were made in the 1970 Yemeni constitution to protect the rights of women and stress their equality with men (articles 7, 29, 34, 36, 37 and 58). Article 13 endorsed the Universal Declaration of Human Rights. The first Yemeni woman judge was appointed during this period.

In 1970 universal suffrage was awarded to women in the south, and several national political associations were created to represent women's interests and link them with the ruling party. In January 1974 traditional family law, based in the Sharia, was the subject of nationwide debate, which resulted in numerous reforms celebrated in the first general congress of Yemeni women on 15 July 1974. This congress of the GUYM, led by Fatiha Abdalla, Nur Baabad, and Fatma Saeed El-Hag, stressed the legal measures taken to advance women's position. The strengthening of women's rights included the restriction of polygyny, raising the age of marriage to sixteen for women and twenty for men, requiring free consent for marriage, curtailing of unilateral divorce, expanded access to divorce for women, and the reduction of bridewealth to a token level. A national program of literacy and technical training was instituted for women. Women also took part in military training for the neighborhood defense militia. Thus, through the 1970s the traditional leaders and their value system were restricted. Under specific attack were all measures and means that reinforced inequality of women. The revolutionary constitution called for the mobilization of women as significant producers in the national economy. One reason was that large-scale labor migration of males to oil-producing nations demanded reconstruction of the Yemeni labor force. Another reason was the presence of ultraimpoverished, very low status *akhdam* (servant) women who were economic refugees from the countryside, desperate for employment.

In a 1975 visit to PDRY, I recall meeting women's groups in factory settings, handicraft cooperatives, and local defense militias. By 1977 women candidates were competing for electoral office, something unimaginable in neighboring Saudi Arabia. Inevitably these radical steps provoked some of the traditional Islamic leaders, who projected the new rulers as "anti-Muslim atheists" and who kept alliances in North Yemen, where socialist policies were not practiced. Interestingly, a number of other Muslim leaders in PDRY accommodated the reforms, and Islam remained the official state religion.

In the Yemen Arab Republic (YAR), or North Yemen, the traditional values and practices were left basically intact. The country became a republic in 1962 and soon fell into a long civil war. The war itself devolved into Egypt's "Vietnam" when Egypt backed the republicans against Saudi-backed Royalists led by Iman al Badr. Amidst these conflicts the YAR managed to steer a slow-moving course between Saudi feudalism and PDRY radicalism. Perhaps as many as 250,000 men from the YAR emigrated to oil-rich nations in the Arab peninsula in search of cash employment to sustain their families. Their absence from home played a role in their wives' independence and liberation, while the men's foreign experiences and disposable income added momentum to the forces of change. According to the YAR Ministry of Civil Service, women's share of government employment rose from 6.1 percent in 1975 to 11.1 percent in 1983.[59] Of these few employed women, most were in the ministries of health and education. Women were legally prohibited from positions in medicine and in the judiciary, according to Thaira A. Shaalan.[60]

In 1990 the dream of all Yemenis, a unified Yemen, seemed to be achieved, but the political differences were challenging and a new civil war resulted. Despite the efforts of the GUYW, it remained subordinate to the nationalist movement and did not fully articulate its urban-based program in the countryside, although advance was made on a literacy program targeting women.

The crushing weight of Yemeni poverty has placed a very heavy burden on the shoulders of the country's women. Mortality and fertility rates are still high, although declining. Fertility differentials are noted by class and region, and use of contraception is slight. Yemeni women have begun the march toward progress, but the way ahead is long indeed.

The contribution on Yemen by Delores Walters (chap. 3) is based upon her research in 'Abs and near Ta'izz, (North) Yemen, during 1982–84. Walters surveys the complex intersection of gender and economic relations, then goes beneath the surface to study the akhdam women who survive at the lowest levels of economic invisibility. In her fascinating research, Walters reminds us that ethnicity and race must be seen as part of the equation, especially for those at the margins of society. As an African-American woman, Walters brings critical sensitivity to the topic of a pariah population.

As elsewhere in the Middle East, women in Yemen are generally deval-ued by society, as reflected in the levels of compensation for their work in social and municipal services, clothing manufacture, and agriculture. Walters's special message is that she compels us to see Arab society in its full reality from the bottom up, not only the male imams and sheikhs but the full, gender- and race-based hierarchy that has launched the akhdam into the urban informal economy of Yemen. The hardships they have faced have added to an incipient spirit of social solidarity that allows a degree of optimism for the future.

Summary

The level of participation in the labor force is an important, but not always consistent, indicator of the general status of women in society. Especially is this true in the Middle East, where class, ethnic, and racial variables must be considered and where religion generally legitimates tradition. There is great change underway through industrialization, labor migration, civil strife, and the effects of tourism and petroleum in certain cases. Yet it is broadly recognized that the general participation of women in the labor force in the Middle East is at one of the lowest levels among all global regions. Without great change, the gap between the Middle Eastern nations and, for example, the Pacific rim nations will only be widened as the posi-tion of Middle Eastern women becomes more anachronistic.[61] The articles in this book suggest that the process of transformation is well underway but hardly uniform.

Turkey, not represented in the following chapters, is the most industrial-ized and diversified of the Middle Eastern, or at least Islamic, nations. Turkey has likewise progressed farthest in respecting religion while cautiously removing it from matters of state, beginning with the reforms introduced early in the century by Kamal Ataturk. The anthropological work of Jenny White[62] on women's labor in poor, working-class neighborhoods in Istanbul is rich documentation that money unites and liberates women to an unprecedented extent. The small family-based enterprises that White observed were often built upon kinship ties, required low capital, and had low risk. Such means allow women an active role in transforming themselves, their identity as producers, and their status, despite the complex interconnections of international finance, regional power, and patriarchy that restrict their advances.

Clearly the portion of economically active women in Turkey is at one of the highest regional levels; there is a particularly high level of women in agriculture and carpet making, where they participate largely for informal compensation. The comparative position of women in Turkey can be taken as a vanguard of overall development. As their role increases in the formal economy, especially manufacturing and the professions, the national labor force is expanded and diversified, and the nation progresses in import substitution, expanded tax bases, broad democratic empowerment, and improvements in social services for all. The role of Islam and its value system of patriarchy can be one of partnership with these changes; otherwise, the risk is one of winning power with icons but failing to provide a model for economic development, technological innovation, and a globalized world in the decades ahead.

This work on women in the Middle Eastern informal economy provides evidence of diversity in women's experiences. It shows that women in this sector have become involved as a creative survival mechanism, stranded between traditional commerce and services and a modern state with a capitalist market economy. This situation can lead to economic stagnation, or it can provide the thin, entering wedge into the wider public arena—monopolized by men, denied to women—that is a doorway to the future of women and to overall national development for both genders.

Clearly the nature of the subject of this book is a moving target. The definitions have not been pinned down to everyone's satisfaction, but a common understanding has guided us. The methodology is inconsistent because ethnographic, quantitative, and various qualitative approaches all have their place. The historical evolution of the informal sector has neither a precise beginning and certainly no imminent end. The activities of women in the shadow economy are problematic in strict research terms.

Without question, women are vastly underrepresented in formal statistical surveys, and the endless labor that they perform is diminished by a patriarchal and gender-based division of labor that has placed unusual burdens upon working women. Yet among Middle Eastern women there is important variation by class stratification, by national and regional origin, by educational level, and by the nature of training and employment.

Neither is the role of Islam and its supposed unitary value system a homogeneous factor. It has such range in application that it is as much a traditional effect as it is a cause of Middle Eastern social values. The values themselves are in a state of remarkable ferment. Women's creative responses to complex and varied circumstances, their engagement in the Middle East as their own history makers, warrant optimism for the future. It is hoped that this book is more than simply good social science but also that the contributors have assisted in revealing the successes and the difficulties ahead in struggling for a region, and a world, of greater gender equality.

Notes

1. Nawal El Saadawi, "The Political Challenges Facing Arab Women at the End of the 20th Century," in Nahid Toubia, ed., *Women of the Arab World* (London: Zed Press, 1988), 8–26, quote on p. 16.

2. UNESCO, *Social Science Research and Women in the Arab World* (Dover, N.H.: Francis Pinter Publishers, 1984).

3. K. Hart, "Informal Income Opportunities and Urban Employment in Ghana," *Journal of Modern African Studies* 11 (1973): 61–89.

4. Stuart W. Sinclair, *Bibliography on the "Informal" Sector,* Centre for Developing-Area Studies Bibliography Series no. 10 (Montreal: McGill University, 1978).

5. Alan Gilbert and Josef Gugler, *Cities, Poverty and Development: Urbanization in the Third World,* 2nd ed. (New York: Oxford University Press, 1992), 94–100.

6. Some of the works that have brought this topic into focus are R. Bromley and C. Gerry, *Casual Work and Poverty* (New York: Third World Cities, 1979); D. W. Drakis-Smith, "Socio-economic Problems, the Role of the Informal Sector," in G. H. Blake and R. I. Lawless, eds., *The Changing Middle Eastern City* (New York: Barnes and Noble, 1980), 92–119; *Supporting the Informal Sector in Low Income Settlements* (Nairobi: United Nations Centre for Human Settlements, 1986); A. Portes, M. Castells, and L. A. Benton, eds., *The Informal Economy: Studies in Advanced and Less Developed Countries* (Baltimore: Johns Hopkins University Press, 1989), 11–37; S. V. Sethuraman, *Basic Needs and the Informal Sector: The Case of Low-Income Housing in Developing Countries* (Geneva: International Labor Office, 1985); and John D. Sullivan, ed., *Building Constituencies for Economic Change: Report on the International Conference on the Informal Sector,*

Center for International Private Enterprise and USAID (Washington: U.S. Chamber of Commerce, 1987).

7. Janet Abu-Lughod, "Migrant Adjustment to City Life: The Egyptian Case," *American Journal of Sociology* 67 (1961): 22–32.

8. Richard A. Lobban, ed., "Studies in African Urbanization: Class Formation," *International Journal of Sociology* 7, no. 2 (Summer 1977).

9. Richard A. Lobban, "The Dialectics of Migration and Social Associations in the Urban Sudan," *International Journal of Sociology* 7, no. 2 (Summer 1977): 99–120.

10. Jacques Charmes, *Methods et résultats d'une meilleure évaluation des ressources humaines dans le secteur non structure d'une économie en voie de développement* (Tunis: Institute national de la statistique de Tunisie [INS] and Office de la recherche scientifique et technique outre-mer [ORSTOM], 1983); Jacques Charmes, "Employment and Income in the Informal Sector of the Maghreb and Mashreq Countries," *Cairo Papers in Social Science* 14, no. 4 (1992): 21–45.

11. This chart first appeared in Michael E. Bonine, ed., *Population, Poverty, and Politics in the Middle East* (Gainesville: University Press of Florida, 1997), 90.

12. Leila Ahmed, *Women and Gender in Islam: Historical Roots of a Modern Debate* (New Haven: Yale University Press, 1992).

13. Ibid., 248.

14. Judith E. Tucker, ed., *Arab Women: Old Boundaries, New Frontiers* (Bloomington: Indiana University Press, 1993).

15. Evelyn Aleene Early, "Getting It Together: *Baladi* Egyptian Businesswomen," in Tucker, *Arab Women: Old Boundaries, New Frontiers;* Evelyn Aleene Early, *Baladi Women of Cairo: Playing with an Egg and a Stone* (Cairo: American University Press, 1993).

16. Carolyn Fluehr-Lobban, "Toward a Theory of Arab-Muslim Women as Activists in Secular and Religious Movements," *Arab Studies Quarterly* 15, no. 2 (1993): 87–106.

17. Fatima Mernissi, *Beyond the Veil: Male-Female Dynamics in a Modern Muslim Society* (New York: Schenkman Publishers, 1975).

18. Ibid., 84–89.

19. Elizabeth Warnock Fernea, *A Street in Marrakech: A Personal View of Urban Women in Morocco* (Prospect Heights, Illinois: Waveland Press, 1988).

20. El Amouri Institute, "Women's Role in the Informal Sector in Tunisia," in Joycelin Massiah, ed., *Women in Developing Economies: Making Visible the Invisible* (Providence, R.I.: Berg Publishers and UNESCO, 1993), 135–65.

21. Valentine M. Moghadam, *Modernizing Women: Gender and Social Change in the Middle East* (Boulder: Lynne Rienner Publishers, 1993), 15.

22. Khalid Ikram, *Egypt: Economic Management in a Period of Transition,* World Bank Country Economic Report (Baltimore: Johns Hopkins University Press, 1980), 110.

23. Arlene Elowe MacLeod, *Accommodating Protest: Working Women, the New Veiling, and Change in Cairo* (New York: Columbia University Press, 1991).

24. Ibid., 50.

25. Heba Handoussa and Gillian M. Potter, *Egypt's Informal Sector: Engine of Growth,* paper presented at the October meetings of the Middle East Studies Association, Portland, Ore., 1992.

26. Earl L. Sullivan and Karima Korayem, "Women and Work in the Arab World," *Cairo Papers in Social Science* 4, no. 4 (1981): 17.

27. Deniz Kandiyoti, ed., *Women, Islam and the State* (Philadelphia: Temple University Press, 1991).

28. Sullivan and Korayem, "Women and Work," 10.

29. Ibid., 215–17.

30. El Saadawi, "Political Challenges," 9–11.

31. Ibid., 24.

32. Margot Badran, "Competing Agenda: Feminists, Islam and the State in Nineteenth- and Twentieth-Century Egypt," in Deniz Kandyoti, ed., *Women, Islam and the State* (Philadelphia: Temple University Press, 1991).

33. Moghadam, *Modernizing Women,* 158.

34. Ibid., 44–47.

35. CAPMAS stands for the Central Agency for Public Mobilization and Statistics, the the main governmental statistical survey body for Egypt.

36. Mahmoud Abdel Fadil, "Informal Sector Employment in Egypt," *Cairo Papers in Social Science* 6, no. 2 (1983): 55–89.

37. Sullivan and Korayem, "Women and Work," 29.

38. Ibid., 35.

39. Barbara Ibrahim, "Social Change and the Industrial Experience: Women as Productive Workers in Urban Egypt" (Ph.D. dissertation, Indiana University, 1980).

40. Mostafa Kharoufi, "The Informal Dimension of Urban Activitity in Egypt: Some Recent Work," *Cairo Papers in Social Science* 14, no. 4 (1991): 12.

41. Helmi R. Tadros, Mohamed Fateeha, and Allen Hibbard, "Squatter Markets in Cairo," *Cairo Papers in Social Science* 13, no. 1 (1990); Georg Stauth, "Informal Economy and Social Life in a Popular Quarter of Cairo" (working paper, Faculty of Sociology, University of Bielefeld, 1986); Gunter Meyer, "Waste-recycling as a Livelihood in the Informal Sector: The Example of Refuse Collectors in Cairo," *Applied Geography and Development* 30 (1987): 78–94; Gunter Meyer, "Employment in Small-Scale Manufacturing in Cairo: A Socio-economic Survey," *British Society for Middle Eastern Studies Bulletin* 14, no. 2 (1988): 136–46.

42. Sarah F. Loza, "Urban Street Food Vendors: Case Study from Egypt," *Cairo Papers in Social Science* 14, no. 4 (1991): 46–52.

43. Nicholas S. Hopkins, "Markets, Marketing, the Market: Informal Egypt," *Cairo Papers in Social Science* 14, no. 4 (1991): 104–26.

44. Carolyn Fluehr-Lobban, "Agitation for Change in the Sudan," in Alice Schlegel, ed., *Sexual Stratification: A Cross-Cultural View* (New York: Columbia University Press, 1977), 127–43.

45. There is a rapidly growing literature on female circumcision, or female genital mutilation, especially among Western feminists and human rights activists. Written by a woman physician, a well-researched book on the Sudanese practice is Asma El-Dareer, *Woman, Why Do You Weep?* (London: Zed Press, 1983).

46. See Nahid Toubia, "Women and Health in Sudan," in Nahid Toubia, ed., *Women of the Arab World* (London: Zed Press, 1988).

47. A comprehensive account of the relationship between women and Islam is found in Carolyn Fluehr-Lobban, *Islamic Law and Society in the Sudan* (London: Frank Cass, 1987), and in Carolyn Fluehr-Lobban, "A Comparison of the Development of Muslim Family Law in Tunisia, Egypt and the Sudan," *Law and Anthropology Yearbook* 7 (1994): 353–70.

48. Nada Mustafa Ali's work was first presented as a paper, "Women's Strategies for Survival during Crisis in Sudan: Five Women from Atbara Talk," at the Third International Meeting of the Sudan Studies Association, Boston, 21–24 April 1994.

49. The relation of balanced socioreligious and political fragmentation in Lebanon is discussed in Kandiyoti, *Women, Islam and the State*, 188–94.

50. Fluehr-Lobban, "Development of Muslim Family Law," 353–70.

51. Moghadam, *Modernizing Women*, 36.

52. Ibid., 33–34, 40, 44.

53. Paula Holmes-Eber, "Women's Visiting Networks in Tunisia: The Informal Social Security System (paper presented at the 35th African Studies Association meeting, Seattle, 1992).

54. Mouinne Chelhi, "The Modern Tunisian Woman between Hysteria and Depression," in Nahid Toubia, ed., *Women of the Arab World* (London: Zed Books, 1988), 116.

55. The original work of Isabelle Berry, "The Informal Sector in the Southern Urban Periphery of the Medina in Tunis," was part of doctoral field research at the University of Tours, Center for Urban Research in the Arab World. I am grateful for the translation of this work by Ghislaine Geloin of the Modern Language Department, Rhode Island College.

56. The data on women presented here are from Richard A. Lobban, "Responding to Middle Eastern Urban Poverty: The Informal Economy in Tunis," in Michael Bonine, ed., *Population, Poverty, and Politics in the Middle East* (Gainesville: University Press of Florida, 1997).

57. Sophie Ferchiou, who wrote "Travail 'invisible,' travail 'a domicile' et condition des femmes en Tunisie" for this book, is well known for her research on this topic.

58. Exceptional cases were the Aden Women's Association, founded in 1958, and the 1959 anticolonial demonstration organized by women. In rural areas in the YAR, agriculture accounted for 98.5 percent of the female labor force, according to the Yemen Central Authority for Planning, *Study on Women's Participation in Economic Activities* (1983).

59. (North) Yemen Ministry of Civil Service, *A Statistical Study on Working Yemenite Women during the Period 1975–1983,* p. 40.

60. Thaira A. Shaalan, "Yemenite Women: Employment and Future Challenges," in Nahid Toubia, ed., *Women of the Arab World* (London: Zed Books 1988), 117–23.

61. Ibid., 30–31.

62. Jenny B. White, *Money Makes Us Relatives: Women's Labor in Urban Turkey* (Austin: University of Texas Press, 1994).

PART I

Strategies for Survival: Women at the Margins

How do women function when survival is the main mission? Anne Jennings tells us about the clever strategies devised by Nubian women in the shadow economy of southern Egypt. They are remarkably productive and control significant wealth, generated in part from tourism. Her observations confront those who barely perceive such women's presence and who imagine that they have no income to control.

Barbara Michael discovers a very intricate system for marketing dairy products among the Baggara women of the western Sudan, who survive within an economy of rural nomadism. They are highly conscious of market costs, rewards, and pricing. They are far more productive and aware than one might imagine.

Delores Walters looks at the margins to describe the North Yemeni women of slave origins, the *akhdam* who survive through handicrafts and by performing tasks that others refuse. Her access to this unique community is penetrating and moving. Her work makes for intriguing interfaces among models of race, ethnicity, and the "invisible" economy.

Nada Mustafa Ali documents the lives of women in Atbara, Sudan, who are at the periphery of the economy and who are suffering from great hardships in the contemporary Sudan. Despite their heavy burdens, they achieve survival.

1

Nubian Women and the Shadow Economy

Anne M. Jennings

The study of female contributions to household economies in the Middle East is a new field, but already it is overturning old stereotypes about the Muslim woman's participation in the economic upkeep of her family. Not only is more attention being paid to the ways in which women support their families with their unpaid labor, but researchers are now also looking at the methods women employ to contribute money that they have earned themselves. In spite of the ideology in the Muslim world asserting that women do not have to earn money outside the home, thousands of women throughout the Middle East do so; nevertheless, the stereotype that the Muslim woman does not work persists.

One of the reasons that such stereotypes have been unchallenged for so long is that Muslim women who do work outside their homes have done so in ways unreported to governmental agencies or tax collectors. This work, in the "informal sector" or "invisible economy," long recognized in the area of male employment,[1] is now being investigated by researchers who are interested in women's work as well.[2] Another reason for the persistence of gender stereotypes concerning the Muslim woman's lack of income-earning activities is that Muslim males have often denied that their female relatives and wives work outside the home, and male anthropologists have often repeated such statements of ideology as if they were a fact of life for all Muslim women.

This paper discusses some of the informal activities by which Nubian village women in southern Egypt make money, as well as the ways they choose to use the money. I believe that, while Nubian women say they work in order to have extra income, one of the unrecognized results of the use of their money is the reaffirmation of gender parity in Nubian village life.

First, however, I want to address the definition of the terms *invisible* and *informal* as applied to the economy, for which I suggest the alternative term *shadow economy.* The informal economy may be defined as a variety of occupations in which people work for goods instead of money or for money that is not reported to the government. It has been used in the literature synonymously and interchangeably with the term *informal sector,* which in turn has been defined as "those activities which are not officially noticed through registration and taxation procedures, and which range from small-scale businesses to sporadic individual and sometimes illegal activities." Formal-sector economic activities, on the other hand, "take place within a visible institutional hierarchy or structure of some kind (a ministry, a firm, etc.) which are licensed, and which (if appropriate) may keep accounts."[3] Most of the investigation into the informal sector in the Muslim world has been carried out with male occupations in mind; thus, questions concerning the definitions of these terms have been mainly concerned with economic and statistical analyses. However, when attention focuses upon female remunerative occupations, other kinds of questions arise.

Such questions arise in part because of the nature of Islamic society, which many investigators have characterized as one of divided gender domains: the "private" sphere and the "public" sphere. The private sphere is considered the woman's domain and encompasses the house and gardens. It is associated with intimate human relationships, the love of close kin, and domestic pursuits. The public sphere, on the other hand, is associated with all that happens outside the home, in the marketplace, the town, the fields, and the mosque. It is the area of business and political activity and of social relationships with nonkin, and it is considered the male domain.[4] It is beyond the scope of this chapter to discuss this model, the misconceptions and controversy concerning the characteristics of these spheres and the accuracy of the terms used to describe them, and the nature of gender segregation in the Muslim world in general. For an overall presentation of the controversy, see Carol Mukhopadhyay and Patricia Higgens.[5]

Controversy notwithstanding, most researchers would agree that the model is accurate as an overall picture of the structure of Muslim societies, and more accurate for some societies than for others. Complicating this problem, these same terms are defined differently by researchers who are interested in the anthropology of work than they are by investigators who are interested in the status of women in Muslim societies. The terms *informal sphere* and *informal sector* have been used interchangeably with the term *private sphere* by the latter, as indicators of the female domain of activity and influence. In like manner, the terms *formal sphere* and *formal sector* have been used synonymously in the literature with *public sphere* as indicators of the male area of influence in Muslim society. The terms *formal sector* and *informal sector,* when employed by economists, were not originally intended to locate actions in any specific physical area; they do, however, involve ideas of physical space when used to discuss women's roles. Thus, the usage of these terms can become confusing and problematical to investigators who focus upon women's work.

There are two reasons for this. First, much of women's work does tend to be located in the private or informal sphere, but it may or may not be informal-sector activity. For instance, a woman who does piecework in her home for a factory that pays her and reports these payments to the government in an above-board manner may be part of the formal sector, although she works in the private or informal sphere. On the other hand, much of the work that women do in the public or formal sphere (selling on street corners, agricultural labor) is part of the informal sector. Male informal-sector activities, on the other hand, rarely if ever take them into the private or informal spheres of their societies. It is important to define our terms such that the informal sector and informal economy, as economic activities, are distinguished from the informal sphere and private sphere, as physical and social entities. Terminology must reflect the areas where these coincide and where they diverge. The same is true for the definitions of formal sector and formal economy as distinct from formal sphere and public sphere.

Second, the discussion of the nature of gender-defined spaces and areas of influence in the Muslim world has not yet led to definitions that are totally accepted. Terminology is at best fuzzy, and it depends upon the particular situation involved and the inclination of the researcher. For instance, women who work as domestics might be said to be working in either the public-formal sphere or the private-informal sphere, depending upon the definition of these spheres. While some investigators might say that they are working in the public-formal sphere because they leave the privacy of their homes to go to work, others would argue that they are still in the private-informal sphere because they are working in a home (rather than in the fields), doing domestic chores. Since we have not yet reached consensus on such definitions, the usage of such words as *public/private* and *formal/informal* creates even more confusion when we attempt to apply them in a cross-disciplinary context.

The term *shadow economy,* instead of *informal economy* or *informal sector,* is valuable in the description of women's unreported remunerative occupations because it avoids the assumption that women's work is always located in the private-informal sphere. In fact, this designation will avoid questions concerning the physical areas in which any individual's unreported money-making activities take place. The term *shadow economy* is, in addition, more indicative of the elusive, almost hidden, nature of many of the occupations involved. Although they are not at all secret, of course, to those who use the services provided, they do tend to be hidden from governmental agencies and tax collectors. I will also avoid using the terms *public* and *private* spheres to refer to the male and female domains of Muslim societies. I would prefer to refer to them as gendered domains, in order to highlight their importance as areas of social and economic influence, not simply physical spaces.

Women's Shadow Economy Activities

In spite of the stereotypes of the Muslim woman's lack of remunerative occupations, many thousands of women throughout the Muslim world earn money at various endeavors, ranging from selling matches on street corners to the professional world of medicine, law, and academia. These occupations, in many cases, tend to be denied by male relatives because of the "suspicion, mistrust, and fear that paid employment outside of the home represents for the family and the community at large. The issue at stake for the family head involves more than a challenge to his ability to provide economically for his relatives; more critically it is a challenge to his control over the whereabouts and consequent behavior of his women."[6] Women's labor has, for the most part, continued to be denied easily and to remain hidden because so much of it involves the shadow economy; since much of female life in Islamic societies has been inaccessible to male anthropologists, they have inaccurately repeated the ideology that Muslim women are solely dependent upon their male relatives or husbands. Female anthropologists have, however, told a different story, and it is mainly our research that has brought awareness of the realities of women's work. Among the many examples are the studies of the Hausa of northern Nigeria, whose money-making activities—production of food for sale by their children outside the home; sales of such commodities as soap, sugar, and cigarettes; and the embroidery and sewing of clothing—are carried on while the women remain in strictest seclusion. These women are heavily dependent upon their children to help them in this work, and they use the resulting cash income to invest in goods for their daughters' dowries and to build up capital for reinvestment in their own economic enterprises.[7]

Even when women step out of seclusion in order to earn a living, their occupations tend to be small-scale and undocumented. Moroccan women, for example, have been shown to make money in the female domain as seamstresses, fortune tellers, midwives, musicians, and bath attendants; in the male domain, as field laborers and prostitutes.[8] But their activities are rarely reported to the government or to tax collectors. In Egypt, women's remunerative occupations in the women's sphere include sewing, fortune telling, washing clothing, and midwifery. They enter the male domain to carry water or to sell small articles and food on street corners,[9] yet their work, too, often remains part of the shadow economy. Nubian women of southern Egypt also engage in small-scale occupations that bring them an irregular, unofficial income. Like women throughout the Muslim world, Nubian village women make money as seamstresses, midwives, and fortune tellers in the privacy of their homes, having had the right to earn some income since pre-Islamic times; since the increase of tourism to Aswan, they have expanded their money-making activities to include the tourist trade. This chapter discusses some of the methods by which the women of the village of West Aswan make money through the shadow economy, and how they use this money.

The Nubians

The Nubians are an ancient and important people in this area of the world. The Nubian homeland of the nineteenth and twentieth centuries, before the building of the Aswan High Dam, extended some 700 miles along the Nile River from the First Cataract, near Aswan, to the Fourth Cataract, in the Republic of Sudan. In ancient times, it continued as far as the Sixth Cataract, beyond the site of ancient Meroë, almost to what is now Khartoum. Archaeological evidence indicates that the Nile corridor has been continuously inhabited since the Late Paleolithic, and it is at this early time (25–16,000 BP) that we see evidence of the beginnings of a uniquely Nubian culture.[10]

Ancient Egypt, the other great power in this region, became a nation state somewhat earlier than did Nubia, then known as Kerma, but when Kerma became the Kingdom of Kush, it endured as a political entity of remarkable stability. Kushite monarchs reigned for close to 1,200 consecutive years, far longer than any of Egypt's three periods of unified kingdoms. Ancient Kush and pharaonic Egypt were entwined in a symbiotic relationship that lasted for millennia. They alternately traded and warred with each other, exchanging human knowledge and expertise as well as gold, copper, ivory, and other material goods, for almost 5,000 years. Nubians lived, farmed, and worked in the Nile valley as administrators at the court of the pharaoh, as priests and priestesses in Egyptian temples, and as mercenaries in Egypt's armies. During times of dynastic upheaval in Egypt, northern Nile valley peoples fled to Kushite kingdoms, where they too worked as administrators and craftspeople at court, as clergy in the temples, and as soldiers in southern armies. The periods of Nubia's greatest prosperity came when Egypt was weakest, and vice versa. Egyptian hieroglyphic texts mention the Empire of Kush as one of the traditional enemies, and Egyptian imperialism devastated Nubia three times throughout their history. In turn, Kush conquered Egypt in the eighth and seventh centuries B.C., when it ruled for almost a century as the Twenty-fifth Dynasty.

Early Christian missionaries wrote about the conversion of Nubia to Christianity in the sixth century A.D., and we know of three Christian kingdoms along the Nubian Nile at the time of the Arab conquest of Egypt in 642. The Nubians at Soba resisted Islam until the start of the sixteenth century, when, through a combination of peaceful intermarriage and conquest, they were brought into the fold of the Islamic polity.

The modern Nubian language is divided into three speech groups: "For the first 145 kilometers south from Aswan, the dialect spoken is Kenuzi and the people call themselves Kenuz. . . . The next reach, stretching [425 kilometers,] is occupied by Nubians who speak Mahasi, a language of several mutually intelligible dialects which is sometimes called Fadija. The last Nubian reach of about 350 kilometers is inhabited by persons who speak Dongolawi [or Rotana] and call themselves Danagla."[11]

Today, Nubian villages dot the Nile from Kom Ombo in Egypt to Dongola in the Sudan, as close to the water as possible. Traditionally, their economy involved a combination of subsistence farming, animal husbandry, and date production. But because of the difficulties of farming in such an arid environment, Nubian men had for centuries sought employment outside of Nubia, returning to their homeland only periodically. In pharaonic times they were mercenaries; at other times they were enslaved (meaning that they never returned home), and after the slave trade was outlawed at the end of the eighteenth century, they became personal servants. Although many Nubian men today are servants, waiters, hotel employees, and doormen, they are entering the civil service, professional life, and politics in greater numbers.[12] The majority of Nubians live in the Republic of Sudan.

This chapter discusses research in Egyptian Nubia, the area of southern Egypt extending from the town of Aswan, approximately 560 miles south of Cairo, to the border of Sudan, a further 193 miles. Most of this territory is now under the waters of Lake Nasser, as a result of the construction of the Aswan High Dam in 1964. Most of the people of Egyptian Nubia, who are Kenuz, were relocated when their homeland was flooded. Approximately 50,000 were resettled in the thirty-three villages that were built to accommodate them near the town of Kom Ombo. A sizable population still remains in the villages surrounding Aswan, which, being north of the High Dam, is in no danger of inundation. In one of these villages, West Aswan, I conducted fieldwork in 1981–82 and 1986–87.

The Village of West Aswan

West Aswan lies directly across the Nile from Aswan and extends north-ward along the river for approximately seven miles. It is divided into eigh-teen hamlets, the southernmost being Gubba. This hamlet, where I lived, is the closest to Aswan. The men of Gubba still do some farming, but they depend heavily upon wage income from jobs at the nearby chemical fertil-izer plant; the High Dam; the airport and train station; and hotels, restau-rants, and hospitals. Others are teachers or office workers. The people of Gubba make most of their money, however, from the tourist trade.

Visitors have been coming to the west bank of Aswan for many centuries in order to see the pharaonic tombs and the monastery of St. Simeon. Nubians have been meeting tourists there in order to offer aid and advice, or simply to satisfy their own curiosity, for almost as long. It wasn't until the High Dam at Aswan was built that the tourist industry began to bloom. In 1986 between thirty and forty tourist cruise ships sailed up and down the Nile between Luxor and Aswan, the largest of which carried 200 people. In addition, visitors came to Aswan by airplane, train, tour bus, and hired car. They came to see the tombs, the monastery, Abu Simbel, Philae, the High Dam, and the Nubian villages.

Nubian men make tourist money most directly as cab drivers, boatmen, and tour guides, and women open their homes to visits by tour groups. Traditional Nubian houses are quite large, with several rooms opening onto a central, sandy-floored courtyard. The older homes have several of these room-and-courtyard complexes, the whole surrounded by a high wall. The better homes are built of mud brick, plastered over with clay and then painted, similar in appearance to the pueblos of the Southwestern United States. At some point in the past, the Nubians learned that foreign visitors were surprised and delighted to behold these structures; pride in their homes, coupled with Islamic traditions of hospitality, resulted in invi-tations to have "real Nubian tea." How and when women decided to earn money from this practice, I don't know. Furthermore, while most of the women I knew in Gubba sought to earn money when they could, only a minority of them invited tourists into their homes. There was no single explanation for them to do so, other than the desire for money. These were not destitute women, lacking males to turn to, nor were they considered immoral for inviting tourists into their homes. Although Nubian men said that they adhered to Islamic ideology involving women's money-making activities, few of them prevented their wives and sisters from engaging in them. One explanation is simply changing times: "Gamal Abdel Nasser decreed that women could go to work," replied one husband to my question. "So why not?" he shrugged.

Another reason may be Nubian women's traditional right to earn money under certain circumstances. Because men have in times past sought work outside of Nubia, women were often left on their own in the villages, in this way "passively" gaining a measure of economic independence. Men regularly sent money home to their families, but these remittances were not always sufficient to make ends meet. It seems there was an understanding

Nubian woman of West Aswan. Photo: Anne Jennings.

that women could supplement their incomes through their own efforts, in at least two ways. First, they could sell what they had raised or grown. They raised sheep and goats, which they sold to neighbors or to men who came to the village expressly for the purpose of buying. The women grew produce in their fields, which they took to market. Second, women could be partners in the ownership of date palms: "The ownership of a palm tree was usually based on a three-way partnership between a land-owner, the owner of a palm-shoot, and the person (usually a woman) who watered the shoot constantly over the many months before it got its growth and could draw sufficient moisture through its own roots."[13] When part of the crop from these trees was sold, the woman who had watered the shoots got a share of the proceeds. This was probably a pre-Islamic practice that continued into modern times because of the women's need to supplement the income received from their husbands.

Since the building of the Aswan High Dam, many more jobs have been available for men in the Aswan area. Even though a woman's husband may now be living at home and working in Aswan, however, she may still seek money for her own uses. Village women still take their harvests of produce and farm animals into Aswan, to the Nubian women's market on Thursday mornings. They gather to sell mainly eggs and fowl, as well as vegetables. Women also crochet small Nubian caps and small round bags in brilliant colors, sold from stalls lining the streets of the market area where tourists congregate. While women do not sell these objects directly to tourists in the marketplace, they do not hesitate to sell them to the tour groups that come to the village, their "gendered territory." They also attempt to sell ropes of beads they have bought wholesale (or received in exchange for their caps and bags) from vendors in Aswan.

Throughout the year, but most heavily in the winter and spring, groups of tourists are brought to Gubba by boatmen to see the village, the houses, and the people. The tour group leader always speaks first with the *rayyis* (the man who owns the boat), who then tells the boatman where to take the tour group—which village and which house. The rayyis sends the groups to the houses of his relatives, usually his sisters, who have agreed in advance to receive them. These women serve the tourists *karkaday* (tea made from the *Hibiscus sabdariffa*) or tea with mint, then take the group on tours of their large and spacious homes. More substantial meals may be prepared and served if a tourist has contracted a boat for the entire day, or if the rayyis recognizes the tourist from previous trips, but this is rare. The women who make tea or meals and conduct the tours hope for an ample tip from the tourists, as well as selling them ropes of beads and crocheted

Nubian woman and daughter crocheting bag for the tourist trade. Photo: Anne Jennings.

items. They also receive a percentage of the fee that the group pays the rayyis.

The volume of tourist traffic differs from month to month. The high season, from December to April, brings an average of three groups per day into Gubba. In 1986 political turmoil in the Middle East led directly to a decrease in tourism in Egypt, but some visitors made trips to Gubba nonetheless. During December, the heaviest month, I counted approximately 400 people visiting various houses in the village. One informant told me that she might earn an average of 3 £E (Egyptian pounds) per day, including her share of money from the rayyis. This is a considerable sum for a village woman—about 90 £E per month.[14] Not every woman in Gubba is engaged in this activity, however; of the twenty-two women I knew well there, only ten invited tour groups into their homes on a regular basis, although fourteen of them sold caps, bags, and beads to tourists in the village square.

What do the women of Gubba do with their money? Ideologically, the money that women make is their own, to spend as they want, but the appropriate purchases are little luxury items for themselves—perfumed soap, a new dress—so as not to challenge the role of their husbands as family providers. Women told me, however, that generally the money went for necessities: food or clothing and schoolbooks for their children. One of my informants bought medicine for her sick mother with her earnings. With any money left after necessities, a woman may make two kinds of investments: gold jewelry for herself or enlargements for the home that she and her husband own.

The most efficient way for a woman in Gubba to save enough money for future investment is through a money-making group, the *jam'iyya*. This is a rotating credit association into which a woman pays a fixed amount for a certain period of time (for instance, £E5 per month for twelve months). At the end of that time, one of the women is designated to receive all of the money, which she may spend as she chooses, and the system begins again. The jam'iyya continues in operation until each of the women has received her share. Many of these women use their jam'iyya money to buy jewelry. For instance, one of my informants sold her old bracelets for new ones in a more contemporary pattern, paying the difference in the prices of the two sets with money she had earned from the tourist trade and saved in her jam'iyya. A woman may use jam'iyya money to buy items for home improvement, like a new door, rather than gold jewelry. On the other hand, the gold most often is itself an intermediate investment against the time when she may need to spend the money on something larger and more substantial, such as the custom called "building the house."

"Building the House"

One of the most important activities of a married woman begins after she moves into her husband's home. Some years after she and her family settle in, she begins to think about enlarging or improving the home in some way. The purpose varies—possibly greater convenience, as in the installation of plumbing, along with faucets and sinks, or beautification of the home, as by adding tiles in the courtyard. When the Nubian wife supervises the construction of additional rooms or floors, she does so for another reason, however: "building the house." In their interviews with me, the women of Gubba used that phrase when they proudly pointed to the additions they had made over the years. They took the major credit for so doing, even though most of the expenses were covered by their husbands' paychecks.

A major investment of time and capital, "building the house" is customarily a right and duty of a married woman. Among the Nubians, when a young woman marries, she and her new husband first move in with her parents. They live there for the first several years of marriage, or until the husband has earned enough money to build his own home. During this period of neomatrilocal postmarital residence, the mother-in-law and son-in-law observe an avoidance relationship. A young married couple must therefore have a private apartment in her parents' house, with a separate entrance if at all possible. Thus, when a daughter reaches marriageable age, and often several years before that, her mother hires and supervises workmen to add a separate wing onto the house. In addition to paying them, she must also provide meals twice a day for them and tea three times a day while they are employed. In this way, five or ten, and in one case twelve, rooms had been added to family domiciles in Gubba during the past ten to fifteen years. These apartments, which in newer houses tend to be on the second floor and in older ones are built within the courtyard of the parents' home, all have at least two rooms and a kitchen.

Nubian women are intensely house-proud, and justifiably so, but not only because their homes are large and beautiful. The investment made in "building the house" expresses to the community the level of seriousness with which a woman takes her maternal role. Whereas the purchase of jewelry benefits chiefly the woman who buys it, the improvement of a house benefits the entire family. A woman demonstrates in this way that she and her husband have in mind the future security of their children, who will inherit the house, and whose property increases in value as a result of her work. When a woman of the community lets it be known that she is saving toward "building the house," her friends allow her to suspend participation in their sharing networks temporarily. Her relatives may also occasionally send foodstuffs, helping her to save a little grocery money. Support and approval is sought, and is forthcoming, from both her family and her friends; when the improvements are finished, the entire community visits in order to look at the house and congratulate her.

Conclusion

This chapter shows how women in Gubba engage in remunerative shadow economy activities of various sorts. They may sell produce or animals in the market or sell crocheted bags and caps to men who have stalls there, for resale to tourists who flock to Aswan. Women may also sell these items directly to tourists who visit the village in groups. In addition, women make money by opening their homes to tour groups on a regular basis. Thus many—though not all—of Gubba's women earn undocumented income in both the male and the female domains of their society. When I questioned them, these women asserted that their purpose was to be able to buy necessities such as clothing, schoolbooks, and medicine. Their earnings also went to buy jewelry, which is in many cases a security against hard times, and to enlarge their houses, a custom of long standing that is a source of pride and self-esteem.

One of the less recognized results of "building the house" is the maintenance of gender equity in the village. Beautiful, imposing, and "built" by the wife, the Nubian house demands that the inhabitants of the women's domain be acknowledged. Although most of the money for the house comes from the husband, it is the wife who takes full responsibility for its construction, and it is she who is congratulated when the house is finished. It has been stated that domestic duties are considered to be of less importance than are public duties in Islamic societies and that women's activities and pursuits, and even women themselves, are devalued.[15] The results of fieldwork by female investigators have challenged these assertions, however, reporting that in fact women and their roles are highly valued in Muslim life.[16]

My research also indicates that Nubians generally do not consider the male domain to be superior to the female domain, and I believe that Nubian houses are visual indicators that the inhabitants of the female domain are important to Nubian social life. Part of the reason may be that Nubian village life is still "domestic centered." That is, the family unit is still the economic, political, and social core of the community.[17] As such, it is highly valued, and the importance of its inhabitants is understood. Both females and males in the village are enmeshed in networks that provide information and other resources and that work both separately and interdependently to maintain traditional Nubian values and social organization.[18] Women's networks allow them control over certain kinds of information vital to the functioning of village society.[19] Since many of the most important decisions in village life are made in the women's sphere, Nubian women are not prevented from engaging in decision-making processes but are in fact expected to contribute to them. Nubian men freely admit that they depend upon their wives, mothers, and sisters to help them in tangible as well as intangible ways; "building the house" can be interpreted as a village custom that demonstrates the continuing importance of the occupants of the female domain.

This theory remains untested. Although the houses that women "build" may be an important symbolic statement of the contributions of women to the village, there are still not enough data to make an accurate assessment of women's actual economic contributions. Only further research will give a fuller picture of the importance of women's earnings to the village economy as a whole. A comparison study of women in urban areas would also be of value: Is the role of the Nubian woman as highly regarded in areas where she does not "build the house"?

A larger sample of women, of the kinds of work they do and the amounts of money they make, would help in estimating the percentage of the village economy made up by women's earnings. The difficulty lies in obtaining accurate information from a large sample of women on this topic. While the women whom I knew and saw every day were open about the amount of money they earned, women who hardly knew me were not so forthcoming. This is a sensitive subject, not only because of the contradiction of Islamic ideology concerning proper feminine behavior but also because any admission of need casts discredit upon male relatives. Furthermore, activity in the shadow economy is purposefully unreported; these are poor people, trying to make a little extra money, and the last thing they want is to have to pay taxes on their earnings. In a situation like this, an anthropologist asking questions might be seen as a spy for the government.

Another difficulty lies in the fluctuating nature of the tourist trade—good in some years but not others—to which the women must adjust. Some of the women leave the area; in 1986 my major informant was heavily involved with the tourist trade but then moved to Cairo with her husband, and such activities no longer concern her. Such fluctuations make it hard to generalize from the data at hand and to predict future behavior. Yet the shadow economy or invisible economy is important in the field of the anthropology of work as well as in the study of women in Muslim societies. We must adjust our data-gathering techniques and methodology if we are to overcome the difficulties peculiar to this subject, so that we may continue to challenge the stereotypes about women's work throughout the world.

Notes

1. Nicholas Hopkins, "The Informal Sector in Egypt," *Cairo Papers in Social Science* 14, no. 4 (Winter 1991).

2. Susan Feldman, "Still Invisible: Women in the Informal Sector," in R. Gallin and A. Fergusen, eds. *The Women and International Development Annual* 2 (1991): 59–86; Andrea Singh and Anita Kelles-Viitanen, *Invisible Hands: Women in Home-based Production* (New Delhi: Sage Publications, 1987).

3. Hopkins, "The Informal Sector in Egypt," 1.

4. Mary Douglas, *Natural Symbols* (New York: Random House, 1970); Cynthia Nelson, "Public and Private Politics: Women in the Middle Eastern World," *American Ethnologist* 1, no. 3 (1974): 551–63.

5. Carol Mukhopadhyay and Patricia Higgens, "Anthropological Studies of

Women's Status Revisited: 1977–1987," *Annual Review of Anthropology* (1988): 461–95.

6. Audrey Smock and Nadia Youssef, "Egypt: From Seclusion to Limited Participation," in Janet Giele and Audrey Smock, eds., *Women: Roles and Status in Eight Countries* (New York: Wiley, 1977), 35–79.

7. Catherine Coles and Beverly Mack, eds., *Hausa Women in the Twentieth Century* (Madison: University of Wisconsin Press, 1991); Enid Schildkrout, "Dependence and Autonomy: The Economic Activities of Secluded Hausa Women in Kano, Nigeria," in Edna Bay, ed., *Women and Work in Africa* (Boulder, Colo.: Westview Press, 1982), 55–81.

8. Susan Davis, *Patience and Power: Women's Lives in a Moroccan Village* (Cambridge, Mass.: Schenkman Publishing Company, 1983).

9. Andrea Rugh, "Women and Work: Strategies and Choices in a Lower-class Quarter of Cairo," in Elizabeth Fernea, ed., *Women and the Family in the Middle East* (Austin: University of Texas Press, 1984), 273–88.

10. Fred Wendorf, *The Prehistory of Nubia*, vols. 1 and 2 (Dallas: Southern Methodist University Press, 1968).

11. Alan Horton, "The Egyptian Nubians," American University Field Staff Reports, Northeast Africa Series 11, no. 2 (United Arab Republic, 1964).

12. Elizabeth W. Fernea and Robert A. Fernea, with Aleya Rouchdy, *Nubian Ethnographies* (Prospect Heights, Ill.: Waveland Press, 1991).

13. Robert A. Fernea and Georg Gerster, *Nubians in Egypt: Peaceful People* (Austin: University of Texas Press, 1973).

14. In 1986, the rate of exchange for Egyptian pounds was 1 £E = $0.75.

15. Richard Antoun, "On the Modesty of Women in Arab Muslim Villages: A Study in the Accommodation of Traditions," *American Anthropologist* 70 (1968): 671–97; Safia Mohsen, "Aspects of the Legal Status of Women among the Awlad 'Ali," *Anthropological Quarterly* 40 (1967): 220–33.

16. Soraya Altorki, "Family Organization and Women's Power in Urban Saudi Arabia," *Journal of Anthropological Research* 33, no. 3 (1977): 277–87; Hildred Geertz, "The Meanings of Family Ties," in Clifford Geertz, Hildred Geertz, and Lawrence Rosen, eds., *Meaning and Order in Moroccan Society* (Cambridge: Cambridge University Press, 1979), 315–91.

17. Susan Rogers, "Female Forms of Power and the Myth of Male Dominance: A Model of Female/Male Interaction in Peasant Society," *American Ethnologist* 2, no. 4 (1975): 727–56.

18. On urban networks among Nubian men, see Richard Lobban, "Alienation, Urbanization, and Social Networks in the Sudan," *Journal of Modern African Studies* 13, no. 3 (1975): 491–500; and Fernea and Fernea, *Nubian Ethnographies*. On networks among village women, see Anne Jennings, *The Nubians of West Aswan: Village Women in the Midst of Change* (Boulder, Colo.: Lynne Rienner Publishers, 1995).

19. Jennings, *Nubians of West Aswan*.

2

Baggara Women as Market Strategists

Barbara J. Michael

In Middle Eastern folklore there is a story about Goha, the trickster, who one day asked his mother to prepare all sorts of tasty foods. Then he lowered her into a nearby well, passed down to her all of the prepared food, and told her, "Whenever I ask for something, you attach it to the rope and let me draw it out of the well." Soon some Bedouins came along to water their camels. They saw Goha, who had set up a table near the well. Goha was tossing his rope down into the well and saying, "Rope, O rope! Give me rice." He drew up the rope, along with a bowl of rice. He repeated the procedure, saying, "Rope, O rope! Give me meat . . . give me soup" until the table was laden with delicious food.

The Bedouins were amazed by the fantastic rope. They asked Goha to sell it to them, but he was reluctant. Finally, after much bargaining, Goha agreed to sell them the rope for a very high price.[1]

In literature as well as life, nomads have been regarded as either country bumpkins or noble savages. Famed Arab historian Ibn Khaldun writes: "They are the most savage human beings that exist. Compared with sedentary people, they are on a level with wild, untamable animals and dumb beasts of prey. Such people are the Bedouins."[2] However, he writes also that the Bedouin are the antecedents of civilization—the sedentary dynasties:

> If one compares sedentary people with Bedouins, one notices how much more insight and cleverness sedentary people have. One might, thus, come to think that they really differ from the Bedouins in the reality of humanity and in intelligence. This is not so. The only reason for the difference is that sedentary people have refined technical habits and manners as far as customary activities and sedentary condi-

tions are concerned, all of them things that are unknown to the Bedouins. Sedentary people possess numerous crafts, as well as the habits that go with them, and good [methods of] teaching the crafts. Therefore, those who do not have such habits think that they indicate an intellectual perfection possessed [exclusively] by sedentary people. This is not so. We find Bedouins whose understanding, intellectual perfection, and natural qualifications are of the highest order. The seeming [superiority of] sedentary people is merely the result of a certain polish the crafts and scientific instruction give them.[3]

To some degree these attitudes toward pastoral nomads are still found today. Many townsmen aspire to the purity, nobility, and freedom of the pastoral nomadic way of life, but they also believe that lifestyle produces an unsophisticated person, incapable of competing in the modern world with themselves. My purpose is not to refute this position but to relate the response to a market economy among pastoral nomads I investigated. Even though the symbiotic relationship of the peoples of "the desert" and those of "the sown" has been much written about, the two modes have been seen as separate, if not polarized.[4] Pastoral nomadic participation in some aspects of the sedentary way of life has even been seen as an indicator of a process of sedentarization.[5] In fact, elements of both have merged, effectively expanding, so to speak, the pastoral mode. This study focuses on Baggara women as market strategists.

Other papers of mine discuss how Hawazma Baggara women seem to have a high degree of autonomy in decisions regarding the allocation of economic resources.[6] The Baggara are pastoral nomads of the Sudan; the Hawazma are one of the five main subgroups located in southern Kordofan, where they herd cattle. Baggara women exercise managerial decisions regarding the allocation of milk, they sell surpluses, and they bring in up to two-thirds of the annual household cash budget. But how do they fare in the marketplace? What are women's strategies? Do they in fact negotiate or manipulate to get the best price for their milk and milk products, or are they the passive receivers of whatever price is given by the sedentary market? Investigating these questions should give some insight into several issues of wider concern, including the dynamics of gender interaction and therefore the interaction of gender and economics, as well as issues of power and resistance within Baggara society and pastoral nomads' "invisible" participation in a cash economy.

Several factors formed the basis for undertaking the investigation of marketing strategies. Data from my first fieldwork with the Baggara, from

1982 to 1984 (twenty-four months), revealed that Baggara women were making major contributions to household budgets through sales of milk and milk products (primarily *semn,* or clarified butter, and *roob,* or liquid yogurt). They were milking, managing, and marketing. Two points seemed particularly salient, especially given the reports about other pastoral nomadic groups that I found in the literature and in communications with other anthropologists.

First, contrary to such reports, women's participation in these activities did not appear to me to be a recent development. Cunnison makes a passing comment on women's milk marketing in his book based on fieldwork in 1952–55.[7] Doxiadis's reports indicate that there were commercial outlets for pastoral nomadic raw milk at least as early as 1930.[8] Lacking adequate documentation, my test for the embeddedness of women's milk marketing was the possibility of conflict over women's marketing activities. Neither probing questioning of both men and women nor long-term observation revealed any conflict within the household regarding either the activity or the right of Baggara women to undertake the role of milk marketers. Nor was there any conflict over their allocating and controlling either any raw resources or the profits from their sales.

Second, the case of Baggara women marketers seems to be unusual in a pastoral nomadic setting. While it is not unusual for pastoral nomadic women to be important economic producers, nor for them to have more autonomous roles than sedentary women, it does appear unusual for them to participate and control all the various stages of this "invisible" economic activity. Qashqai' women, for example, make rugs, but their husbands market them and pocket the cash.[9] Other pastoral nomadic women who milk and produce milk products lose control of their labor at the point of marketing and right to profits.[10]

In Kordofan province the Ministry of Animal Resources operates seasonal cheese factories that produce an uncooked white cheese and a cooked rope cheese. In addition to various town markets and private cheese factory operators, the ministry's cheese factories are a primary outlet for raw milk during the rainy season, when milk surpluses are great. One part of my research plan for 1989 centered on joining a *fariq,* or camp, that I knew, and collecting data on the women's daily milk sales at one of the seasonal cheese factories serving fariqs in the area. The purpose was to investigate the extent and impact of seasonal milk sales. Rains generally begin in June and end abruptly in late September or early October. Since the trek requires travel over about a month's time each at the beginning and end of the rainy season, cheese factories operate only about two months out of the year. While some of the cheese factories follow fariq movement from South to North Kordofan, most do not begin operation until the fariqs reach the locus of rainy season pastures in an arc around the town of El Obeid. Each cheese factory typically serves ten to fifteen fariqs.

While doing preliminary research, gathering statistics on the twenty years of the ministry's involvement in cheese making, I discovered the ministry's joint project with UNICEF for teaching nomadic Baggara women to make white cheese. The aim of that project is twofold. One is to shift white cheese production from ministry cheese factories to nomadic camps to allow the ministry to specialize in cooked cheese production. Second, the project is part of a broader initiative under the Integrated Women's Development Programme to improve women's access to the means of production, thereby increasing disposable income and home production; to enhance existing skills and teach new ones; and to assure food supplies for the household, particularly maternal and child nutrition.[11]

When the UNICEF director for El Obeid learned what my research interests were, he asked me all sorts of questions. It developed that marketing was one of the weakest aspects of the cheese-making training project. Personnel from the Ministry of Animal Resources, who are also the project trainers, make a circuit of cheese-producing camps, picking up the cheese and paying the women for it. During the 1989 rainy season, twelve camps (out of seventy-two trained) consistently produced cheese. However, there was concern that when the total number of camps trained in cheese making reached the 1992 goal of 240, it would no longer be feasible for the ministry to provide the primary marketing outlet. For the long-term stability and strength of this new economic scheme, it was necessary for the cheese producers to develop their own marketing strategies. Success of the project would require that Baggara women retain control over marketing, as well as production, of milk and cheese.

The incentive for milk marketing has existed since at least the 1930s, surging in intensity over the last twenty years. One of the first cheese factories established in Kordofan opened in Abu Haraz in about 1930. Other privately owned cheese factories followed, and in 1960 the Sudanese Veterinary Department (now the Ministry of Animal Resources) began operating cheese factories. In 1984 there were five government-operated cheese factories and approximately forty privately operated cheese factories. In 1989 there were seven cheese factories operated by the government agency. By 1989 the number of privately owned cheese factories had increased to

100, but since the camps had started making cheese only in 1987, it was too early to see a shift in cheese production, from government and small private production to a female-dominated cottage industry.

When they make decisions about the allocation of milk, Baggara women must take many social and nutritional needs into consideration. Everyone, adults and children, wants plenty of milk available for home consumption. Milk with tea is standard fare for everyone in the morning and often in the evening as well. Milk is used in a number of sauce recipes or is served as the only accompaniment to *assida* (a stiff millet or sorghum mush) for the evening meal. The value of milk for good health, particularly for children, is clearly understood. The greater availability of milk during the rainy season is given as one reason why the rigors of the trek from South to North Kordofan and back, a distance of about 200 miles each way, are worthwhile. In comparing fariq and village life, almost everyone I have met says that fariq life is better, with milk availability cited as the first reason, along with fresher air and cleaner living spaces. Mothers make sure that there is enough milk for their children to drink at various times throughout the day, often at the demand of the child. During the dry season, children's needs for milk are often met by milking goats. During the rainy season, cow's milk is plentiful.

Milk is also an important item in social affairs. A visitor to a fariq will likely be given a refreshing drink of roob. A large bowl of foamy fresh milk may also be offered to guests present at milking time. Milk is churned into butter and made into semn, valued both in the diet and for sale. Women largely control what portion of a cow's milk production is allocated to any calves, in addition to what is taken for household, hospitality, and market purposes. Even though women might be most concerned about household nutrition, they must also be sensitive to the effect of their allocation decisions on household status as reflected by men's ability to be hospitable. All these uses and demands make milk allocation a heavy responsibility.

Once women have allocated milk between home use and sale, they move into the realm of the market economy. Hawazma (Baggara) women are astute analyzers of market conditions. Information travels quickly and widely about prices being paid for raw milk and milk products in various markets or at cheese factories along the trekking route and the rainy season camping areas. In 1989 the two topics that dominated women's conversations in the camps were milk prices and security conditions in South Kordofan. Women influence men's decisions on where to camp so as to have access to the most profitable markets. In fact, in 1983 the women complained that the rainy season camp selected by the men was too far from the closest cheese factory, thus forcing the men to move the camp.

During the 1989 rainy season women also wielded a great deal of economic power in their relations with cheese producers and marketers. There were at least fifteen fariqs in the area of the one in which I was living, within easy walking distance of a privately owned cheese factory. Prior to the 1989 rainy season, none of these camps knew how to produce cheese, though some women from several of them received training in September 1989. The training did not affect their marketing of raw milk while I was there, as they did not become cheese producers in the 1989 season. With each camp averaging eight adult, home-owning women, there were approximately 120 milk suppliers in the area.

On the first day that I visited the cheese factory, I identified thirty-two women producers bringing milk to the cheese factory. At the end of ten days, three to fifteen women were patronizing the cheese factory, and in twenty days the number had dwindled to five or six women. Finally, the cheese factory closed because it was taking in only about three *safiha* (twelve gallons) of milk per day. The lack of milk intake did not reflect a decrease in milk production or the movement of camps from the area. Women were selling their milk elsewhere, their primary consideration being the price paid for raw milk.

Close to the camps in the area were several lorry routes serving El Obeid, and Baggara women from camps near the one where I lived could travel and transport milk on the lorry services; several of them were operated by young Baggara men, sons of pastoral nomads. The cheese factory was paying £S40 (40 Sudanese pounds) per safiha (four gallons), but in El Obeid the women could sell milk for twice that amount. The women told me that if the cheese factory owner had agreed to pay even £S50 per safiha, they would have sold to him rather than travel to El Obeid. It took about forty-five minutes to walk to the cheese factory from the camp where I was, or a round-trip total of about two hours. In order to make sales in El Obeid, women left camp about 6:00 A.M. and returned around 5:00 P.M. Even though their cost accounting for such expenditures of time is not weighted as it might be from our economic perspective, the difference between two hours and eleven hours for marketing milk was a consideration. Still, women chose to spend most of the day in El Obeid and to pay transport costs for themselves and their milk containers in order to reap the economic advantage of the considerably higher price.

Part of the women's strategy to increase the profits from marketing was

Middlewoman (center) and Baggara supplier. Photo: Barbara Michael.

an incipient self-generated cooperative. Each Baggara woman took turns taking milk from four or more women on the lorry to El Obeid. Thus, while the cost of transporting the containers remained constant, the personal transportation cost for the one woman marketer was spread among all the women cooperating. The cooperative shared the burden of keeping up with household and child-care tasks as well. While one or two women were marketing the milk, and perhaps shopping for themselves and the women left behind, the women who stayed in camp took care of the children of the marketer.

The strategy also solved another potential conflict for individual marketers that, if left to fester, might have cost women their control of marketing: the problem of preparing *fitur* (breakfast) for a household. Feeding children would not be a problem, as children frequently eat at a household other than their own. But feeding the menfolk might have been a problem if the task of marketing had not been shared and rotated. If every woman head-of-household had gone every day into El Obeid, leaving just after sunrise and not returning until dusk, men might have been left with no food for communal meals under "the men's tree." The rotating arrangement ensured that, except for one or two days of the week, each man had a bowl of food to share at communal meals. Given marketing cooperation, enough women and teenaged girls were left in camp to cook for the men.

Even daily communal meals are linked to hospitality and status, but since only a few women were unable to fulfill their role in male hospitality on any given day, men were satisfied with, and in fact proud of, their wives' economic productivity.

Several times I accompanied the Baggara women on the lorry into El Obeid, where they sold milk at one or two milk-collecting points in the suq, or market. At the lorry stop there was also a great, cacophonous rush of townswomen toward the lorries, wanting to buy milk wholesale from the Baggara women to sell at retail prices.

Toward the end of the rainy season, Hakmula's household, with which I was living, moved out of camp, but I stayed on in another part of the camp to finish some work. I had told Hakmula I would go into El Obeid to meet her in the suq, but I couldn't find her there. I asked townswomen marketers in the suq if they had seen Hakmula. One woman who knew her said that the lorry had left early and Hakmula had been on it. Hakmula would be back within the next couple of days, but in the meantime I was stranded. The market woman, whom I recognized as having been in a crowd around the Baggara women's lorry, negotiating to buy milk, said that I could go home with her. She said Hakmula would visit the suq in the next day or so and would be seeking her out. That townswoman and several others were selling milk by the *rutl* (pound), but I recognized the significance of that only after I spent some time talking with them there in the market before they went home for the day.

They were in fact middlewomen, buying Baggara raw milk and roob in quantity and selling it by the rutl to local customers. Some of them were also selling larger quantities of milk to shopkeepers. Each of the middlewomen had developed a set of dyadic relationships with Baggara women, ensuring a steady supply of milk for themselves and a steady outlet for the nomadic women. Some of the middlewomen encouraged these links by offering Baggara women access to goods or services. In 1989 a number of commodities—sugar, tea, coffee, soap, oil—were quite scarce, but middlewomen, through contacts with a wider range of merchants, helped Baggara women obtain what they sought. They operated primarily through a black market network, selling from their houses. They also provided contacts for services such as sewing clothing, another cottage industry. Through these marketing links Baggara women supplied their households with essential commodities that men were often unable to find in markets in El Obeid, Kasgeil, or Abu Haraz. More important, the steady, higher prices middlewomen offered, along with access to scarce goods, were the reasons why Baggara women were willing to travel four hours round-trip to sell milk.

Indirectly, the middlewomen were also the reason that the cheese factory I had intended to study went out of business.

Clearly Hawazma women are knowledgeable about market prices. During the trek north to rainy season pastures, they visit perhaps three or four markets and encounter several cheese factories, both private and government-owned. At their rainy season camps, they receive visitors from across the arc formed by camps and cheese factory locations, thus gathering market information from a wide area. They understand the principle of supply and demand, expecting higher prices at the beginning and end of the rainy season, lower prices at peak season. Baggara women negotiate with milk buyers for a price agreeable to both parties. Negotiation is not as likely with cheese factories, though, as I learned, the women may let a cheese factory owner know that his price is too low by refusing to sell, even when the location is convenient. Negotiation is typical of relationships between Baggara women and direct buyers or middlewomen. In 1989 several middlewomen told me that although the standard price for raw milk in El Obeid was £S80 per safiha, the Baggara women who supplied them asked £S90. Finally, in the late rainy season when milk supplies were dwindling, the middlewomen agreed to pay £S85 per safiha.

Perhaps the market behavior reported here seems predictable. Asante and Hausa market women also wheel and deal, as do other Sudanese mar-

Middlewoman selling to town customers. Photo: Barbara Michael.

ket women. These groups, however, are town dwellers,[12] while Baggara women are pastoral nomads. Among pastoral nomadic women, the Baggara are the only ones, as far as I am aware, who do marketing, as well as milking and managing.

Those who posed the problem of cheese marketing to me suggested that Baggara women probably lacked the skills necessary to deal directly with merchants and would require the intervention of the Ministry of Animal Resources. However, as I discovered, Baggara women were already using a variety of market links to dispose of milk surpluses. Although those with whom I have worked most closely do not make cheese at this point, cheese marketing strategies can build on their experience in marketing milk. Baggara women are aware of price structures. They know how to establish links with outlets in larger town markets such as El Obeid, and when such outlets are not available, they sell milk to cheese factories or direct to customers in smaller periodic markets. The women told me that if they were making cheese, they could market it through established links with middlewomen, and one woman said her middlewoman had already asked her for cheese to sell.

Women in the single cheese-producing camp I was able to visit did not yet seem to have such links. As their camp was not near a lorry route to El Obeid, they were marketing cheese through the Ministry of Animal Resources, whose personnel picked up the cheese. Despite their relative lack of experience, though, they are not totally dependent on the ministry as an outlet. At one point, when no cheese had been picked up for several weeks and they did not know when to expect the next pickup, they had sold their cheese to a privately owned cheese factory nearby—where they had refused to sell raw milk because of the price offered. For the cheese, the women had negotiated for the same price paid them by the Ministry of Animal Resources. I find it remarkable that these women wouldn't sell milk to the cheese factory owner but were able to convince him to buy the cheese they produced: clear evidence that they are quite capable of surviving as marketers in the marketplace.

Conclusion

Milk marketing is a widespread phenomenon among Baggara women, vital to the existence of the many cheese factories, which in turn stimulates the production and marketing of raw milk. Data collected from 1982 to 1984 showed that women who sold milk were typically able to contribute as much as one-third of the annual household budget. Women indicated that more milk cows in their herds and higher prices in 1989 would enable them to support their households for as much as two-thirds of the year. Table 3 compares production and profit data from 1984 and 1989.

Much of the women's money from milk sales goes for food. In 1989 I saw a greater variety in the camp diet. Important new items including cucumbers and fruits such as bananas, grapefruit and guava, and dates had been added. Cucumbers were prepared with peanut sauce, another high-protein food, not common in the diet during my previous studies (1982–84). The woman of the household allocates many of these new foods primarily to herself and the other women and to the children. While both men and women are concerned about each other's well-being and that of their children, the control of buying goods, especially foodstuffs, is very important. Women's higher incomes mean that the dietary supplements noted here, formerly considered luxury goods, are now used in greater quantities.

Women's incomes have the potential for further increases if they become cheese producers and marketers. Table 4 compares the various options, including several marketing outlets for milk and cheese. The present marketing structure for raw milk includes (1) women producers; (2) privately owned cheese factories; (3) merchants (middlewomen); and (4) the Ministry of Animal Resources. There is every indication that women cheese producers will expand these links to include outlets for their new product.

One of the payoffs of higher income through cheese production may be improvement in herd quality. My previous research has shown that women are likely to provide the stimulus for herd improvement, to achieve higher milk production levels from their cows. While herd management has traditionally been a male concern, Baggara women have become involved in herd management decisions. Specifically, they frequently use the earnings

Table 3. Comparison of Production and Profit

| | Production | | Net Profits | | | |
| | Safiha per week | | 1984 | | 1989 | |
	1984	1989	£	$	£	$
Zeinab	2.79	14.00	24.38	12.19	1,088.00	89.91
Khadija	2.44	10.50	21.35	10.68	780.50	64.50
Average*	2.03	9.15	17.71	8.86	684.85	56.60
	Increase:	450%			Increase:	640%

* Individuals in 1984 and 1989 samples not the same because of shifts in residence. Figures represent averages for individuals in respective samples.

from milk sales to buy feed supplements for milk cows, particularly during the dry season. Herd improvement has implications not only for the volume of milk production but also for herd size; larger herds may not be needed. In turn this has implications for environmental degradation.

One concern, expressed by some of the Baggara women themselves, is control of the profits from cheese making. Women now have the right to allocate milk usage and to retain any income from sales, of either milk or cheese. If women are able to convert their milk marketing links, particularly middlewomen, into outlets for cheese, they will be able to retain the right to allocation of profits. Indications of improvements in diet related to increased milk sales suggest that cheese sales will bring further improvements in diet and health, including more frequent decisions to seek health care for women and children. Even now, Baggara women simply announce their intention to go to a hospital or clinic; they don't ask their husbands' permission. Greater availability of cash will undoubtedly mean greater use of whatever health care facilities are available.

Table 4. Profit analysis of milk and cheese sales

	Production		Net Profits (£S per week)			
			Raw Milk Sales		Cheese Sales	
	Milk	Cheese				
	(Safiha	(Kilo per	Cheese	El Obeid		Open
Person	per week)	week)[1]	Factory[2]	Market[3]	Ministry[4]	Market[5]
Naima	14.00	44.87	560.00	1,088.00	1,011.00	1,523.85
Zainab	14.00	44.87	560.00	1,088.00	1,011.00	1,523.85
Um Kallam	12.25	39.20	490.00	910.00	881.46	1,325.26
Irah	7.00	22.40	280.00	511.00	504.32	761.92
Hakuma	3.50	11.20	140.00	241.50	252.16	380.96
Khadija	10.50	33.60	420.00	780.50	756.49	1,142.89
Aisha	7.00	22.40	280.00	511.00	504.32	761.92

[1]3.12 safiha milk = 10 kg cheese.
[2]Based on 1989 prices of £S40 per safiha. No costs for transport.
[3]Based on 1989 prices of £S80 per safiha. Lorry costs: £S23/day; £S3/safiha/day. However, this group shared the lorry costs, with usually only two people taking all the milk. Therefore, weekly costs have been prorated, based on total number of trips and total number of safiha transported.
[4]Based on 1989 prices of £S235 per 10 kg. Production costs include salt @ £S50/lb; rennet tablets @ £S3 each; transportation costs £S66 @ £S3/safiha plus £S20/person. Ministry personnel sometimes pick up cheese, at no transport cost.
[5]Based on 1989 prices of £S350/10 kg paid wholesale by merchants who purchase cheese from factory owners. Production and transport costs are calculated as in note 4.

Baggara men are also interested in women maintaining a high degree of autonomy in their economic affairs. Women's greater self-sufficiency and greater autonomy free men to participate in international wage labor for periods of a year or more.[13] As long as women can support the household, men need not be concerned about sending remittances. Men's incomes can be used instead to increase herds.

Clearly the participation of women in the Sudanese cash economy is intensifying. How far can women increase their incomes before demands beyond household maintenance are made on them? Where will the points of tension arise? From a broader anthropological perspective, one hoped-for result of following the developments in this situation will be a better understanding of the political aspects of gender versus the "invisible" economic aspects of gender.

Notes

1. Barbara J. Qandil [Michael], "A Comparative Study of a Near Eastern Trickster Cycle," *Southern Folklore Quarterly* 34 (1970).

2. Ibn Khaldun, *The Muqaddimah* (Princeton: Princeton University Press, 1966), 93.

3. Ibn Khaldun, *Muqaddimah,* 342–43.

4. For example, see Mohammed Abbas, "The Nomadic and the Sedentary: Polar Complementaries—Not Polar Opposites," in Cynthia Nelson, ed., *The Desert and the Sown* (Berkeley: University of California, Institute of International Studies, 1973), 97–113; Fredrik Barth, *Nomads of South Persia: The Basseri Tribe of the Khamseh Confederacy* (London: Allen and Unwin, 1964); Fredrik Barth, "A General Perspective on Nomad-Sedentary Relations in the Middle East," in Cynthia Nelson, ed., *The Desert and the Sown* (1973), 11–21; William Lancaster, *The Rwala Bedouin Today* (Cambridge: Cambridge University Press, 1981); Mustafa Abdel Rahman Mustafa, "A Comparison of Sedentary Cultivators and Nomadic Pastoralists and Their Market Integration in the Radoam Area of Southern Darfur," *Occasional Papers in Social Anthropology* 19 (1980): 107–32; Cynthia Nelson, "Women and Power in Nomadic Societies of the Middle East," in Cynthia Nelson, ed., *The Desert and the Sown* (1973), 43–59; Philip C. Salzman, ed., *When Nomads Settle* (New York: Praeger, 1980); Brian Spooner, "Nomads in a Wider Society," *Cultural Survival Quarterly* 8, no. 1 (1984): 23–25; Nina Swidler, "Sedentarization and Modes of Economic Integration in the Middle East," in Philip C. Salzman, ed., *When Nomads Settle* (1980), 21–23; W. W. Swidler, "Adaptive Processes Regulating Nomad-Sedentary Interaction in the Middle East," in Cynthia Nelson, ed., *The Desert and the Sown* (1973), 23–41.

5. See, for example, Barth, *Nomads of South Persia;* Salzman, *When Nomads Settle;* N. Swidler, "Sedentarization."

6. Barbara J. Michael, "Cows, Bulls and Gender Roles: Pastoral Strategies of Survival and Continuity in Western Sudan" (Ph.D. dissertation, University of Kansas and University Microfilms, 1987); idem., "Milk Production and Sales by the Hawazma (Baggara) of the Sudan: Implications for Gender Roles," *Research in Economic Anthropology* 9 (1991): 105–41; "The Impact of International Wage Labor Migration on Baggara Pastoral Nomadism," *Nomadic Peoples* 28 (1991): 56–70. Research was carried out as a member of the Western Sudan Agricultural Research Project, 1982–84, and in 1989 with a grant from the Social Science Research Council.

7. Ian Cunnison, *The Baggara Arabs: Power and Lineage in a Sudanese Nomad Tribe* (Oxford: Clarendon Press, 1966), 30, 39, 48.

8. "Agronomy, Land and Water Use Surveys in Kordofan Province of the Republic of the Sudan," Report on the Hawazma Tribe (Doxiades Associates, Athens, 1966).

9. Lois Beck, "Women Among the Qashqa'i Nomadic Pastoralists in Iran," in Lois Beck and Nikki Keddi, eds., *Women in the Muslim World* (Cambridge: Harvard University Press, 1978), 351–73; Andre Bourgeot, "The Twareg Women of Ahaggar and the Creation of Value," *Ethnos* 52, nos. 1–2 (1987): 103–18; Daniel A. Bradburd, *Ambiguous Relations: Kin, Class, and Conflict among Komachi Pastoralists* (Washington, D.C.: Smithsonian Institution Press, 1990); Dawn Chatty, "Changing Sex Roles in Bedouin Society in Syria and Lebanon," in Lois Beck and Nikki Keddi, eds., *Women in the Muslim World* (1978), 399–415; Jean E. Ensminger, "Economic and Political Differentiation among Galole Orma Women," *Ethnos* 52, nos. 1–2 (1987): 28–49.

10. "Integrated Women's Development Programme" (El Obeid, Sudan) (UNICEF, unpublished manuscript, 1989).

11. W. R. Bascom, *The Yoruba of Southwestern Nigeria* (New York: Holt, Rinehart and Winston, 1969); Paul Bohannan and G. Dalton, *Markets in Africa* (Evanston: Northwestern University Press, 1962); Polly Hill, *Studies in Rural Capitalism in West Africa* (Cambridge: Cambridge University Press, 1970); R. Lystad, *The Ashanti, a Proud People* (New Brunswick: Rutgers University Press, 1958).

12. Michael, "Milk Production and Sales."

3

Invisible Survivors

Women and Diversity in the
Transitional Economy of Yemen

Delores M. Walters

The sisters at Bayt Hadrami (House of Hadrami) transform their sitting room into a virtual sewing factory after the midmorning meal. Babies are washed, fed, and placed in hammocks for a nap. Then the sewing machines (German and Japanese imports) appear. Nura says that she makes about five *qumsan* a day, or roughly twenty of the dresses a week! Amina is also at a machine. While 'Aisha adds the neck embroidery by hand, the threads she uses are typically held by Sabah, a servant. I judged Sabah to be of ex-slave ('*abid*) ancestry, rather than menial laborer (*akhdam*) status, based on several criteria, including the lightness of her skin and the intimacy of the women's association.[1]

Racial Differences: An Overlooked Factor in Gender-Based Production

This vignette, taken from my field notes, is just one example of diverse women's engagement in longstanding, mutually beneficial economic enterprise. This chapter explores economic production relationships involving women in various social categories within what was formerly known as the Yemen Arab Republic, or North Yemen. In the new state order resulting from reunification of conservative North Yemen and Marxist South Yemen in 1990 and a two-month civil war in May 1994, transformations in the roles and status of women are occurring.

This analysis is based on eighteen months of ethnographic fieldwork conducted during 1982–84 and a three-month stay at the end of 1994. During the initial research, I lived in two locations: a southern farming village, Wadi Dabab, near Ta'izz, and the northern coastal (Tihama) town of 'Abs.[2] The introductory vignette took place in the Abs field site, but the relevance of racial and gender differences to women's visibility is applicable throughout the Yemeni economy.

Women are visible in the Yemeni economy to varying degrees. It is the failure to fully recognize diverse women's contributions to the economic system in Yemen that accounts in part for the extreme levels of invisibility to which certain women are subjected. "Nontribal" peoples and members of various racial groups have long been integral to production relations in Arabian Peninsula societies. Yet to date the relevance of gender categories to women's changing social status is most fully elaborated for women in elite and majority groups.[3] Especially persistent is an ethnographic bias against examining the socioeconomic roles of ex-slaves and other racial or ethnic minorities.[4]

Members of the group that until recently was assigned to the social category called the akhdam are the focus of this article.[5] Socially, the akhdam, literally servants, are considered by other Yemenis to be even lower than ex-slaves ('abid). Both groups are considered to have origins in East African countries. Whereas the origins of the akhdam are placed in the mythical past, the East African ancestry of 'abid is both more recent and more often acknowledged by group members themselves.

As a group, the akhdam are relegated to work that is considered demeaning by those in more respected social categories. Akhdam women, however, are invisible in economic production to an extent exceeding that of women in higher social positions. Furthermore, while akhdam is a racialized servant category in popular perceptions, images of the female members of the group are also exploited sexually. In the mid-1980s akhdam women acted as low-commissioned selling agents for grain farmers or sold certain vegetables, especially leeks (karrath), that were both culturally and commercially devalued. They were also agricultural workers, market women, musical entertainers, and domestic servants. Yet, despite their undeniable participation in various sectors of the economy, akhdam women tended to be stigmatized and stereotyped as prostitutes.

Women born into the lowest-status group, presumed to be of African descent and routinely stigmatized, envisioned themselves differently from the perceptions of most others within and outside of Yemeni society. Accordingly, akhdam women did not necessarily exclude key considerations of family honor and personal dignity from their calculations of self-worth. Akhdam women who resolved to preserve their cultural integrity were doubly peripheralized. They defied their invisibility in the face of both indigenous and ethnographic presumptions.

Akhdam women negotiate their identities and transcend verbal and other forms of discrimination routinely in their daily encounters. Often, in deflecting negative categorization, akhdam women seemed conscious of their roles as agents of socioeconomic change. The term *invisible survivors* refers to women who occupy various positions in the social hierarchy, particularly the lowest, and whose strategies as subsistence, household, and commercial producers are potentially transformative for the entire social economy.

In Yemen, the values that people attach to racial differences are evident in the relationships of women as economic producers. As in other Middle Eastern countries, Yemeni ideas and attitudes about such phenotypic variations as skin color and hair types are intertwined with other culturally defined categories of difference. Consequently, the intersection of racial and gender differences within the social and sexual hierarchy helps shape the cultural dimension of women's work relationships.

"Fields" of Invisibility: The Racial Dimension

Proper depiction of akhdam women's invisibility in production relationships requires the consideration of race as an analytic and cultural category. Although the principal locations of my fieldwork were a southern farming village and a northern coastal town, the term *invisible,* with respect to complexly related racial and gender categories, applies most starkly to a third location. In the northern capital of San'a, the shadowy figures of beggars and street sweepers, mainly women and children, blended with the dusty city streets. Ironically, the most visible persons on the streets of the northern highlands capital are these beggars and street sweepers. Though they are all Muslims and are not necessarily darker-skinned than other Yemenis, the social dimensions of akhdam women's marginalization could, however, be understood in terms of race. As Audre Lorde states, referring to the United States: "Within this country where racial difference creates a constant, if unspoken, distortion of vision, Black women have on one hand always been highly *visible,* and so, on the other hand, have been rendered *invisible* through the depersonalization of racism" (emphasis mine).[6]

In Lorde's assessment, African American women's identities are not envisioned even though their racial difference makes them visible. Similarly, akhdam women on Yemeni streets have been both more and less visible to other Yemenis and even to outsiders.

In Yemen, racial designations tend to blur the distinctions among low-status groups. In the village, as an African American, I was intrigued by what became a playful ritual between non-akhdam women and me.[7] When I pointed out to them that my own brown skin color nearly matched theirs, non-akhdam women then laughingly held their wrists to mine to confirm the likeness. Thus, Yemenis from different social groups are not always distinguishable on the basis of the color of their skin or other racial features such as hair types. Still, all akhdam are referred to as "black" (aswad) even though the complexion of all groups in the region tends to be a variation of chestnut brown. Interestingly, villagers corrected me when I referred to myself as "black," saying that I was "brown" (samra').

Throughout Yemen, "nontribal" servant groups, namely the khaddam, who are not African-identified—as well as those whose African origins are real ('abid) or reputed (the akhdam)—are all referred to as black by people in other social categories.[8] In line with this practice, upon hearing that I planned to relocate from Dabab to 'Abs, villagers inquired, "Why do you want to go there?—All of them [Tihamis] are black." Villagers thereby denoted their awareness of the high ratio of dark-skinned coastal residents. Tihamis themselves designated nonservants as "white" (abayd). Thus, one's position in society is less a matter of race in Yemen than in the United States, but Yemenis use culturally defined racial terms to denote social status.

Racial differences were most pronounced in coastal Yemeni society. There, the consequences of contacts with African cultures, dating back to antiquity, were readily observed in contemporary work relationships. Such contacts were apparent in the physical appearance of residents whose skin coloring ranged from light to near black and whose body types covered an equally wide range. Architecturally, Tihama houses, with their mud-and-thatch roofs, called 'ushash, largely account for a landscape that is strikingly similar to that found on the other side of the Red Sea. Although slavery was legitimate in (North) Yemen until the early 1960s, and although various Africans (and Asians) continue to supply cheap labor (usually women) as well as technical assistance (usually men), most Yemenis take for granted the diversity of the country's workforce. The racial component of Yemeni social inequality generally, and of akhdam women's invisibility specifically, must nevertheless be evaluated within the broader context of gender roles and social relations.

Hierarchical Social Institutions

Attitudes affecting relationships between akhdam and non-akhdam, though state-supported, are also influenced by the modernization of Yemeni social identities. Following the revolution of 1962, which overthrew the conservative Zaydi imams, all social categories including slavery were officially abolished. Although it was outlawed, Yemenis remained dependent on this intricate hierarchical system, based on birth status and occupation, to define social status. Yemeni racial, ethnic, and gender ideologies, as we have seen, have also remained implicit in the social categories.

Servant groups (khaddam, 'abid, and akhdam) are still regarded as deficient (*naqis*) by Yemenis who claim an honorable descent status. "Deficiency" signifies that individuals are social, not racial, inferiors who are not entitled to use the term *qabili* (fem. *qabiliyah;* pl. *qaba'il,* tribespersons) for self-reference. Similarly, servant categories are differentiated from elite categories, especially *sayyids* (literally, descendants of the Prophet) and *qadis* (Islamic judges and administrators). In the 1980s the services provided by the three servant groups overlapped considerably. But only low-status individuals served as barbers, butchers, and wedding and circumcision specialists. Depending on region, these specialists were also known by the various titles of their occupations. Thus, Yemenis attach greater significance to an ancestry in which both lineage and occupational status are understood than to race per se. However, Yemenis construe race (or color) to represent positions in the social hierarchy—not the other way around.

Nevertheless, the official rhetoric of the postrevolutionary republic in the north proclaimed in the preamble to the Constitution of 1970, "We the Yemenis are an Arab and Muslim people." Neither the unique social hierarchy nor the component groups were named. It was the explicit connection, however, between being Arab and being of honorable descent, in both official and nonofficial views, that ensured that Yemeni groups who were denied tribal ancestry would remain less than fully acknowledged citizens.[9] The deeply ingrained perceptions of racial differences were sanctioned by the government even though discrimination against certain groups was not necessarily attributed specifically to race.

(North) Yemen's commitment to the egalitarian ideals of a Muslim state has been reaffirmed since reunification. In the decade before reunification, opportunities for economic advance were not equally accessible to the various members of the society. Overt signs that the rigid system of ranked social categories was being dismantled were apparent only among the more privileged groups. In urban settings, in the highlands capital of San'a, and in the coastal plains town of 'Abs, akhdam women and men as subordinate laborers remain under the control of their municipalities.

Invisible Shadows in Urban Life

During the 1980s akhdam women in San'a were engaged both in a regulated sector of the economy (street sweeping) and in an unregulated sector (begging). Thus, like Yemeni women generally, akhdam women were not limited to unregulated "informal" activity. Invisibility, therefore is not synonymous with informality. The emphasis on fluid boundaries between formal and informal income-generating activities, while useful, has limited application in the Yemeni case.[10] The labels *informal* and *formal*, therefore, do not describe the extent to which the akhdam, including both women and men in various work, are ignored by state authorities.

During the 1980s government-sponsored changes in the jobs traditionally performed by akhdam of both sexes provided the group with certain limited advantages. Street sweeping was "elevated" by titles such as *muwazzafin lil baladiyah* (municipal employees) or *'ammal al-nazafah* (workers of cleanliness). These jobs, most visibly performed by women and children, paid well relative to the standards of the day. But the work was not always voluntary. Even after the social categories were outlawed, akhdam individuals were brought from the coastal plains areas to San'a for street cleaning. Public water and sewer officials denied that coercion was used.

Forced displacements of akhdam were perhaps more common in the more distant past. Fifty years ago, a group of akhdam was forced to relocate to 'Abs in order to service the market, according to non-akhdam residents of the town. These involuntary resettlements indicate that municipal authorities persistently disregard the rights of akhdam citizens for the sake of expediency. Because *qaba'il* (tribespersons) could not be enticed to engage in occupations they deemed unacceptable, certain workers—street sweepers and people of the market (*ahl-as-suq*)—are considered indispensable by the authorities. Qaba'il males might work as garbage truck drivers, but even akhdam males usually are not observed as sweepers. The akhdam benefit from others' refusal to perform socially demeaning work. However, the financial rewards could not be realized beyond certain limits.[11] Local authorities, therefore, regarded the akhdam as a "reserve army" who could be commandeered to provide essential services that are refused by others. To ensure that sanitation standards are met, local officials justify the violation of akhdam human rights by offering them financial compensation.

In 1994, when I returned to Yemen, government-supported projects aimed at incorporating akhdam women or families were underway in certain northern highland cities. These programs suggested that akhdam women are not now viewed as nonpersons by state officials. However, akhdam women's invisibility continues within the economy, as does their subjection to sexual stereotyping, based on the presumptions by non-akhdam males that akhdam families are weak associations that are incapable of protecting their members.[12] Despite seeking various employment opportunities, akhdam women in particular remain a mythological presence—a kind of cultural chimera[13] on the Yemeni landscape.

Social Contexts of Economic Relationships: Village Women's Interactions

An examination of akhdam social and economic interactions with other Yemenis appeared virtually impossible in the more urban settings of the country. In San'a, the akhdam lived on the outskirts of the city, crowded together in a compound that was often described (accurately) as a heap of garbage. I elected instead to live in a village where the akhdam were integrated into daily life with the Yemeni majority—tribespeople and farmers—and with non-African-identified servants (khaddam). In this setting, it was possible to observe the extent to which women in general recognized their potential as contributors to local economic relationships.

Wadi Dabab contained scattered villages of a hundred persons or fewer in the southern agricultural midlands region of the country. Houses of the different groups were interspersed. Most people referred to themselves as farmers (ra'iyah) rather than as tribespersons (qaba'il). A family of barbers-circumcisers (khaddam) lived in the village area. One extended akhdam family were client farm laborers for the household of the village administrator (qadi). However, with the exception of local leaders (shaykhs, or sheikhs by other contributors and shayuk in the proper Arabic plural, as well as qadis), residents belonged to non-landowning families and lived in conditions that were meager even by Yemeni standards. Non-landowning tribespersons/farmers were either renters, sharecroppers, or occasionally day-laborers. Interdependence between landless farmers, servants, and landowning elites was represented by a patron-client village organization.

In other small villages, the benefits of remittances from male out-migration were markedly in evidence by the mid-1980s, but most men in Dabab, regardless of social category, could not afford exit visas. The akhdam had been prevented from owning land until the 1960s, although by 1994 some had acquired a small piece of rain-dependent land. Labor migration, the major avenue for upward mobility, for the most part remained closed to them. Thus, while the transition from subsistence agriculture to cash-based economy was underway, in Wadi Dabab it seemed a slower process than in other small villages in the country.

Women's traditional roles had not changed drastically. No girls and very few boys were attending school in nearby Ta'izz in the mid-1980s. As in other rural areas, however, women's work in the field, the home, and the marketplace in Dabab was essential to the local economy. Furthermore, women's participation in various sectors of the economy preceded Yemen's entry into the global market.[14] Typically, agricultural, domestic, and commercial production units consisted of women belonging to the groups of elite (sayyids or qadis), tribespersons/farmers (qaba'il/ra'iyah), and servants (khaddam and akhdam), whose roles were based on mutual obligations. As in most rural villages throughout Yemen, women in both "tribal"/farmer and servant groups also contributed to family and local economies by selling homemade foodstuffs in the market.

Women in all social categories routinely worked unveiled. In contrast to San'a, where veiling was the norm, women in Dabab wore headscarves rather than covering the face. It was only on special occasions, such as a

Suq ad Dabab, market women, 1983. Photo: Delores Walters.

woman's wedding day or a rare trip to Ta'izz, that women wore the traditional full-length *sharshaf*. Even women in landowning or elite families
who lived in relative seclusion had workloads comparable to those of their
less affluent sisters. Only comparatively wealthy, high-status women, or
sometimes women of marriageable age, were restricted from selling their
foodstuffs in the market. Most households in Dabab simply could not economically afford to impose such limits on women's activity.

Most village residents lived at subsistence level. The integration of the
houses belonging to the various groups perhaps underscored this fact.
Obligatory interactions *between* groups were governed less by economics
than by considerations of social status. This may explain the strict adher-
ence to cultural convention when conducting certain social relations across
categorical lines. One of my encounters as revealed below strikingly con-
veys the ideal of social separation:

> On a rare rainy day in the village, I go down to our former landlord's
> house to borrow a shovel for re-digging our outhouse. Ni'ama and a
> small group of men and women in the qaba'il category are squatting
> around a pot of *fatut* and *samn* (sorghum porridge and clarified but-
> ter) in her new kitchen. Zakia 'Ali, who would soon be attending to
> the special work of an older *khadima* [washing Ni'ama's new baby],
> is eating off to the side by herself, as is the young couple's toddler son.
> I am invited to join the main group.[15]

This example demonstrates the measures taken by most villagers to
maintain their social distance from the akhdam (in this instance, a khadima, fem. sing.). The meal served to Zakia 'Ali was in part her fee for
rendering infant care services. Clearly, as an impoverished individual, she
could not refuse this form of payment simply because it was degradomg to
do so. Thus, while the women shared an impoverished existence, they were
not united by class. Rather, women in the various social categories were
committed to culture-bound prejudices.

> Consequently, women organized their work within their respective
> social categories, rather than across categorical lines. Chores were
> performed in groups based on kin networks. Women of the same
> household and from adjoining houses of agnatic or affinal kin rou-
> tinely joined one another in collecting firewood and in performing
> other chores outside the home. The older daughters of the qadi and
> those women related by blood or marriage to the qadi's brother and
> sons could be seen embarking in twos and threes to gather wood in
> the late afternoon. Women of the smaller akhdam and qaba'il house-

holds joined other women of their own groups to gather wood or to perform such tasks as washing clothes. Young women teamed up to fertilize the fields that were owned or, more often, rented by their kinsmen. Joining them in the fields meant backbreaking work—not the party that their enthusiastic invitations suggested.

Women in the village did not intimate that their work teams provided them with mutual support and companionship. Such information was given only vaguely and implicitly. Passing by Ni'ama's house one evening, she says, "Three years ago, before the *hawd* [covered, piped water source] was constructed, we young girls (she was unmarried then) used to go to the wadi in the *suq* or at Mawkhaza on such a moonlit night. During the day, it was too hot." Her nostalgic reminiscences bring a smile, revealing that a good time must have been had by all.[16]

Such memories of camaraderie were more than just pleasant interludes sparked by the weather. While they understated it, women appreciated the supportive environment that their work units provided. Women's most explicit concern was for their reproductive responsibilities. Yet child care, which was also built into their work groups, was merely taken for granted. Consequently, in Dabab, despite a daily routine that included farming and household chores—lifting and hauling water, firewood, and fodder—a woman's response to the question of what she was doing on a given day invariably was *"jalis"* (sitting; women used the masculine active participle). To a certain extent, the reality of Yemeni women's roles as producers was unrecognized even by themselves.

The social significance of women's work and of collaboration for this purpose was most vividly demonstrated in akhdam families. The atmosphere was emotionally supportive of akhdam women's work, similar to that of the kin groups of women in other social categories. Zuhra, one of our neighbors in Dabab who was designated a khadima by others, illustrated this in her relation to her paternal family. Not long after reminiscences with Ni'ama confirmed how valuable women's work collectives were to them socially, Lee and I took one of our first trips with Zuhra. On leaving the village, I noticed that Zuhra's mood visibly changed as we headed for her parents' home:

It is a half-hour's ride going south to the pilgrimage center of Yufrus. Zuhra was reluctant at first to accompany us [Lee and me]. She had concluded on the basis of our past trips with her neighbor, Sa'ida, that we did not seek any other companions, and Sa'ida had insinu-

Wadi Dabab, 1983. Photo: Delores Walters.

ated as much. During the ride, Zuhra, who is not usually enthusiastic, has indeed become less somber. Then, when we get to her house, which is situated at the bottom of the hill before reaching the town, she becomes almost ebullient. She is obviously delighted to be able to offer her sisters the bottled water we have brought. (Yemen has two modern mineral water plants, but not the facilities to dispose of the plastic containers, which now litter towns and countryside.) When we return from our visit to the shrine, Zuhra greets us on the road, taking me by the hand to the lunch she has helped to prepare.[17]

It was clear that Zuhra's family was not surrounded by goodwill from their neighbors. Zuhra had to endure taunts from taxi drivers—which she ignored. A self-appointed guide in Yufrus was incredulous that we had been invited to lunch with that "bint" (girl). He then rescinded his own invitation and advised us to move our American friend's car, parked in what, from his point of view, was "the wrong side of town." Such occurrences illustrate not only the persistence of prejudicial attitudes against the akhdam, but also the role of akhdam homes as a haven from hostilities.

Another dimension of women's work and of women's work groups was also exhibited in this encounter. Although Zuhra spoke mainly of the superior environment at her father's place in terms of material comforts, including a more substantial daily diet, she undoubtedly derived a great deal of

Zuhra (d. 1995), Wadi Dabab. Photo: Delores Walters.

satisfaction from less tangible factors. She was not a guest at her father's house but a contributing individual to a large household. Members of this family had been servants for the shaykh over generations, a fact they cheerfully acknowledged when I mentioned on one occasion that we had visited their town leader. Such immediate verification of their connection to the shaykh suggested that they were proud to serve an important household, service that in turn confirmed their stature, at least in their own eyes. Furthermore, according to qabili (tribal) codes of honor, subordinates were considered protected clients of a shaykh in return for their domestic service.

On my subsequent visit, Zuhra had returned to her parent's home, leaving the house in the village that had been provided for her and the two sons by her husband, who lived in Ta'izz with another wife. It was clear that Zuhra received positive reinforcement of her self-image from her natal family. It was also apparent from her inquiry about Sa'ida that she had derived emotional support from her qabiliya neighbor in Dabab. Women depended on others—actual kin, close neighbors, or faithful servants—to complete household chores and for child care. In some instances, familial relations overlapped with the mutual obligations that were expressed in patron-client bonds. Women bonded together in carrying out essential chores, which for most households were virtually the same. Generally, as previously mentioned, these tasks were accomplished in cooperation with other women of the same social grouping. However, exclusivity in these working relationships was not strictly maintained. Still, neighborliness extended only so far. Sa'ida claimed that she was a shaykh's daughter (*bint al-shaykh*) and identified herself as a qabiliya. (Her claims invariably were discounted by those who claimed equal or higher status.) She played the role of the good neighbor but rejected the possibility of her children marrying a *khadim* or *khadima,* below their status.

Women's Interactions in a Coastal (Tihama) Town

In part, women's lack of recognition of their own organized work efforts explains women's tendency to see their various responsibilities—whether

Wadi Dabab, 1983. Photo: Delores Walters.

in the household, field, or market—as inseparable. On the other hand, women's work has typically been underrecognized in official circles because the services rendered to social superiors by a domestic team such as Zuhra's were not income-producing. In the town of 'Abs, women generated an income from work they performed at home. Work and social activity incorporated the various social groups.

'Abs is located inland in the Tihama or coastal plains region. It lies to the north of the port city of Hudayda, and south of Jizan in Saudi Arabia. The beginning of economic growth resulting from Saudi remittances was evident in 'Abs during the 1980s. Transformations of this kind were typical of small towns all over Yemen at that time. Unlike the women in Dabab, those in 'Abs were rarely seen carrying twenty-liter *dubbas* (plastic water jugs) on their heads uphill to their homes. Donkeys and wheelbarrows were used for this purpose. Though not atypical, villages such as Dabab existed on the fringes of Yemen's economic expansion.

Another notable difference was that residents of 'Abs spoke more openly about their qabili (tribal) origins than in Dabab, where such information, even after a year, remained largely piecemeal. According to a recognized historian in the town who was a qabili (tribesman), people in 'Abs were descended from the Bani Thawab, who after moving down from the mountains lived in the foothills just east of 'Abs. The qabili agreed that both 'abid and akhdam followed or belonged (*tabi'a*) to the same territorial domain, but neither they nor the Hunud (natives of India with whom the qaba'il intermarried) were indicated on the genealogical chart he had drawn. Oral traditions, rather than written genealogies, revealed the interrelationships among various groups.

In the past, the town of 'Abs was divided into multiple overlapping sections designated according to the various ethnic, tribal, social, and economic production communities. In the 1980s the town consisted of two main sections: the suq (market), where the akhdam lived, surrounded by the medina (town), where tribespersons (qaba'il) and ex-slaves ('abid) were the primary residents. Houses were evenly divided between the mud-and-thatched roof dwellings and the newer cinder block constructions. Households of prominent families, shaykhs, for example, continued to rely on domestic servants, who were formerly slaves ('abid). Elite women, such as the merchants' daughters in Bayt Hadrami at the beginning of this chapter, also relied on servants and nonservants of both genders to supply them with imported cloth and to market the finished garments. Akhdam women acted as sellers or buying agents. Akhdam and 'abid males acted as suq managers for prominent families.

In both the village and town where we lived, women's productive and procreative labors were performed both within the home and outside it, as if they were merely extensions of one another. Social visiting was also not strictly distinguishable from economic and other kinds of activity. Thus, while one of the Hadrami sisters was working on a dress (*qamis*), sewing by hand, another sister was referring to certain events at the time a certain baby had been circumcised, or to trips taken to various cities for medical care; still another was choosing and purchasing dress material.

In 'Abs, where there was more time for leisure, women engaged in the more formalized socializing prevalent in Oman, for example, and other

Tihama household, 1983. Photo: Delores Walters.

parts of the Middle East.[18] In Dabab, almost constant interaction occurred between persons of the same and differing social categories. However, women in the village merely incorporated stops at each other's houses for a chat into their farming and household chores. The distinction between work and socializing was more blurred in 'Abs than in Dabab. Because social and work relations of ex-slaves in the households of former masters often overlapped, it was difficult to determine the social rank of intergroup and interfamilial participants. Also, since sociability was a dominant feature of women's gatherings, it almost seemed inaccurate to describe their activities as "work."[19] Thus, while I described the household of the merchant's daughters in the opening vignette as a "sewing factory," they did not designate it as such.

The various aspects of the Hadrami household production followed certain social norms with respect to gender identity, and there was a clear division of labor according to social status as well. None of the women, all within childbearing age, was ever seen in the suq. This included the seamstresses' assistant, Sabah, whom I judged to belong to a family of former slaves. The seamstresses, being the daughters of an elite merchant, were prevented by their high status from having a public market role. In Sabah's case, her age, rather than her social background, may have been the most important factor in preventing her from performing public duties. Other women in the region, usually older and often from bordering mountain villages, came regularly to the market to sell various items on the weekly market day. Restriction of the Hadrami sisters to the domestic sphere did not curtail their economic enterprise. It simply necessitated that a salesman bring imported cloth to their home. The sisters negotiated prices directly with this middleman, who also marketed the completed garments.

I viewed the businesslike way in which the self-reliant Hadrami sisters handled their sewing operations as analogous to their father's business acumen in manufacturing *shamma* (snuff). Our landlady explained that the father of the sisters was a "big" merchant. Unlike her own husband, who sold merely food and petty goods, Hadrami employed men who ground tobacco on hand mills in the mud-walled structures reserved for that purpose. High-status males also engaged in market transactions indirectly through trusted agents. Similarly, high-status women's income-producing activities were out of public view.[20] Their production was not devalued simply because the producers were females who worked in a social atmosphere.

Clearly, the sisters were serious producers whose aim was to make a profit, albeit in the context of traditional responsibilities as wives and mothers. Obviously, too, the women recognized the remunerative value of their work even though it was home-based. However, working at home also allowed them to uphold the cultural ideal of being a secluded, leisurely class. Therefore, their stature as high-status Muslim women was not compromised by doing business with men and allowing their goods to be sold to strangers.

In the Middle East generally, one measure of upward mobility was the reduction of women's physical labor outside the home.[21] In Yemeni cities, a move up the economic ladder, even for akhdam women, meant greater confinement. Village women in Dabab identified with the ideal of not having to work, but their idealizations contrasted with women's experiential reality. 'Absi women, adhering to a standard of leisure and seclusion, confronted an equally strong incentive—the desire for economic autonomy. In neither location was women's industriousness ever in question.

Women's Self-Images Reinforced?: The Political Sphere

Whether paid or unpaid, Yemeni women worked in groups that reflected their participation in a network of reciprocal obligations and exchanges. By joining together to carry out domestic, agricultural, and social responsibilities, women contributed to community productivity. Their work groups, an expression of group identity, provided social, not political, solidarity. Thus, women who organized their labor did not necessarily constitute a united front for social change. Moreover, the system of ranking individuals according to the hierarchical social categories continued to operate in women's work and social relationships.[22]

On the other hand, there was also evidence that women in both subordinate and superior groups were challenging the system of social and sexual inequality in various ways. In one household in Dabab, women explicitly rejected being categorized as akhdam. They considered themselves bound by the moral codes of Islam and adamantly opposed even innuendos suggesting otherwise. While these women expressed their outrage, on moral grounds, at being labeled as akhdam, they also resisted cultural limitations on their gender roles and sexual identities. For example, one young woman who contributed to her family's income by selling produce in the town market refused to accept her father's commitment to marriage and childbearing as a woman's only viable option.

Women in other social groups were conscious of their subordination based on gender, but unlike akhdam women, they rarely acknowledged other forms of social inequality. Thus, a divorced landowning qabiliya refused to remarry because of the possibility that she would lose her land rights. Yet her interactions with her female akhdam neighbors were a vociferous attempt to keep them in their place. Gender inequities were more often the basis for a non-akhdam woman's social consciousness.

Although women in the village were negotiating social or sexual boundaries for themselves, akhdam women in particular had few reference points for reestablishing their identities. Government initiatives are only beginning to address akhdam women's social marginalization. There was also little evidence that akhdam women were utilizing external sources for self-validation. Indeed, village women who rejected the label *akhdam* also disavowed any association with practices attributed to the akhdam. Specifically, the *zar* exorcism rituals, widely considered to be of African origin and usually thought to be the special province of the akhdam, were ridiculed by these women.[23] Akhdam women only vaguely identified with other African images or practices.[24] Thus, women who disassociated themselves from the akhdam label did not look beyond Yemen for positive self-images.

Conclusion: Envisioning Women in the Development Process

In the mid-1980s, it was apparent that women at the very bottom of the Yemeni social scale had the potential to stimulate new social, political, and economic relationships. To regional planners, however, low-status women's contributions to local and family economies remained a largely unacknowledged resource. Despite continued government depersonalization and despite varying degrees of exclusion from respectable social circles and economic competition, akhdam women were nevertheless in the process of renegotiating their social status.

The intersection of race with other, culturally defined categories of difference played a significant role in the construction of women's production relationships in the mid-1980s. An analysis of akhdam women's invisibility in the Yemeni social economy requires the inclusion of issues of race as well as gender. As street sweepers, akhdam women are a conspicuous reality. Racial conceptualizations are a lens through which their marginal status could be viewed. In the village and town where I worked, racialization and sexualization of akhdam women as workers ensured their continued subjugation. It is not yet clear whether the racial ideologies built into a particularly rigid social hierarchy will also facilitate definitions of self and social agency by akhdam women.

Further, while Yemeni women generally have been essential contributors to family and local economies, their work also is not fully recognized. Part

South Yemeni women of slave origin in handicrafts association. Photo: Richard A. Lobban, Jr.

of the explanation is that women have not seen themselves as "workers." In addition, women's commercial labor often took place within the socially oriented atmosphere of the home. Women in general remained hidden within production relationships; akhdam women were virtually invisible.

The particular needs and contributions of diverse women in various sectors of the economy warrant recognition by regional and state planners. In an increasingly globalized economy, policy makers may take one of two routes: They may unwittingly reinforce deeply ingrained beliefs about marginalized and racialized groups, or they may incorporate the self-help efforts of stigmatized peoples into development objectives. Yemen's postrevolutionary ban on the system of social categorization may be seen as a step toward the latter. Greater inclusion of women and minorities in the unified and post–civil war Republic of Yemen may be achieved by adopting the approach of former South Yemen in dealing with social inequities. Under the Marxist regime, people were reeducated about discrimination, and liberal reforms with respect to women's status were instituted.[25] It was evident in the south that redefinitions of self by Yemenis having little power to resist state-fostered images and representations of themselves require official and public sanction. In the north, only Yemenis whose sense of self is consistently legitimized have received such support. Still, whether or not a state-sponsored discourse is enacted, women's initiatives are occurring, not just at the top and middle of the hierarchy but at the lowest ends of the social spectrum as well.

Notes

I wish to thank Mahyoub Anaam, Phillip Richards, Lee Maher, Najwa Adra, and Paula Johnson for their support and editorial comments.

1. Excerpt from my field notes dated 12 November 1983. All names of individuals in this and subsequent excerpts are pseudonyms.

2. My research was supported by the Fulbright-Hays and Social Science Research Council Dissertation Fellowships during 1982–84. An American Institute for Yemeni Studies (AIYS) Fellowship funded my research in 1994.

3. See Soraya Altorki, "Women, Development and Employment in Saudi Arabia: The Case of 'Unayzah," in Joseph G. Jabbra and Nancy W. Jabbra, eds., *Women and Development in the Middle East and North Africa* (Leiden: E. J. Brill, 1992); Susan Dorsky, *Women of 'Amran: A Middle Eastern Ethnographic Study* (Salt Lake City: University of Utah Press, 1986); Christine Eickelman, *Women and Community in Oman* (New York: New York University Press, 1984); Cynthia Myntti, "Yemeni Workers Abroad: The Impact on Women," *Middle East Report*, no. 124 (June 1994): 11–16. A contrast is provided by Valentine M. Moghadam,

Modernizing Women: Gender and Social Change in the Middle East (Boulder, Colo., and London: Lynne Rienner, 1993). She concludes that middle-class women in the Middle East are in the vanguard of social change.

4. African cultural and historical identities tend to be subsumed under Arab identities. Exceptions include Fredrik Barth, *Sohar: Culture and Society in an Omani Town* (Baltimore: Johns Hopkins University Press, 1983); Abdalla S. Bujra, *The Politics of Stratification: A Study of Political Change in a South Arabian Town* (Oxford: Clarendon Press, 1971); R. B. Serjeant, "South Arabia and Ethiopia: African Elements in the South Arabian Population," in *Proceedings of the Third International Conference of Ethiopian Studies* (Addis Ababa: Haile Selassie I University, 1966). For a study of the impact of nonindigenous racial-ethnic labor migrants on women's identities, see Anh Nga Longva, "Kuwaiti Women at a Crossroads: Privileged Development and the Constraints of Ethnic Stratification," *International Journal of Middle East Studies* 25, no. 3 (August 1993): 443–56. Also, gender and class inequities are considered in Joseph Jabbra and Nancy Jabbra, eds., *Women and Development in the Middle East and North Africa* (Leiden: E. J. Brill, 1992).

5. For an extended discussion of the position of the akhdam within Yemen's social organization, see Delores M. Walters, "Perceptions of Social Inequality in the Yemen Arab Republic" (Ph.D. dissertation, New York University, 1987).

6. Audre Lorde, "The Transformation of Silence into Language and Action," in *Sister Outsider: Essays and Speeches by Audre Lorde* (Trumansburg, N.Y.: Crossing Press, 1984), 42.

7. During this field study, I was also fortunate in having as a companion Lee Maher, a fair-skinned European American whom Yemeni women referred to as my *rafiqah* (escort), considering her to be my mother, thus ignoring the obvious racial differences.

8. The terms *akhdam* and *khaddam* are both derived from the same triliteral Arabic root, *kh-d-m,* meaning to serve.

9. Most Yemeni denials that race had any bearing on how groups were defined appeared to apply mainly to their perception of past attitudes. The effect of increasing exposure to Western media images on Yemeni racial consciousness has not been explored.

10. See, for example, Manuel Castells and Alejandro Portes, "World Underneath: The Origins, Dynamics, and the Effects of the Informal Economy," in Castells Portes and Lauren Benton, eds., *The Informal Economy: Studies in Advanced and Less Developed Countries* (Baltimore and London: Johns Hopkins University Press, 1989), 12.

11. When akhdam sewer cleaners (males) demanded wages considered excessive by officials in Ta'izz, they were replaced by migrant Pakistani and Indian workers.

12. Until the revolution, the symbolic display of one's status as protector of subordinates, especially the highlands custom of wearing the ceremonial dagger (*jambiya*), was denied to low-status groups.

13. My thanks to Huda Seif for this expression.

14. Oil was discovered in North Yemen in the mid-1980s. However, as Altorki discusses in "Women, Development and Employment in Saudi Arabia," the significance of women's commercial activity has been underestimated in Arabian peninsula economies before globalization and before oil development.

15. Entry taken from my field notes dated 23 January 1983.

16. Field note entry dated 27 April 1983.

17. Field note entry dated 1 May 1983.

18. See Eickelman, *Women and Community in Oman.*

19. Similarly, Jenny B. White, "Women and Work in Istanbul: Linking the Urban Poor to the World Market," *Middle East Report* 173, vol. 21, no. 6 (November–December 1991): 18–22, discusses women's home production in Turkey as being "disguised as social relations based on reciprocity." See also Lourdes Beneria and Martha Roldan, *The Crossroads of Race and Gender: Industrial Homeworking, Subcontracting, and Household Dynamics in Mexico City* (Chicago: University of Chicago Press, 1987), and Maria Mies, *The Lace Makers of Narsapur: Indian Housewives Produce for the World Market* (London: Zed Press, 1982), who illustrate women's inclination to consider work and leisure as overlapping categories in other Third World contexts.

20. As Cynthia Myntti has discussed, women in Yemen were valued as much for their productive as for their reproductive capabilities; see her "Women and Development in Yemen Arab Republic" (Federal Republic of Germany, German Agency for Technical Development, 1979), 11.

21. For a discussion of the Yemeni case, see Shelagh Weir, *Qat in Yemen: Consumption and Social Change* (Dorchester: British Publications Ltd., 1986).

22. Janet Bujra, "Female Solidarity in the Sexual Division of Labor," in P. Caplan and J. Bujra, eds., *Women United, Women Divided* (London: Tavistock, 1979), 31–33, found that the effect of sex-segregated work groups may actually contribute to perpetuating women's subordination.

23. It was not clear, however, whether the zar was rejected by akhdam women in Dabab as being non-Islamic or non-Yemeni, since it was often considered to be peripheral to Islam or was publicly devalued, especially outside the Tihama.

24. Despite the fact that akhdam women in the village admired my Afro hair style, and often had woolly hair types themselves, they made no effort to adopt any but the most common hair style among Yemeni women generally. Obviously, more data are needed to draw any conclusions regarding akhdam individuals' attitudes toward "race."

25. See Maxine Molyneux, "The Law, the State and Socialist Policies with Regard to Women: The Case of the People's Democratic Republic of Yemen," in Deniz Kandiyoti, ed., *Women, Islam and the State* (Philadelphia: Temple University Press, 1991); and Sheila Carapico, "Women and Public Participation in Yemen," *Middle East Report* 173, vol. 21, no. 6 (November–December 1991): 15.

4

The Invisible Economy, Survival, and Empowerment

Five Cases from Atbara, Sudan

Nada Mustafa M. Ali

The entrapment of the Sudanese state and society in a multidimensional crisis is a well-documented fact. Civil war, political instability, ecological disasters, refugee influx, economic devastation—all are features of this crisis. Above all it is a crisis of representation and interpretation. I argue in this chapter that for historical, socioeconomic, and political reasons, the power center in the Sudan has been dominated, since independence, by the Northern Sudanese male elite, with the result that the visions of the Arab northern male have defined Sudanese history, culture, and identity. Contributions of "other" identities have been considered inessential.

Although women have played important roles in Sudanese society and the economy, their contributions are usually invisible.[1] The ongoing crisis in Sudan, especially in its economic dimension, has highlighted the great value of "women's work" and of coping mechanisms hitherto taken for granted as women's economic activities have become vital for the very survival of many households, particularly in the poor urban areas. In the current state of affairs, there are possibilities for rethinking the Sudanese culture and identity, and it is time for women's voices to be heard. What are women's perceptions of the current crisis, and what are the mechanisms they use in facing this crisis? We need to learn whether women's economic activities have contributed to a change in their self-perceptions, or whether they are still trapped in the dominant patriarchal discourse of "common sense" that relegates women to the position of superfluous "others."

Challenges to the Sudanese State and Society

The Sudanese state has a unique setting among Middle East and African countries: Separated from the Arabian Peninsula by the Red Sea, it covers about 1 million square miles of Africa. The state has been subject to circumstances experienced by other African states—that is, being a colonial creation, with a restricted resource base and structurally distorted economic structure, dependent on the international community for most of its needs.

At the same time, because of its Arab and Islamic ruling class, the country is part of the Middle East. As a result of political, socioeconomic, and historical factors, the elite that has dominated the country since its political independence has been culturally affiliated with the Middle East, and has inherited the "neopatriarchal" nature of this social formation, in the words of a prominent Arab writer, Hisham Sharabi.

Neopatriarchy is identified by Sharabi as the sociopolitical structure resulting from the combination of patriarchy and a system of dependency, as has been the case in Arab society during the last century. Neopatriarchy, Sharabi explains, refers to a specific form of traditionalism that has been absorbed into dependency of a unique character, having a dimension of cultural-intellectual dependency in addition to economic and military dependency.[2] Major threats to such a sociopolitical structure are innovation, consciousness raising, and cultural change.[3]

According to Sharabi, "neopatriarchal society is incapable of repressing new awareness once it penetrates the existing ideological barriers. Social and ideological change in the context of neopatriarchy inevitably lead to some form of structural disintegration, [as happened] in the late Ottoman Empire."[4] In such societies any attempt at innovation or at rethinking history, culture, or the role of women as being socially constructed would be contested by ruling bodies.

Given this framework, one can conclude that being situated in Africa initiated many dimensions of the Sudanese crisis, and being part of the Middle East intensified the country's problems and made their solution a difficult task. The intelligentsia adhered to Western ideas, and the combined forces of patriarchal society and intellectual alienation prevented new ways of thinking. That is why some scholars have stated recently that Sudanese studies are in a crisis that is in some ways no less profound than the other crises in the country at present.[5] One strategy toward reconstructing the Sudan is to look at the daily experiences and perceptions of ordinary men and women.

The analysis in this chapter is based on extensive interviews in March and April 1992 with five women in Atbara, a town three hundred kilometers to the north of Khartoum. Atbara is one of the towns most affected by the economic crisis in the Sudan. As the town is a railroad center, most of its employed inhabitants are linked to the public economic sphere, which is currently deteriorating.

Four of the narrators described here are petty traders in a small market, and the fifth is a housewife. Four of the women belong to northern Sudanese ethnic groups, and the fifth is of West African origin, a Fellata. As all five live in northern Sudan, they do not directly experience the war-

Can handicrafts secure her needs? Photo: Yasmin Bedri.

related destruction taking place in the southern and eastern parts of the country. The stories of women living in the south, for example, would definitely take a different form.

Women's Perceptions of the Crisis

All of the informants acknowledged the existence of a crisis in the country. Based on their daily experiences, they saw mainly an economic crisis: price increases, shortages of certain basic household commodities, impoverishment, and destitution. The five narrators provided comparisons of present and past prices. Their real-life statistics make more sense than the frozen figures produced by official agencies.

One of the women used the term *azma* (crisis) to describe the shortages and the rising costs of goods and services. The narrators perceive the crisis in Sudan in terms of its effects on people's material survival and well-being. They do not see it as being connected to the quest for military superiority, for example, or to import restrictions, or to modern economic theories mainly concerned with profit.

Survival Strategies: "Need Is the Mother of Innovation"[6]

Trading

For Sudanese women, who are disqualified from many formal jobs, informal trading remains a significant option. Women in poor urban areas have long participated in the invisible economy, but their efforts have gone unnoticed. Because of the economic crisis, their presence in the invisible economy is increasing; for example, petty trading and domestic production are gaining importance.

The choice of petty trading as a coping mechanism is conditioned by many factors. In the northern parts of Sudan, women generally have restricted mobility, or their activities are limited to the household domain. The location of a submarket in a *hilla* (village or residential area) makes the woman trader feel that she is part of the domestic sphere, still doing housework.

Through their daily activities, the women interviewed have learned how to address economic crisis in a way that makes them distinct from the males of their class. The women can thus be seen both as victims of crisis and as depositors of knowledge about coping mechanisms.[7] For example, in order to minimize costs and raise profits, the women followed strategies such as small-scale processing and time reallocation.

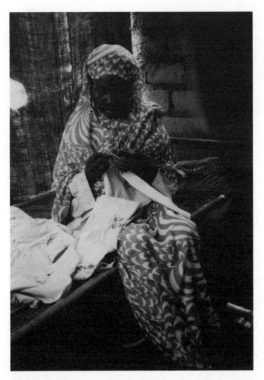

Atbara girl sewing at home. Photo: Yasmin Bedri.

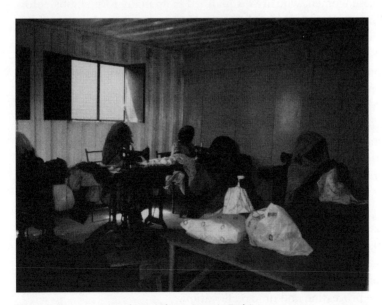

Women's Center sewing classes. Photo: Yasmin Bedri.

The narrators in this chapter stated that they go to the central market in Atbara at times when the vegetables they purchase are low in cost. They are very conscious of the additional value that some commodities gain when milled, ground, or sorted.

Networks for Saving and for Barter

Most of the market women participate in a *sanduq* (literally, a box or container), the popular name for a method of saving money through a rotating credit association—a practice generally associated with women in the Sudan.[8] The sanduq first appeared in the Sudan in the 1940s, a period of economic depression.[9]

The money accumulated in a sanduq is used to buy either materials for resale or foodstuffs needed in the everyday diet of the household. The market women have traded long-term security for survival. The women also exchange goods and services with each other. Community exchange networks are a tradition in various Sudanese communities. Under the prevailing economic conditions, these networks have gained in value, becoming necessities, not simply sites for social interaction.

One of the five narrators constructed a mud oven that is used by the rest of the neighborhood without charge, but users generally donate their leftover flour, or they bring food or fuel for the woman's household. Such items are appreciated more than payment would be at present, because of extreme inflation and because the items themselves are not easily found in the market. As one of the women interviewed stated, "Now, *objects* are more valuable than money."

Another woman performs free medical services for the neighborhood, and these services are gaining in regard, given the lack of medicines and the high costs of medical services. Another woman said that she exchanges medical advice and witchcraft knowledge in return for pastries, tea, and old clothes.

Changing Cultural Patterns

Some cultural practices are either fading away or taking different forms. The ritual of serving *jabana* (coffee), which gave women an opportunity to exchange news and views about social life with each other, is rare at present because of both limited time and economic constraints. The scarcity of sugar and coffee restricts their use for entertainment.

The ceremony of *wadi* (forecasting) is also fading away because of the lack of time. Wadi had often served as psychological relief from the troubles of life by forecasting what the women wished to occur or what the solution would be for a dilemma that had no immediate answer.

Another ceremony that is disappearing is the practice of *zar*, which is considered heresy and nonsense by the regime in power. The zar is a mechanism that was used by Sudanese women and men as a cure for various types of psychological illness. It has provided women with opportunities to escape, resist, and challenge dominant cultural constructs. For example, talking about her experience in zar ceremonies, one of the women said, "I have the *khawaga* [foreigner] thread on me [whenever the khawaga thread was called]. . . . I would go to the center of the circle. I would do whatever came into my [mind]. I could pull my hair, jump up and down, I could say anything; no one would blame me, all the women knew that it was not me, it was a *khawaga*." Stopping zar ceremonies deprived women of the relief they found in articulating frustration, relief not possible through other means of sociopolitical expression.

Another important change in cultural patterns concerned the ancient ritual of *Rahmatat* (the deceased's supper). In many parts of northern Sudan, it is believed that the dead can taste food given on their behalf by their relatives to children and to the poor on the last Friday of Ramadan. As a result, most households in these areas used to distribute certain kinds of food to groups of children of the *hilla* (neighborhood). This ceremony has in fact been given up by the narrators, although it was shameful (according to one of the narrators) for any family not to provide Rahmatat in the past, even if they themselves had very little food.

In the five women's narratives, positive cultural changes were also clear. One is related to segregation and food consumption: In the past, women and men used to eat separately, each gender group using a special tray. The "men's tray" usually was served first and usually contained more food, of better quality, than women and children received. Food shortages, ironically, affected women's position positively. Trays for men and women are now usually combined for economic purposes, eliminating gender-based differences in quantity and quality. As one of the women put it, "*al-mulah* [the stew] cannot be divided into two plates now. Life has changed the people."

Disengagement and Resistance

An important strategy that the narrators pursue, consciously or unconsciously, is disengagement. As a subordinate group, the narrators, along with other women, have developed "subaltern discourses," which help in coping with uncertainty and in explaining events within the women's social network which recognizes that "women are excluded" from the ruling or dominant circles.

Selling petty commodities in a district market is in itself a form of material and psychological disengagement from the deteriorating public sphere. The neopatriarchal nature of the ruling apparatus does not encourage innovation, but in the shadow there is room for innovation. Being part of the "invisible" economy also relieves women of the fear of being dismissed. As one of them said, "Nobody can fire me. I only have these vegetables of mine, and if they [the government] took them, let them take it."

These are empowering aspects of petty trading for women, on both the material and the political level. The material rewards are not very high. Nonetheless, within the context of the current economic crisis, coping mechanisms are of great value, not in terms of abstract monetary gain but of basic human survival.

Consumption and Saving

"We used to throw out the remaining food and bread or give it to the animals, but times have taught us how to keep things," said one of the narrators. The five women have adjusted in various ways to the rise in prices and the shortages of basic household commodities. Alternative commodities and service institutions have been invented by these women.

The quantities of food consumed have been adjusted in a way that satisfies the needs of the whole household. "Now, a half-kilo of meat is divided into two quarters of a kilo, a quarter of a kilo is divided into two parts." These women have learned from their experiences to minimize the impact of severe shortages of basic commodities. For example, remnants of bread, which were not saved for meals in the past, are now kept for emergencies; to quote one of the women, "I have a *shawaal* [big sack] in which I store any remaining pieces of bread after I dry it. If I don't have the money to buy bread, . . . I would cook a very hot *maraga* [soup cubes] with onions. I would then wash the dry bread and pour the *maraga* over it."

The narrator said that she had learned this cooking tip during the floods in many parts of Sudan in 1988. Before that, her dried bread had gone to her neighbor's hens. The storage places of necessary commodities have also changed. Sugar, a commodity that is highly valued, is not stored in the kitchen, as formerly, but is usually "hidden" somewhere in the "mother's" room among other precious materials.

One of women's additional tasks in the hard economic times is that of conserving sugar in the daily *sarfa* (distribution) and making sure there is enough money to buy sugar. Long before Ramadan, an occasion when extra sugar is consumed, housewives begin to save small amounts by reducing daily consumption. These realities contrast with the government's official statement that the country has reached self-sufficiency with regard to sugar and wheat.

One of the narrators adjusted to the rise in transportation costs by walking to and from the market. "The bus driver used to charge two piasters, now four pounds [is the fare]. . . . I don't pay anything. I come on foot. It is too far and I carry those things [her commodities] on my head."

The narratives also indicate that women were able to subvert the institutional constraints by creating their own institutional schemes. As men-

Women basket makers battling poverty. Photo: Yasmin Bedri.

tioned earlier, neighbors shared a mud oven, constructed "just like our grandmothers used to do." This oven lifted the burden of waiting to use the public bakery, where the neighbors had baked bread and pastries in the past years. Moreover, the fuel they used in the mud oven consisted of wood remnants, old clothes, dried orange peels, and dried sugar cane. All cost nothing—in abstract money. Their fuel conserved energy, and it paid off in terms of survival.

Another narrator stated that she dried tomatoes when they were low in cost, then used them for cooking instead of processed tomato paste. This indicates the revival of some valuable traditional ways that might have died out because of the use of expensive modern technology. Self-sufficiency and indigenous ways are lessons to be learned in seeking to reconstruct the public, visible economy.

The narrators found ways to preserve patterns of self-decoration by using less expensive alternatives to customary items that have increased in price. Instead of *mahlabiya,* an oil that darkens henna dye decorations drawn on the skin, women now use lemon juice. One of the women interviewed used nail polish to renew her old sandals; another made slippers for her daughters from old car tires. Both found solutions to the restrictions imposed by the money economy and by factory production.

To what extent are these and other economic contributions recognized in the narrators' self-perceptions? Do these women still hold the cultural views constructed by the hegemonic neopatriarchal order, or have they constructed alternative views—discourses of resistance—based on experience? How can these narratives help in setting the agenda for managing the crisis in Sudan and empowering women?

Conceptions of Self and of Women's Roles

In effect, the five narrators' perspectives combined two forms of consciousness: one emerging out of their activities in the everyday world and the other internalized from the dominant traditions of culture and thought in the northern parts of Sudanese society. From the two forms of consciousness, paradoxical narratives of both subordination and empowerment emerge.

A clear example of the gap between experience and expressed self-perception can be found in the account of one of the narrators who was an authority in preparing certain local medicines for various types of disease. Such treatments are gaining credit at present because of the rising costs of medical services. The narrator, whose husband had divorced her, supported herself through the returns from her medicinal preparations. She was able to maintain the house where the two had lived, although it belonged to her ex-husband's family. Despite all this, the narrator thought of herself as a *miskina* (a "poor" person). The word has many implications besides economic need, including powerlessness and sometimes a tendency toward avoiding problems.

The opposite of the word *miskina* is *shadida*,[10] which in Sudanese colloquial Arabic refers to women who are knowledgeable and powerful, at

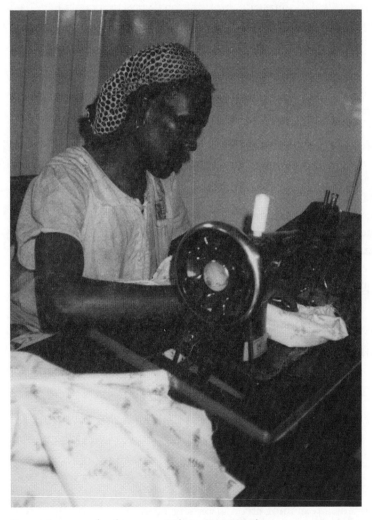

Can sewing secure family expenses? Photo: Yasmin Bedri.

least in terms of the knowledge that they have, through which such women can usually overcome critical situations. The use of these two words, *shadida* versus *miskina*, suggests two conceptualizations of the terms *powerful* and *powerless*.

In this sense, the way in which the five women react to various situations, as well as their major contributions to household survival, brands them as *shadidat* (pl.). Yet they hold the socially hegemonic view and thus call themselves *masakin* (powerless), in contrast to men or formally employed women. Asked if she perceived herself as a *shadida* or not, one of the women said that she was "a sick, old woman, living on the edge of survival." This self-perception contradicts the narrator's reality, because she is considered a knowledgeable person and is often consulted by other women when they buy various commodities from the market.

Another example of the gap between experience and self-perception can be found in views expressed about women working in the formal sector of the economy—in the court system, for example. One of the five narrators, who was divorced, complained that her husband was not providing for the weekly food needs of his family as required by law and expected by Islam. It was her opinion that men in powerful institutional settings, such as judges in court, are unjust, like her ex-husband, and that men do not help women who are poor like herself. However, she did not like the idea of women working as judges. The same view is expressed in the pervasive male discourse.

To sum up, when asked to define themselves in the abstract, the narrators parroted the socially constructed beliefs that women are "passive," "weak," and "idle" creatures. There was hence nonconformity between experience and self-perception. When the women were talking about their experiences and interaction with crisis, the talk often turned into a narrative of empowerment. After talking about strategies for coping, one of the women said, "At present, you might have money but still not be able to buy what you need. Men can only bring us government money. If money stops, the men stop [become useless], too."

Conclusion

In conditions of crisis, there are many options for redefining culture, identity, and the sociocultural value of women's work. Crisis brings to light things that are usually taken for granted; this might threaten the status quo. The narrators' everyday activity in coping with poverty and shortages of basic necessities poses a challenge to the hegemonic concep-

Selling handicrafts in the Atbara market. Photo: Yasmin Bedri.

tual order, which has alienated Sudanese women from their own experiences and has reduced them to superfluous "others."

The narrators' practical contributions to survival are based on knowledge accumulated throughout their daily routines. In the past, these contributions were hidden and were undervalued by the hegemonic order.

Under conditions of crisis, when people on the lower rungs of the social hierarchy cannot meet their basic needs, there are openings for changing social relations. Women's work may get consideration because mere subsistence is no longer a given and has stopped being a marginal element in people's lives. In the long run, this situation leads to suspicion of the "commonsense" beliefs about women and their role in society, history, and culture as the very survival of poor households depends on the work that women do. This situation is likely to change the terms of the pervasive discourse.

In Sudanese history, the prevailing crisis could be an opening in which the self-manifesting of women could occur in various forms, especially if survival and empowerment options offered by "invisible" spaces are self-consciously recognized as spaces for resistance and transformation. Such a development could lead to the dismantling of the whole neopatriarchal system that has set the definition and value of Sudanese identity and culture since the country's independence, and that is our quest.

Notes

This chapter is based on research conducted in Atbara, Sudan, in March–April 1993. Thanks are due to Cyrus Reed, director of the African Studies Center; Cynthia Nelson, dean of the School of Humanities and professor of anthropology; and Enid Hill, professor of political science at the American University in Cairo.

1. See Dorothy Smith, *The Everyday World as Problematic: A Feminist Sociology* (Boston: Northeastern University Press, 1989); and G. Lerner, *The Creation of Patriarchy* (Oxford: Oxford University Press, 1987).

2. Hisham Sharabi, "Patriarchy and Dependency and the Future of Arab Society," in H. Sharabi, ed., *The Next Arab Decade: Alternative Futures* (Boulder, Colo.: Westview Press, 1989).

3. Ibid., 2.

4. Ibid., 3.

5. See, for example, Alex de Waal, "Sudan: Searching for the Origins of Absolutism and Decay," *Development and Change,* no. 24 (1993); and "Introduction," *Dirasat Sudaniya* (Sudanese Studies) (Cairo), no. 1 (1992).

6. A Sudanese proverb, to which one of the narrators referred. The domain defined as "household" differs in range and nature from culture to culture in Sudan. In the context of this study, household refers to the house itself.

7. See Bina Agrawab, "The Gender and Environment Debate: Lessons from India," *Feminist Studies* 181, no. 1 (Spring 1992).

8. F. Rehfish, "A Rotating Credit Association in the Three Towns," in I. Cunnison and W. James, eds., *Essays in Sudan Ethnography* (London: Hurst, 1972), 189.

9. S. Kenyon, *Five Women of Sennar: Culture and Change in Central Sudan* (Oxford: Clarendon, 1991).

10. Ibid. Kenyon refers to these two concepts in the context of *al-Qala (Sennar).*

II

Women and Work: The Invisible Economy of Egypt

The unusual tale of the informal health practitioners in Alexandria by medical anthropologist Marcia Inhorn carries the study of the "invisible" economy to new domains. These women venture into an area conceptualized as an exclusively formal-sector profession. Inhorn reveals how the invisible economy is highly creative in accommodating modern needs within traditional society.

Evelyn Early offers rich detail in four biographies of crafty women entrepreneurs from Cairo. These female "wheelers and dealers" operate with limited capital resources but nevertheless achieve remarkable success and independence of action.

The contribution by Barbara Larson focuses on the rural side, studying women from Beni Suef in Upper Egypt. She finds that they are highly connected to both urban markets and weekly rural markets as domains of their commercial activities. They are engaged in a great diversity of pursuits, including crafts production, agriculture, sewing, and poultry sales.

Marie Butler gives detailed data and analysis of development assistance to home-based microenterprises in Kalyubia in the Egyptian Delta. They build on traditional strengths of the roles of women in small-scale farming and show how chicken and egg batteries can be very successful indeed. Butler's probing analysis of policy and practice extends the focus of this section on Egyptian women in the informal economy.

5

Urban Egyptian Women in the Informal Health Care Sector

Marcia C. Inhorn

This chapter begins with the story of Siham,[1] an Egyptian women's healer who practices unofficially from her home in the crowded back alleys of a poor neighborhood in Alexandria. Siham is a plump, middle-aged woman who, dressed in black with a colorful kerchief tied around her head, looks like any one of the legions of poor women residing in the ancient city. But those who know Siham hold her in high esteem, for within her poor neighborhood she is known as a talented *daya* (traditional midwife), who not only delivers babies but also provides abortions and female circumcisions and helps infertile women overcome their plight through a wide range of folk remedies.

Siham's introduction to midwifery came when she moved into her husband's family's home as a bride. The multiple-story structure was known in the neighborhood as *bait id-dayat* (house of the midwives), for all of the women of Siham's husband's family, including his grandmother, great-aunt, mother, and married sisters, were practicing midwives. Indeed, Siham's mother-in-law was an "educated" daya, one who practiced midwifery "by certificate."

At first, Siham had no interest in the deliveries of infants that occurred in the family's compound and to which her female in-laws were constantly being called. But when she came to work as an all-purpose aide in a gynecologist's private clinic, Siham, an uneducated but highly intelligent woman, began observing the doctor and learning to "circumcise and deliver and do abortions and everything." Siham worked in the doctor's clinic for eight years, when her knowledge of obstetrics and gynecology grew tremendously. Thus, when her mother-in-law died, Siham decided to quit her job at the doctor's clinic and take over the family midwifery business, where she introduced female circumcision and abortion into her practice.

Today, Siham, who is in her mid- to late forties, has a thriving practice because, as she claims, she "knows everything" about helping women overcome their reproductive problems. She is called upon to deliver two to three infants a day, although she is unable to assist all of the women who request her midwifery services. Furthermore, she sees at least two infertile women a day, having developed a reputation in her neighborhood and beyond as a highly skilled infertility specialist. Through physical manipulation of the reproductive organs, through herbal vaginal suppositories, cupping, and a wide range of therapeutic rituals (which make use of fresh placentas and miscarried fetuses, for example), Siham is able to cure her infertile patients. Their afflictions include malpositioned uteri, utero-ovarian *rutuba* (humidity), *dahr maftuh* (open back), *khadda* (shock), and *kabsa* (a.k.a. *mushahara,* or pollution leading to reproductive binding), all considered to be major causes of infertility by Siham and her clients.

Nevertheless, Siham knows that some infertile women and those with other gynecological complaints must be treated by physicians. She explains, "There are injections and lots of things from the pharmacy. Now, medicine is not like before. It is more enlightened." But she adds, "With doctors, you pay a lot and buy medicines and pay for operations. And some people are very poor, and they're scared of doctors. That's why they go to folk remedies. [Doctors'] treatments are surgical operations, like *nafq* (tubal insufflation) and *kaht* (dilatation and curettage) and *kawi* (cervical electrocautery). They just do nafq and such things to get money. Believe me, I'm frank. They get £E 500 or 600 [$200–240]. The doctor I worked with did that, and the cure is from God. . . . There are lots of treatments from doctors, and there are some very good doctors. And there are doctors who only want money and don't help you. They ask for more and more money and nothing happens."

According to Siham, she sends her infertile patients to physicians only when all of her remedies fail to cause pregnancy. However, "thanks to God," she estimates her success rate to be 60 percent.

The "Invisible" Nature of Women's Health and Healing in Egypt

Siham is one of thousands of women healers practicing unofficially in the urban areas of Egypt. Their exact numbers are unknown, and their activities have been largely unaccounted for. Nevertheless, urban Egyptian women healers—primarily older, postmenopausal women with little formal education—are meeting the reproductive health care needs of Egypt's poor urban female populace. They do so through an "informal economy of health care" that remains largely invisible to the authorities (scholarly ones included).

In Egypt, as in most other societies throughout the world, women are expected to assume responsibility for meeting the health care needs of their children and those close to them, often through the direct provision of remedies and other health services in the home.[2] Some women extend their domestic therapy management skills to nonkin, and they may eventually have paying clients and lucrative practices. Today in Egypt, large numbers of women seek the services of women healers, who are often more affordable, sympathetic, and understanding of women's health care beliefs and needs than the mostly male obstetrician-gynecologists (ob-gyns) who practice in urban areas.

Indeed, "modern" medicine itself serves as a major force of therapeutic diversification in Egypt. Because many female patients fail to obtain high-quality health care within the modern medical sector, they tend to fall back on the services available from women healers operating in the informal health care sector. Why do poor urban Egyptian women often prefer the services of healers such as Siham? The reasons lie in both the formal and informal health care sectors in urban Egypt, as well as the dynamic tension operating between them.

Following a brief methodological discussion, this chapter begins by characterizing the formal health care sector in Egypt, focusing on the colonial legacy of biologically based, Western medicine (so-called biomedicine) in Egypt and on some of biomedicine's contemporary deficiencies. The approach in this section is one of cultural critique,[3] since I am interested in examining critically the ways in which the formal health care sector fails to meet the needs and expectations of Egyptian women as health care consumers.[4] This chapter then characterizes the informal health care sector in urban Egypt, including a typology of female "ethnomedical" practitioners. Most important, I examine the reasons why so many poor Egyptian women patients choose healers such as Siham—who dedicate themselves to helping their fellow women but whose services go officially unrecognized—over treatment in the formal biomedical sector.

Methodology

The anthropological research upon which this chapter is based was carried out between October 1988 and December 1989 in Alexandria. This historic seaport city, located on the northwestern tip of the Nile Delta where it meets the Mediterranean Sea, is today a markedly class-stratified city of an estimated 3 million to 5 million inhabitants, many of them poor migrants from rural areas of both Upper and Lower Egypt.

This research was carried out in Alexandria's poor urban and periurban neighborhoods. Women who participated in this study were first contacted at the University of Alexandria's Shatby Hospital, the public ob-gyn teaching hospital serving mostly lower- and lower-middle-class women from the Alexandria vicinity. Participant observation and semistructured interviews were conducted in the hospital with 190 reproductive-aged women, 90 of whom were fertile and 100 of whom were infertile. The vast majority were poor women from migrant families. Most were illiterate, uneducated, and unemployed (given the stigma surrounding women's nondomestic work in this population).[5]

It was through these women, many of whom invited me to their homes, that I gained a tremendous amount of information and insight about the nature of the formal and informal health care sectors in urban Egypt. Additionally, it was through these women that I met the informal-sector women healers who participated in this study. Over the course of the study, I interviewed and/or observed eleven women healers, only one of whom had any formal health care training. All of the healers, as middle-aged or older women of the lower class, were illiterate and uneducated, Seven women had acquired their midwifery or other healing skills from relatives, most often grandmothers, mothers, and aunts who were practicing dayas. All of them either practiced out of their own homes or visited the homes of their patients. None of them had clinics, shops, or even telephones, which meant that their patients (or emissaries from their patients' families) always contacted them in person.

Although these women were widely known for their obstetric and gynecological skills throughout their communities, they were nonetheless "invisible" on an official level, as they were not members of professional organizations, nor listed in directories of any kind, nor known to the governmental authorities or health care professionals in the area. Thus, I could meet these women healers only through an intermediary. Generally, once contacted, these healers were enthusiastic participants in this study, sharing freely, via tape recorder, information about their belief systems, *materia medica,* and healing practices, as well as their views on modern Egyptian medicine.

In addition to this informal-sector research, interviews with physicians were conducted in various formal-sector health care settings, including the university teaching hospital, public maternal and child health (MCH) clinics, Islamic clinics associated with mosques, and physicians' private offices in the Alexandria vicinity. I conducted semistructured, tape-recorded interviews with seventeen ob-gyns, all but one of whom practiced in the Alexandria metropolitan area. I also conducted library research, in both Egypt and the United States, on the formal health sector in Egypt.

The Formal Health Care Sector in Egypt

Contemporary Egyptian biomedicine is, unfortunately, best characterized as the victim of its British colonial heritage. Despite health care reforms instituted under Nasser following the expulsion of the British from the country in the early 1950s, reforms have failed to transform the basic character of Egyptian biomedicine, which today bears the indelible mark of late-nineteenth-century colonization and anglicization.[6] Perhaps most discouraging, contemporary critics charge that the British colonial legacy has thwarted the potential excellence of Egyptian biomedicine as a system responsive to the *needs of its own citizens.*[7]

What, exactly, are the colonially induced ills plaguing contemporary Egyptian biomedicine? And how do they relate to Egyptian women's health care?

First and perhaps most important, the British thoroughly privatized Egyptian medicine.[8] Instead of encouraging health for all in Egypt, the British exported their own brand of fee-for-service, private medicine, practiced by physicians as a profession for financial gain. Excessive entrepreneurialism in biomedical practice was the result, and Egyptian physicians—"second-class citizens" to the European doctors imported by the British after they occupied Egypt in 1882—were forced to compete in sometimes unseemly ways in order to make a living. Furthermore, biomedical services were no longer accessible to the Egyptian masses under the private, fee-for-service system; thus, the public health of the Egyptian populace suffered dramatically during the period of British domination.[9]

Today, more than a century after British occupation, the foreign physicians are gone, and health care reforms have again brought public-sector medicine to the masses. However, the effects of colonial privatization have been profound in Egypt and have resulted in a major chasm between public and private health care services. To wit, purportedly "free" medical care is available to all Egyptians through Egyptian Ministry of Health hospitals (including university teaching hospitals) and clinics constructed under Nasser's aegis. Yet, as apparent in poor Egyptians' many complaints about public health care, this system of free clinics and hospitals is "crumbling under the weight of the huge demand and lack of resources."[10] Public hospitals are in disrepair, and many patients' stays are unnecessarily extended because physician manpower and crucial equipment and supplies are lacking.[11] Similar problems plague Ministry of Health outpatient clinics, including MCH clinics, where the hours of operation are short, the waiting lines are long, and drugs and other materials are often in short supply. The result is serious underutilization of public, primary health care services—underutilization fueled by the pervasive feeling among patients that it is wiser to spend hard-earned money on a visit to a private clinic.[12]

Private care is available only to those who can bear the full cost of medical intervention without the help of insurance. Yet, despite the economic hardships associated with seeking private medical care, many Egyptians, including the poor, prefer to seek out private clinics and hospitals, which have proliferated in Egypt in recent years. The reasons for this proliferation are considered to be threefold:

1. The significant glut of un- and underemployed Egyptian medical school graduates who, after completing mandatory government service in often remote rural areas, cannot find substantial, well-reimbursed positions in the more desirable (that is, urban) areas of the public-sector system;[13]

2. The significant numbers (75 to 80 percent) of active public-sector physicians, including university medical professors, who attempt to supplement their meager government salaries through afternoon and evening practice in their own private, fee-for-service clinics;[14]

3. Sadat's capitalist call for "open investment" in Egypt, including targeting private "investment" hospitals, described as the "medical Hiltons and Sheratons" of Egypt but considered by some critics one of the most prominent "diseases" of the free-market economy.[15]

The result today is a schizophrenic medical landscape in which many Egyptian "biomedicines" are practiced according to patients' abilities to pay. For most Egyptians, who despise the quality of service and treatment in the overtaxed, underequipped public medical sector, private medical care is the first choice, given sufficient out-of-pocket funds. Even private biomedicine is pluralistic, however, lacking uniform standards of quality. Thus, as it now stands, even patients who can afford to pay private physicians have no guarantee of appropriate care for what ails them.

Second, after privatization, the British, true to their heritage in industrializing Europe, exported to Egypt a brand of Western biomedicine enamored with technology for the "repair" of broken-down bodily "machines." Instead of developing prevention-oriented public health care services, which were desperately needed throughout the disease-ravaged Egyptian countryside, the British promoted high-tech, curative, urban, hospital-based health care, which was frankly unresponsive to the pressing medical needs of Egypt's largely rural populace.[16]

Today, the biomedical system in Egypt remains biased in similar directions. Namely, urban areas are favored over rural by health care personnel. Curative care is privileged over preventive services. And invasive high-tech medicine is often practiced at the expense of noninvasive lower-tech medicine, even though the standards of technological medicine in Egypt often lag far behind developments in Western medicine.[17]

Third, when the British took over medicine in Egypt, the quality of medical education deteriorated dramatically.[18] Medical school admissions of Egyptian students were cut drastically to make room for the European physicians who were soon allowed free rein in the country. Furthermore, the cost of medical education, which had been free to any bright (male) Egyptian student, became prohibitively expensive under the British, who thus restricted medical education to the wealthy elite. Language became an additional barrier; Arabic, the original language of Egyptian biomedicine, was replaced by English, which became a prerequisite for medical school admission. Finally, in Egyptian medical schools the British quashed altogether critical scientific inquiry and innovative medical research, encouraging instead traditionalism in education based on the rote learning of imported materials.

In Egypt today, the state of medical education differs little from a century ago. Although Egyptian medical education has been opened up to the point of overextension, the quality of medical education is still seriously deficient.[19] Classes are filled well beyond capacity, leading to a shortage of seats, textbooks, and opportunities for more individualized training, especially in critical clinical skills. Faculty are often absent and, when present, encourage students to adulate them as "demigods" in a system that is blatantly paternalistic, hierarchical, and authoritarian.[20] Furthermore, faculty encourage medical traditionalism by failing often to take their own research mandate seriously; by relaying sometimes outdated knowledge and standards of practice to their students, yet expecting unquestioning acceptance; and by failing to encourage the efforts of up-and-coming junior physicians who want to engage in biomedical innovation. The result is the graduation of thousands of poorly trained physicians, who forget much of what they were forced to memorize for exams, who are not proficient in current clinical or research skills, who are underspecialized, and who may never be forced to update their knowledge or standards of practice, given the lack of continuing medical education requirements in the country.[21]

Furthermore, Egypt has no system of physician self-monitoring (for example, board exams or medical ethics review boards), and no system against medical malpractice. Physician graduates thus are essentially free to do as they please once they enter community practice, with little surveillance or scrutiny of their capabilities or services. Such deficiencies, according to critics, have led to poor-quality care in many instances and the lack of a well-developed medical morality in Egypt (which, in fact, can be traced to the British, who scuttled early ethical reforms).[22] However, given the absence of health activist and consumer advocacy groups in Egypt today, individuals have little recourse when they feel their rights have been violated or their cases mishandled. The outcome is lack of trust in and ambivalence toward physicians, who as a group are often criticized by angry consumers for their incompetence, ineffectiveness, and avarice.

Lack of trust is perpetuated also by medical elitism of the worst kind, another byproduct of British medical domination. The British promoted the idea that everything European was superior to everything Egyptian, thus encouraging Egyptian physicians to speak only English and to look down upon the Egyptian masses, including the ethnomedical specialists who had practiced for centuries in their country.[23] Early efforts to train ethnomedical practitioners, such as dayas, as ancillary medical personnel were entirely suspended under the British,[24] and these healers were deemed "quacks" and "charlatans," sought out only by "ignoramuses" among the poor folk.

In this area, too, the situation in Egypt is little improved from a century ago. Attempts to incorporate ethnomedical practitioners into the biomedical system have been feeble at best and limited to dayas, whose services remain officially illicit. Furthermore, ancillary medical personnel of all kinds—nurses, medical technicians, paramedics, medical social workers, psychologists, and others—are undervalued, undertrained, and in chronically short supply.[25] Instead, only physicians are accorded professional prestige (although it often outstrips their real contributions), and their attitudes toward other health care personnel and toward their patients remain supercilious at best.[26] Indeed, the patronizing attitudes and lack of cultural sensitivity of many Egyptian physicians toward their patients—especially poor, uneducated patients presenting at public facilities—has been noted by a number of scholars, who have described the untoward effects of medi-cal paternalism on doctor-patient communication.[27]

Today, most biomedical practitioners in Egypt lack the overt antipathy toward their ethnomedical counterparts displayed by many Egyptian phy-sicians at the turn of the century. However, the reason is largely that most contemporary Egyptian physicians, especially those practicing in urban areas, have no idea of the extent to which ethnomedicine and ethnomedical practitioners continue to influence the actions of their patients. For ex-ample, urban ob-gyns tend to be wholly unfamiliar with all of the follow-ing: their patients' ethnomedical beliefs regarding the causes of women's health problems; the ethnomedical practices women engage in, including the types of ethnomedical practitioners from whom they seek help; and the significant degree to which poor urban Egyptian women participate in the ethnomedical world, claiming faith in its beliefs, practices, and practitio-ners.

Most urban ob-gyns admit that they possess no knowledge of ethno-medicine, given their lack of interest and resultant failure to inquire about "such superstitions" from their patients. However, others are adamant that such beliefs and practices have "disappeared" altogether in the urban areas of Egypt and are found only at a low level, if at all, among ignorant people living in the countryside of the Egyptian Delta or in Upper Egypt. Further-more, those who dismiss the significance of ethnomedicine contend that only desperation would drive a woman to believe in and undertake ethno-medical practices—and then only after prior biomedical treatment had failed to provide a cure for her affliction.

Egyptian physicians who show little or no interest in the subject of ethnomedicine—deeming it irrelevant in the modern world—grossly un-derestimate the degree to which ethnomedicine is still present in urban Egypt in a vast informal health care system that parallels their own. Fur-thermore, little do they realize that the actual pervasiveness of ethnomedi-cine in urban Egypt is, in part, a reflection of the contemporary character of Egyptian biomedicine and its tendency to repel patients who might oth-erwise avail themselves of biomedicine exclusively.

To reiterate an earlier point, biomedicine itself serves as a force of thera-peutic diversification, given the characteristics of biomedical practice that cause many patients to reject it. Such factors include economic and social class barriers to access and utilization of biomedical services; asymmetrical power relations between biomedical practitioners and their patients, which are maintained through physician authoritarianism, paternalism, and un-dermining of patients' self-esteem; utilization by physicians of purportedly

therapeutic, invasive procedures that are in reality biomedically un-
founded, often health-demoting, and perceived by patients as profit-making ventures for physicians; and the resultant inability of many patients to
find solutions within the biomedical system.

For some Egyptian women, ethnomedicine might be less appealing were
biomedicine to offer more certain cures. However, given the deficiencies of
Egyptian biomedicine described here, seeking solutions within the informal
health care sector becomes compelling for many women, especially those
who uphold ethnomedical notions of etiology, diagnosis, and treatment.

The Informal Health Care Sector in Egypt

Indeed, most poor urban Egyptian women accept the expertise of ethnomedical healers and the validity of their healing practices, which counterpose the formally legitimated, but nonetheless problematic, tenets of biomedicine as it is practiced in Egypt today. Women's acceptance is evident in
many patients' serial or simultaneous utilization of both the formal and
informal health care sectors. Egyptian women's tendency toward holistic
health-seeking has been characterized as curative eclecticism and is regarded as a strategy for maximization of therapeutic benefits.[28]

In fact, poor women seeking health care in Egypt now have a number of
options from which to choose: (1) private, fee-for-service medicine administered by a physician; (2) public, purportedly "free" health care administered by a physician, nurse, or nurse-midwife in a government health care
facility; (3) free or low-cost medicine administered by a physician in an
Islamic clinic associated with a mosque;[29] (4) or ethnomedicine administered by one of an assortment of traditional healers, whose beliefs and
practices derive in large part from three major literate medical traditions
dating back approximately five thousand years in Egypt.[30]

With respect to the last category, poor urban neighborhoods of Egypt
are replete with ethnomedical practitioners who cater to the masses, pro-
moting in many cases health care beliefs and practices that derive from
Egypt's ancient medical traditions. Yet, because of shifting historical hege-
monies, unified "schools" of ethnomedicine rooted in ancient traditions
are entirely absent in the country today. Rather, most contemporary ethnomedical practitioners offer services that can only be described as markedly
eclectic in nature. Moreover, because they are not stringent adherents of
any particular historical medical philosophy, most ethnomedical practitioners are not book-taught, learning instead by observation or apprentice-

ship. Furthermore, lacking professional associates and associations, they tend to operate independently.

Interestingly, subspecialization is just as common among ethnomedical healers as it is among Egyptian physicians. Ethno-obstetrics and gynecology is a particularly active area of ethnomedical practice. The reasons are Egypt's high total fertility rate, 4.6 births per woman;[31] the maternal health problems that accompany such high fertility; the concern with fecundity among childless women; and the various barriers, both social and economic, that prevent Egyptian women from seeking biomedical care. In Egypt, the vast majority of poor rural and urban women consult an ethno-obstetrician or gynecologist, usually a daya, at least once in their lifetimes and usually much more often. However, ethnomedical specialists other than dayas also treat women's reproductive health problems.

Sittat kabiras

In fact, in urban areas of Egypt it is possible for women to visit healers who specialize in the treatment of only one or two specific "female conditions." These healers are typically postmenopausal women, or *sittat kabira* (literally, elderly women), who distinguish themselves from dayas because they do not perform deliveries or other roles traditionally associated with midwifery. Rather, these women perform various cures for miscarriage, infertility, excessive uterine bleeding, or other reproductive problems, especially cures requiring ritual healing objects. Because these objects are often difficult to obtain, originating as they normally do in Saudi Arabia, women who own them may begin to specialize in the treatments associated with them and become recognized for this specialized knowledge.

Dayas

In addition to sittat kabiras, Egypt is home to thousands of dayas, or lay midwives such as Siham, who throughout the centuries have delivered the infants and cared for the health of Egypt's women. In Egypt today, it is estimated that approximately ten thousand dayas are active practitioners of midwifery, conducting between 80 and 90 percent of all deliveries among the rural and urban poor.[32]

Formal, six-to-twelve-month practical obstetrics training of dayas was initiated in the 1940s in Egypt. However, in 1969 the Egyptian Ministry of Health changed its policy by discontinuing all daya training; revoking all previously issued licenses; warning women by radio against the use of "ignorant, unskilled, and often dangerous" dayas; and encouraging women to deliver with governmentally trained *hakima*s, or nurse-midwives, stationed at MCH clinics and rural health units throughout the country.[33] Because of this governmental effort to wipe out the position of the daya,[34] dayas were essentially forced underground, continuing their practices illicitly without the putative benefits of supervision, training, or hygienic supplies. Not until the 1980s, when the Ministry of Health realized that its program of health modernization had failed to bring about intended changes in the state of Egyptian obstetrics, did it reinstitute limited daya training programs in primarily rural governorates.[35]

Yet, despite recent attempts by the Egyptian government and international health agencies such as the World Health Organization and UNICEF to regulate and professionalize the *obstetrical* practice of dayas,[36] little attention has been paid within the international health and scholarly communities to the *gynecological* services performed by dayas on thousands of Egyptian women. This neglect is serious because dayas are Egypt's truest "ethnogynecologists," performing the greatest variety of the most commonly employed ethnogynecological cures for pregnancy loss, infertility, and other types of gynecological problems.

In fact, it would not be overstating the case to suggest that dayas are perhaps the major force in the effort to treat infertility problems in Egypt. Many dayas, such as Siham, have gained wide recognition in their communities for their infertility services, thus silently but effectively competing with unwitting Egyptian gynecologists for infertile patients. However, to impute competitive motives to Egyptian dayas is unfair, given that the majority of them do not claim to treat the kinds of problems, such as "blocked tubes" and "weak ovaries," that only physicians are able to handle. Because dayas restrict themselves to the treatment of minor conditions, they generally charge their patients relatively little money for their services— usually £E 0.5–5.00 ($0.20–2.00) and rarely more than £E 10 ($4). Some dayas, in fact, refuse payment altogether, in the knowledge that if the infertile patient becomes pregnant, a gift will be forthcoming.

Munaggimas

The same is not true, however, of *munaggima*s (female spiritist healers), a distinct class of healers. Unlike sittat kabiras and dayas, they tend to charge high fees for their services (e.g., £E 10–250, or $4–100). By far the most controversial class of urban Egyptian ethnogynecologists, munaggimas are widely known for specializing in diagnostic clairvoyance and the treatment of the more difficult, socially mediated causes of ill health, primarily those involving angered spirits. Despite cautionary mention of them in the

Qur'an, many munaggimas draw upon "the power of the Book" (the *Qur'an*) to help them diagnose and cure patients. Because of their professed religiosity, munaggimas are often addressed and referred to by the religious title *shaikha.* However, many Egyptians say that munaggimas do not deserve such a title of respect, given that they do not truly "know God," and they refer to munaggimas pejoratively instead as mere *sahhara*s (sorcerers or magicians) or *daggala*s (quacks or charlatans).

Given the suspicion surrounding munaggimas, it is perhaps surprising that they make up significant numbers throughout the poorer areas of Egypt, claiming their fair share of reproductively troubled women. In fact, munaggimas are highly sought after for their ability to tell fortunes concerning matters of reproduction. For example, some munaggimas claim to divine whether or not an infertile woman is suffering from a biomedical problem, such as "weak ovaries," for which she should seek a physician's treatment, or an ethnomedical problem such as reproductive binding. Furthermore, some munaggimas claim to cure ethnomedical infertility problems through vaginal suppositories, herbal potables, cupping, and various healing rituals.

Unlike their male counterparts, female munaggimas generally do not traffic in malevolent sorcery—either its creation or its dissolution. However, they may be deeply involved in the spirit world, either as possessed individuals, who use their spirits to diagnose and treat other spirit-troubled women, or as skillful agents of spirit invocation, who make the wishes of others' spirits known. For women who are infertile or who repeatedly miscarry, female munaggimas communicate with the *akhawat taht il-ard* (spirit-sisters underground), who trouble their earthly sisters by preventing them from having children. However, because these spirit-sisters do not actually possess, or "wear," their earthly sisters, the female munaggimas who treat the infertile for spirit troubles rarely ask them to participate in the communal *zar* spirit placation ceremonies attended by the possessed. Instead, they may perform elaborate, private rituals that usually call for animal sacrifice and a variety of unusual and expensive items.

Because of the large amounts of money involved in undergoing a munaggima's healing rituals, munaggimas are regarded with a great deal of suspicion by most poor urban Egyptians, who view them as avaricious and potentially inauthentic in their claims. Furthermore, because the questions munaggimas ask patients are often indicative of prior knowledge of the patients, many Egyptians are suspicious of munaggimas' strategies of divination, believing that their knowledge must be based on illusive practices and trickery. Thus, munaggimas are often accused of being quacks, tricksters, liars, opportunists, and thieves who take advantage of gullible, desperate Egyptian patients and cheat them of large amounts of money. Even those individuals who complete a munaggima's suggested healing regimen are often unconvinced of its efficacy and may comment that the munaggima "stole my money for nothing."

This ambivalence toward a class of ethnogynecological healers appears to be restricted to munaggimas alone. It also appears to be increasing along with Egypt's contemporary Islamist movement and its attempt to eliminate all unorthodox religious elements, including spiritist healers and their practices. Sittat kabiras and dayas are generally viewed by the poor as being both honest and beneficent healers, even though many of their practices, too, are viewed with increasing skepticism by Egyptian Islamists.

Choosing the Informal Alternative

Despite growing Islamist concern over ethnomedical unorthodoxy, the utilization of ethnomedicine by poor urban Egyptian women continues unabated, for reasons having to do with the positive gender and class attributes of ethnomedical healers themselves, as well as issues of acceptability, accessibility, affordability, and appropriateness.

First, most ethnomedical healers who treat women for their reproductive health problems are also women, whereas most biomedical practitioners are not. Although Egyptian women, rich or poor, will generally seek the care of a male ob-gyn if necessary, the traditional preference for female reproductive health specialists (be they women physicians or healers) remains strong and appears to be increasing as a result of the Islamist movement in contemporary Egypt. Today, more women are refusing to expose their bodies—and especially their genitals—to male physicians, given their belief that this is immodest and *haram* (sinful in the religion). Yet because the biomedical practice of obstetrics and gynecology continues to be one of the most prestigious areas of specialization, it remains a bastion of male domination and frank intimidation of the poor, uneducated female patients who must deal in great discomfort with upper-class male physicians.

Ethno-obstetrics and gynecology, on the other hand, is a markedly gynocentric, female-dominated area of practice, with dayas and other women healers providing the bulk of the health care. "Gender comfort" is certainly one of the major reasons why most Egyptian babies are delivered by dayas. Furthermore, because many ethnomedical illness categories are perceived to be gender-specific, healing rituals are necessarily gynocentric, with women helping other women to effect cures.

Second, the class-based differences that often radically separate Egyptian doctors from their patients are essentially absent in the ethnomedical world. Most healers are themselves drawn from the lower classes and share their patients' social norms and expectations. In Egypt, male physicians tend to treat poor women patients as though they were ignorant: the physicians fail to divulge crucial diagnostic and therapeutic information, and they communicate in obscure and obfuscating medicalese. Women healers, on the other hand, tend to treat their female clients as equals: the healers share with patients their own beliefs and knowledge in familiar colloquialisms, and they bolster, if anything, clients' hopes and self-esteem. Thus, the haughtiness and patronizing attitudes that often typify physicians' care, especially in public facilities, are essentially absent among the women healers, who are themselves poor, uneducated women occupying the same social world as their female clients.

Third, physicians and healers tend to differ fundamentally in their willingness to communicate with their patients. Whereas physicians tend to disclose very little, treating all diagnostic and therapeutic information as being akin to sacred knowledge, ethnomedical healers tend to share information freely with their patients. The process of sharing is largely how ethnomedical beliefs become disseminated and accepted within poor urban communities. Moreover, poor women know that their beliefs concerning reproductive binding, shock, humidity, angered spirits, and the other sources of gynecological trouble will be immediately accepted and likely remedied within the ethnomedical community. Physicians, on the other hand, are known to scoff at such views and attempt to eradicate them. Thus, poor women who visit ethnomedical healers, rather than or in addition to physicians, are in part seeking acceptance of their ideologies of health and illness, which are often at great odds with those of the biomedical system.

Fourth, in addition to compatibility of beliefs about etiology, diagnosis, and cure, poor urban Egyptian women have much easier access to ethnomedical healers, who live within the patients' own communities—perhaps only blocks or doors away. They can often be called upon day or night to assist with deliveries and other medical care in the patient's own home. A visit to a physician's clinic or a health facility, on the other hand, may require a long walk or a difficult and perhaps expensive journey by taxi or bus. Women may view such trips with great trepidation, and their husbands may even forbid them, begrudging the expense and fearing their wives' use of public transportation along with unknown men. Moreover, health clinic hours are usually short, waiting lines are typically long, and time may run out before a patient is seen. Even when health facilities are conveniently located in or near poor neighborhoods, women may shun them because they view health facilities as breeding grounds for both biomedical and ethnomedical illnesses. Thus delivering a baby at home is considered much safer than in a hospital, but only dayas—not obstetricians or even government nurse-midwives—are willing to perform home deliveries.

Fifth, the poor urban woman's major reason for preferring women healers may be affordability. Most women healers (except for munaggimas) charge only nominal fees for services, or they may accept voluntary fees or gifts only if their remedies prove effective. Women who visit healers may be expected to purchase various ingredients of remedies. However, they are spared the expense of office visits, laboratory tests, prescriptions, medical procedures, surgeries, hospitalization, and tips to various health care personnel, which may apply even in public health facilities. For poor patients lacking health insurance, such costs are often overwhelming. Thus, ethnomedical care that is shown to provide relief is often considered a good investment, offering substantial savings to those who can afford little in order to stay healthy.

Finally, as noted by Siham in the introduction to this chapter, many poor patients suspect physicians of avarice—performing inappropriate medical procedures just to gain money. Indeed, the appropriateness of many of the ob-gyn interventions performed by Egyptian physicians has been called into serious question, given the health-demoting potential of the outdated, invasive procedures performed.[37] Furthermore, because ob-gyn is a surgical specialty, its practitioners' surgical bias leads to many unnecessary operations, which is especially frightening given the high postoperative infection rate in Egypt.[38] Thus, women avoid biomedical treatments, which often cause significant pain, prolonged recovery time, and complications without even curing the patient. Such treatments are seen as both financially and physically risky. Ethnomedical treatments, on the other hand, are rarely invasive and often employ familiar ingredients and household objects. Thus, even if they inflict pain, such treatments are usually viewed as more appropriate for a woman's body, given the known risks of high-technology medicine.

Conclusion

For all of these reasons, poor urban Egyptian women are often enthusiastic participants in the informal health care sector—relying on women healers of various types to deliver their babies and help them to overcome their reproductive problems. Not only are women healers such as Siham inherently appealing in many ways, but their methods of health care delivery continue to counterpose those of the colonially molded formal health care sector, where the poor have come to feel unwelcome, silenced, and mistreated. Indeed, the very vitality of the informal health care sector in urban Egypt today is in many ways a direct reflection of the inability of "modern," formal-sector biomedicine to treat the poor as patients needing health care and as human beings deserving of dignity and respect. Until the basic problems afflicting Egyptian formal-sector health care are recognized and reforms are achieved, it is quite likely that informal-sector healers such as Siham will continue to play a major role in caring for Egypt's poor women.

Notes

Parts of this chapter are adapted from Marcia C. Inhorn, *Quest for Conception: Gender, Infertility, and Egyptian Medical Traditions* (Philadelphia: University of Pennsylvania Press, 1994).

1. This name is a pseudonym.

2. Carol Shepherd McClain, ed., *Women as Healers: Cross-Cultural Perspectives* (New Brunswick: Rutgers University Press, 1989), 7–8.

3. John Ehrenreich, ed., *The Cultural Crisis of Modern Medicine* (New York: Monthly Review Press, 1978), 1.

4. Theresa El-Mehairy, *Medical Doctors: A Study of Role Concept and Job Satisfaction, The Egyptian Case* (Leiden: E. J. Brill (1984), 189–90.

5. Marcia C. Inhorn, *Infertility and Patriarchy: The Cultural Politics of Gender and Family Life in Egypt* (Philadelphia: University of Pennsylvania Press, 1996), 70.

6. Peter J. Blizard, "International Standards in Medical Education or National Standards/Primary Health Care—Which Direction?" *Social Science and Medicine* 33 (1991): 1165.

7. Amira el Azhary Sonbol, *The Creation of a Medical Profession in Egypt, 1800–1922* (Syracuse: Syracuse University Press, 1991), 12.

8. Ibid., 106–41.

9. LaVerne Kuhnke, *Lives at Risk: Public Health in Nineteenth-Century Egypt* (Berkeley: University of California Press, 1990).

10. Peter Kandela, "Egypt: Medical Care, Public and Private," *Lancet* (July 2, 1988): 34–35.

11. Institute of Medicine, *Health in Egypt: Recommendations for U.S. Assistance* (Washington, D.C.: U.S. Agency for International Development, 1979), 71–104.

12. Hassan A. Abu-Zeid and William M. Dann, "Health Services Utilization and Cost in Ismailia, Egypt," *Social Science and Medicine* 21, no. 4 (1985): 458–60.

13. El-Mehairy, *Medical Doctors,* 107–8; Institute of Medicine, *Health in Egypt,* 77.

14. El-Mehairy, *Medical Doctors,* 19; Institute of Medicine, *Health in Egypt,* 72.

15. Kandela, *"Egypt: Medical Care, Public and Private,"* 34.

16. Kuhnke, *Lives at Risk,* 162–63; Sonbol, *Creation of a Medical Profession,* 135.

17. Inhorn, *Quest for Conception,* 301–17.

18. Sonbol, *Creation of a Medical Profession,* 108–20, 131–32.

19. El-Mehairy, *Medical Doctors,* 62–69; Institute of Medicine, *Health in Egypt,* 99–100.

20. El-Mehairy, *Medical Doctors,* 66.

21. Ibid., 24, 67–69.

22. Sonbol, *Creation of a Medical Profession,* 89, 110–11.

23. Ibid., 48–50.

24. Ibid., 130.

25. Kim Carney, "Health in Egypt," *Journal of Public Health Policy* 5 (1984): 136; Institute of Medicine, *Health in Egypt,* 85, 102–3.

26. Barbara L. K. Pillsbury, *Traditional Health Care in the Near East* (Washington, D.C.: USAID, 1978): 3.

27. Marie Assaad and Samiha El Katsha, "Formal and Informal Health Care in an Egyptian Delta Village," *Contact* 65 (December 1981): 5; Evelyn A. Early, "Catharsis and Creation in Informal Narratives of Baladi Women of Cairo," *Anthropological Quarterly* 58, no. 4 (October 1985): 175; Sandra D. Lane and Marcia Inhorn Millar, "The 'Hierarchy of Resort' Reexamined: Status and Class Differentials as Determinants of Therapy for Eye Disease in the Egyptian Delta," *Urban Anthropology* 16, no. 2 (1987): 173; Soheir A. Morsy, "Health and Illness as Symbols of Social Differentiation in an Egyptian Village," *Anthropological Quarterly* 53, no. 3 (1980): 159–60; Soheir A. Morsy. *Gender, Sickness, and Healing in Rural Egypt: Ethnography in Historical Context* (Boulder, Colo.: Westview Press, 1993), 178.

28. Evelyn A. Early, *Baladi Women of Cairo: Playing with an Egg and a Stone* (Boulder, Colo.: Lynne Rienner, 1993), 47, 80.

29. Soheir A. Morsy. "Islamic Clinics in Egypt: The Cultural Elaboration of Biomedical Hegemony," *Medical Anthropology Quarterly* 2, no. 4 (1988).

30. Inhorn, *Quest for Conception,* 53–62.

31. *World Population Data Sheet* (Washington, D.C.: Population Reference Bureau, 1993).

32. Assaad and El Katsha, "Formal and Informal Health Care," 7; Amira El Malatawy, *Daya Training Programme in Egypt* (Cairo: UNICEF, 1985), 3.

33. Pillsbury, *Traditional Health Care,* 32; Hind Abou Seoud Khattab, *The Daya: Knowledge and Practice in Maternal-Child Health Care* (Cairo: Report for

Newborn Care Project, 1983), 2; Soheir Sukkary, "She Is No Stranger: The Traditional Midwife in Egypt," *Medical Anthropology* 5 (Winter 1981): 28.

34. Pillsbury, *Traditional Health Care,* 32.

35. Sawon Hong, *Review of Training Programmes for Traditional Birth Attendants in Selected Countries* (New York: UNICEF, 1987), 11.

36. Assaad and El Katsha, "Formal and Informal Health Care," 7; J. Bentley, "Need for Strengthening Managerial, Administrative and Supervisory Capabilities of Midwives in District" (WHO Report EM/CNS.TBA.VLG/9, 1989); Edna Ismail, "Training and Performance of TBAs and Midwives in the EMR" (WHO Report EM/CNS.TBA.VLG/6, 1989); *"Review and Analysis" of Daya Training Programme in Egypt* (Cairo: UNICEF, 1985).

37. Marcia C. Inhorn and Kimberly A. Buss, "Infertility, Infection, and Iatrogenesis in Egypt: The Anthropological Epidemiology of Blocked Tubes," *Medical Anthropology* 15, no. 3 (1993): 227–30; Marcia C. Inhorn and Kimberly A. Buss, "Ethnography, Epidemiology, and Infertility in Egypt," *Social Science and Medicine* 39, no. 5 (1994): 677–79.

38. Inhorn and Buss, "Infertility, Infection, and Iatrogenesis," 228–29.

6

Nest Eggs of Gold and Beans

Baladi Egyptian Women's Invisible Capital

Evelyn A. Early

During my ethnographic research in Bulaq Abu 'Ala, a *baladi* (traditional) quarter of Cairo, during the 1970s and 1980s, I marveled at baladi women's energetic mobilization of social and material resources. Qualitative case studies best capture these resources—the capital that creates and influences work in the baladi invisible economy. Bulaq, a ten-minute walk north of downtown Cairo, was selected as an industrial site by Muhammad Ali in the early nineteenth century, and it rapidly changed from a medieval elite Mamluke suburb to a grimy popular quarter with textile, spinning, iron foundry, and dye factories. Today the small workshops of Bulaq provide lathing and foundry services for Egypt's public and private sectors. Shoppers from all over Cairo crowd the Wikalat al-Balah market in Bulaq to buy spare car parts, scrap iron, and used clothing. In the late 1970s, when the brunt of inflation wrought by post–Camp David "opening up" hit Cairenes, they diversified their activities. More older women sold food, and more traveled to work in the Gulf. Men sought second and third jobs in coffeehouses or workshops. Families devised such extra income sources as renting out a food cart. By the early 1990s, baladi youth worked in tourist and other service sectors, but the invisible economy remained vibrant.

Baladi Women's Work Culture

Urban Egyptian women's historic economic role in household production and landholding diminished with the advent of factories and wage labor.

For example, small-scale home textile production was squeezed out by textile factories established by Muhammad Ali in the early nineteenth century.[1] As the female role in production contracted, "service industries multiplied; by the end of the nineteenth century, working women were concentrated in this world of casual services and informal networks."[2] Throughout the nineteenth century, rural and urban Egyptian women participated in petty trade, selling food, utensils, and cloth, and some wealthier women worked as traders.[3] Today the majority of baladi women workers perform services: vendor, merchant, midwife, seamstress, tattooer, bread baker, henna applier, bath attendant, or (if educated, and usually after a long wait) private or government white-collar work. A few serve in textile, pharmaceutical, and other factories. Older, uneducated baladi women may be forced to work as day laborers, hauling dirt and cement, or as messengers and porters. The lucky ones are chauffeurs. Baladi women augment family capital by arranging favorable marriages or by making contacts in the government and private sectors. Young baladi women are now entering the professional sector of doctors, lawyers, and engineers.

This chapter discusses four women who have mobilized different blends of social and material resources. Social capital resides in any relation—be it

Woman cheese seller in Cairo. Photo: Evelyn Early.

kin, friend, neighbor, or work colleague. Material capital includes private savings nest eggs made up of jewelry or cash amassed from vending and the more sizable income from shops or other family interests. The forms of capital in the invisible economy range from social contacts, expertise, or reputation to grocery profits, jewelry, or government documents. Activity in the invisible economy spans the formal sector of commercial wage earning and marketing (the area of secondary relations), and the informal sector of exchange in kind and primary social relations.

The Nature of a Nest Egg

A highly intricate system of sociability glosses social relations through acts of proffering, accepting, and rejecting. Women give money gifts (*nuqta*) at life events such as circumcision or marriage. Recipients keep track of gifts so that they may return a slightly higher amount for the giver's next occasion. To return the same or less is to signal a break in social relations that can only be reestablished by family reconciliation. Women returning from trips to the village calibrate social closeness when they distribute special breads to relatives and friends. If a woman proffers an inappropriate amount, the recipient may refuse it:

> One day when Badriyya, who had just returned from the village, passed out bread, biscuits, and *futir* . . . she [first] dispatched the best two *futir* to her mother-in-law's house and then she started to divide the rest of the basket with her other relatives and neighbors. When she offered her sister-in-law Suad half a *futir* and a handful of biscuits, Suad refused them and scowled at her daughter Abir when Abir started to pick them up from the table. The *futir* distribution was a ritual litmus test of social ties, in a spontaneous performance. Suad refused her measly share of village breads because she judged them less than her rightful share as the sister-in-law of Badriyya.[4]

Jewelry, like stocks and bonds, ensures against divorce or other disaster; women pawn jewelry for crises and also for investments such as renting a new flat, which requires key money, or buying furniture. Unable to find bank loans, they depend on the invisible economic sector of creditors, savings associations, and neighborly assistance. No one writes promissory notes, but women do calculate "debt balances" out loud for all to hear and corroborate when a neighbor returns a quarter kilo of sugar or a larger debt.

The savings association is a popular way to amass money for large expenditures. A woman pays, say, ten pounds each month to the association organizer, then receives the lump sum of one hundred pounds once during the ten-month cycle. Whoever forms the association determines the order of payment. First in order is not necessarily best. So as to avoid wasting the savings on daily trifles, many prefer to schedule payment just before such a major expense as a wedding.

Casual vending can fund the start of a more substantial form of commerce. Zainab used capital amassed from selling bean sandwiches to launch a village-city cheese and ghee trade. Another vendor becomes a *tagarit ash-shanta* (suitcase merchant), who sells glassware, lingerie, cloth, and other household items. Some women need not suffer through the first stage of petty trade; Rida, the *warsha* (workshop) supervisor, inherited a share in her father's investment. Others are bankrolled by a husband's repair shop or business.

The Household

The household, whether extended or nuclear, is the basic economic unit of activity in the invisible sector. This chapter considers four cases: an urban household supported by extensive commercial-urban social networks; an urban household supported by a workshop and by a salaried daughter; an urban household supported by the wife's rural-urban merchanting network, which in turns props up international migrant labor; a rural extended family household supported by the salaries of Egyptian army members and the wages of unskilled labor in Saudi Arabia, and by livestock and produce sales, orchard crops, and grocery sales.

"Invisible" household production is hard to quantify; dairy, grain, and other products are consumed, sold, or exchanged in patterns determined by season and by social occasion. Market and in-kind payments are intermingled. For instance, household-produced cheese and butter may be sold at market for money used to buy household staples such as tea and sugar; it may also be payment in kind for labor or shared as gifts.

Social dynamics continually modify a household's economy. For example, I knew a toothless Egyptian grandmother who felt restless in depending on the son with whom she lived. Although too decrepit to move at more than a hobble, every day she sold lemons in the lane just outside her front door to raise money for her food. Nevertheless, when this grandmother fell ill, no household resource was spared to obtain the best medical care available. In extended households, daughters-in-law may divert funds to their natal family, sometimes for reinvestment in livestock or other natal family ventures.

A baladi Egyptian household is not a collection of individuals with separate incomes but a complex collection of human, social, and material resources that may be exchanged in kind or for money. A questionnaire can not capture this economic unit's dynamics. Qualitative case studies best shed light on them.

The Sociocultural Setting of the Case Studies

The four case studies here illuminate blends of nonmaterial and material capital; private and public space; and invisible and formal markets. The women studied are Suad, the queen of *baksheesh* (tips); Rida, the warsha (workshop) supervisor; Zainab, the charge account merchant; and Zakiyya, the peasant grocer.

The first three live in the baladi quarter of Bulaq Abu 'Ala. Zakiyya lives in Menoufiyya province, three hours north of Cairo, but her life is touched by the urban baladi culture of work.

The concept of baladi is a rich one, having many aspects. Baladi downtrodden (*gallaba*) people contrast with the *afrangi*, who are pampered (*dala'ain*). There are baladi ways and there are afrangi ways to earn a living, practice religion, celebrate a wedding, cure a disease, talk to a friend, or solve a problem. Baladi people see themselves as authentic, astute, honorable, religious, nationalistic, simple, personal, and hospitable; they see afrangis as spoiled, gullible, dishonorable, nonreligious, foreign-oriented, materialistic, artificial, and stingy. My baladi friends contrasted their society with that of Zamalek, where afrangis care little for others and neglect such social duties as joining a passing funeral procession to signal social solidarity with the family.

Non-zoned baladi quarters such as Bulaq Abu 'Ala in medieval and central Cairo are crisscrossed by narrow lanes lined with warehouses, workshops, markets, and dwellings. Cooking and welding may spill over into the lane from adjacent buildings. Pedestrians navigate baladi quarters by asking directions, not by consulting a map. Famous mosques or restaurants serve as landmarks and are more important than street names. Cairo is changing and by the early 1990s baladi/afrangi distinctions had blurred. Some baladis became consumers, leaving baladi values of hospitality and simplicity behind to buy European-design furniture and to dress in the latest European fashions.

Many of the role models of informal baladi entrepreneurs are congruent with traditional role models of women as mothers and wives. Casual activities can be shaped temporally and organizationally according to family responsibilities and needs. Women dress and interact traditionally because baladi business transactions depend on personal ties, trust, and a familiar language. Theirs is informal, individualized labor where one shows initiative, while afrangi work is formal, uncreative, boringly routine. The women of Bulaq speak of the afrangi schedule kept by a woman office worker who returns home for lunch and a nap—in contrast to the baladi vendor, who works long hours, starting with a predawn visit to the wholesale market. Baladi women see themselves as oppressed, but they are proud of their freedom from afrangi office work. Sawsan Messiri reports a self-description of a baladi *bint al-suq* (woman of the market): "[a character-type] who has foresight and is intelligent. 'One *bint al-balad* equals twenty men in trading.' In contrast, a woman employee in the government is 'bound' to her desk and hence lacks experience and is unaware of the world about her."[5] Mothers are aware that blue-collar salaries are higher than those of the afrangi office worker. One woman exclaimed to me: "What use is a *muwazaff* [office worker] these days! He makes less than a hundred pounds [a month] while a *sana'i* [skilled worker] makes at least four to five hundred. None of my daughters will marry *muwazaffin*!"

The bint al-suq is known today as a *mu'allima*, a knowledgeable, streetwise woman who is respected and feared by all and who is untouched by innuendos of loose morals reserved for other "street women." *Mu'allima* is also the word for teacher, but the two are never confused. A street mu'allima talks rough, curses as if she were a man, and deals sternly with customers. A popular story recounts how an Egyptian coffeehouse proprietress barred an army general from her establishment shortly after the 1967 defeat by the Israelis, with a stream of expletives about how this "pimp of the Israelis" would never darken *her* door. An Egyptian woman engaged in a business venture is first of all a businessperson, and second, a woman. It is this compartmentalization that allows her to run a coffeehouse or to sit in the lane vending fruits and sweets as a respected woman of the community. Tough in the shop and street, a mu'allima reverts to her other, womanly self at home. When I told a woman I encountered that I thought we had met before, she replied: "Oh, you don't recognize me now because the last time we met, you bought bread from me. I was a mu'allima wearing black and acting tough; now you see me as a normal housewife."

Bulaqi women develop strategies for mobility, investment, and credit. They routinely hustle national and international networks in search of a local taxi driving job or a Saudi construction job. A woman may finance work in the Gulf for a family member, or she may obtain documents herself to travel abroad to work as a domestic. Patrons and client women of different status groups exchange information, goods, and services. An "expediter" such as our queen of baksheesh works for patron women creditors, who develop into "quasi-kin." The four cases here blend service and production in varying constellations, and they mobilize material and social capital.

Case 1. The Queen of Baksheesh: Suad, the Clinic Expediter

We often stereotype Third World societies as requiring a tip or bribe to accomplish anything. However, tips occur also in high corporate finance throughout the world; in simple terms, a $1 million gratuity appears more to resemble graft and a five-pound tip more to be payment for social services. Gifts, in money or in kind, are common in government clinics such the one in Bulaq Abu 'Ala. Community women serve tea, clean vegetables, and wash sheets for the clinic staff. In return, the staff assure community women a generous share of powdered milk and other clinic rations, as well as priority treatment in examinations and prescriptions.

Neighbor women tip the clinic midwife for help at delivery and for follow-up visits. Sometimes women invite the clinic midwife to the *subu'a* (the seven-day naming ceremony), and they shower the midwife with sweets and money. Midwives in a clinic and traditional midwives have a well-defined and for the most part noncompetitive relationship. A common adage summarizes their division of labor: "Leave the umbilical cord for the clinic to cut or you will not receive your birth certificate." The traditional midwife supports the mother through the ups and downs of delivery; the clinic midwife cuts the cord, drips in eye drops, and issues the birth certificate.

Raising orphans is both a Ministry of Health service and a business. The social worker certifies foster mothers to take care of orphan infants. This service saves foundlings from the horrors of institutional nurseries and usually provides a loving environment. Baladi women I knew raised orphans with the same care and love as they gave their own children; they sometimes adopted a foster child to avoid losing the child to an orphanage when old enough to be institutionalized. Raising an orphan also has a business face. In addition to their monthly stipend, foster mothers receive a special allotment of milk and other commodities such as flour and oil.

The Ministry of Health bureaucracy needs facilitators. Enter Suad, the Orphan Queen. Suad worked closely with the Bulaq Abu 'Ala clinic social worker Karima as Karima's intermediary to neighbor women. Suad herself raised at least two orphans at any given time (although the limit was supposed to be one), and she essentially determined which women of the neighborhood would receive Ministry of Health orphans. Suad's relationship with her neighbors was mutually profitable. Although I could never prove it, I was sure that foster mothers generously tipped Suad, both in money and in a share of commodities. Suad in turn offered them services based on her special connection with Karima, another mutually beneficial relationship. First, Suad assured Karima a supply of reliable child rearers. Second, Suad saved Karima the bother of interviewing prospective foster mothers and of fending off the press of women eager to join the program. Third, Suad guaranteed order in the clinic; she formed queues of women grown restless waiting for examinations. Fourth, Suad, after listening attentively to the clinic doctor, counseled neighborhood women on inoculation, oral rehydration, and cleanliness.

The act of guaranteeing someone is done in traditional, informal society, by means of "invisible" institutional checks on household standards or credit. What Suad did for Karima, others do for creditors. I knew a woman who guaranteed customers as a good risk for a woman who lent money for furniture and other major purchases. My friend also collected monthly payments for the creditor. In studying an economically marginal society, one must consider multiple measures of multiple resources, including qualitative resources such as social contacts, bureaucratic advantage, and household production.

Case 2. Rida, Warsha Supervisor: Stretching Inheritance

Rida is the daughter of Sakkina, who worked as a nurse in Domyatt, in northern Egypt, before marrying Ibrahim, owner of a machining lathe workshop on Shanin Street in Bulaq. In 1975 Sakkina's husband died. When Rida decided to take over the warsha to prevent her four half-siblings from "spoiling the inheritance," she and her sister, Amal, quickly became experts on inheritance law, escrows, liens, and shares. At the workshop Rida, seated next to the lathe and wearing a pants suit, ordered raw materials by phone, accepted work orders to lathe machinery parts, kept the books, paid workers, and dispensed shares to family "stockholders." It was Rida who paced tasks for the three tradesmen and some half-dozen apprentices, negotiated prices and delivery schedules, and mediated disputes. When Rida traveled to visit village relatives, her mother fussed that "no one but Rida knows how to run the warsha."

To understand Sakkina's family's investment of their inheritance, I needed first to understand the complex web of social/kin and material exchanges that permeated the workshop. All transactions were in cash. Any money not used to pay shares to the six children inheriting the shop was poured back into equipment and raw materials. Here I seek not to untangle the web but to suggest interrelationships through the window provided by Sakkina's exegesis. She updated her saga on each of my return visits.

One day as Sakkina and I cleaned rice, she spoke of the genesis of the "inheritance mess":

[2 November 1975] When my husband Ibrahim was sick, he brought a lawyer to write the will so as to give me one-half of the warsha, saying "This is your money." I told him that I would inherit my share when my husband died, that my children were educated . . . [and] that his children (two stepdaughters and two stepsons) were not educated, and would not be able to make a living. . . . After I made this decision I did not feel so tired. I was always busy caring for my ill husband, but I did not worry about what would happen.

But after he died, you should see the character of his children who are my stepchildren. . . . Now my position has changed. My stepdaughter Nadia's husband told me that Nadia wanted to come to condole me when Ibrahim died, and I said that since my husband's death my house has been open. Where has she been? We will buy from whoever wants to sell their warsha shares. I have already bought my stepson Ahmad's share. My lawyer estimated the warsha's worth at 6,000 pounds, so I paid Ahmad 480 pounds. (100 piasters, or one pound, equaled about two dollars at that time.)

[1 April 1976] Muhammad [the other stepson, who works in the shop] wants to have money in his hand to support his drinking. Yesterday he fought with Rida, claiming that he should receive more than his usual 125 piasters a day. He threatened to tear up the accounts books. . . . We are selling Amal's gold bracelets to make money to buy out Muhammad.

[22 April 1976] Hassan is trying to court Rida. He sits around in the warsha while she works. She tells him that he is a drifter without a job, that he is no good for her because he had been spoiled by his mother, who brings him his socks and everything he wants. Hassan wanted to buy Rida's half-brother Muhammad's share of the warsha from him, but now he has decided to get it via Rida. We don't want Hassan. He was engaged to a girl from the Turgoman district; he got her pregnant and she died while aborting. We don't want him. He has no skill. What good are men with an education? The most you can expect is that they will earn a pitiful clerical salary. I want my girls to marry skilled workers who make a decent income!

These vignettes highlight the commingling of romance and inheritance, the importance of jewelry as quick capital, and the informality of warsha management. Shares were sold officially, but workshop management evolved informally. Rida assumed charge when she felt her half-siblings were ruining the business. As long as Rida paid off half-siblings with regular stipends, they were happy to see her do the work. Rida and Amal grew up in the workshop and knew its inner workings. Ibrahim's other children, who lived across town, knew little about supervising workmen or filling orders. One day while we drank tea, Rida told me her story.

As a child, I came here to watch my father, but I never learned to run the machinery. When my father died, my half-brothers ran the warsha for a year . . . [but] they did not care for it well, so we seized our rights and started to manage the shop.

Our family told us that women should not work in a warsha, that nothing would come of it. I have a commercial diploma, and I knew that we had to look after ourselves. . . . We specialize in making car axles, water pumps, and "motrin" [the piece that turns the dynamo of the car]. . . . Out best customers are representatives of industries in the public sector who need machinery parts replaced. We can often figure out how to duplicate a worn-out part.

Our head craftsman earns 150 piasters a day (plus 25 piasters a day in Ramadan for food), and the boys earn 100 to 300 piasters a week (plus 10 piasters a day for food during Ramadan). Each week I pay the coffee man 70 piasters and my half-brother, 2 pounds.

Rida's technical expertise was impressive as she handled orders for plastic factory molds or machine spare parts. She gauged what to charge and when to deliver. She deftly hired and fired. One day she dismissed a young boy for excessive absences. She told apprentices when to operate minor machines, such as the drill, and when to assist the senior craftsman at the lathe.

When I left Bulaq, it was not clear whether Rida and her sister would try to sell the lathe shop. What was clear was that Rida operated in the gray area of orders from public-sector factory representatives, supplies from official and black markets, kin issues of cooperation and profit sharing, and legal issues of inheritance. It is impossible to construct a model of Rida's family's economic activities without considering the subtle trends that emerge in everyday business narrative accounts.

Case 3. Zainab, Rural-Urban Merchant: Cheese on Credit

Zainab was born in a northern Nile Delta village, three hours from Cairo by train. She left home for Cairo in the 1950s to marry a peasant turned civil servant functionary. In the early 1960s, after the two quarreled, she returned to her village, where she sold bean sandwiches. Using the money earned, Zainab began to sell cheese and ghee house-to-house in Cairo, on credit, in the mid-1960s. Every week she traveled to her home village to buy as much dairy produce as she could carry. By the late 1970s, when I visited the market with her, I noticed a new breed of rural dairy merchants—men leaning against Peugeot station wagons waiting to fill their tin cans. Nevertheless, in the late 1980s Zainab's business was still flourishing, mostly because she served a need: provision of small-scale, informal credit to baladi neighbor women.

Usually she sold a large chunk of ghee to one or two people and the remainder, along with the cheese, to customer targets of opportunity. On her return from the weekly village market, Zainab's room was awash with neighbors dropping by to buy small portions of cheese. For example, on 20 April 1976, Zainab brought back twenty-three kilos of ghee and three and one-half kilos of cheese. She first weighed out fifteen kilos reserved by Um Sabah from the church lane; she sent the rest of the ghee to a neighbor and to a nurse who works in the bilharzia hospital and lives in Shaykh Ali. As for the cheese, a half-kilo went to the woman upstairs; one-fourth to a woman across the street; one-half to a woman in the same house; and one and one-half to a regular customer in the church lane. Zainab had kept a quarter-kilo for herself, leaving one-half kilo. A neighbor quickly took that and asked for another half-kilo for her sister. Zainab told her sternly: "If you had told me when I arrived that you wanted a kilo I would have been glad to save it for you!" That day Zainab told me that she cleared fifteen piasters on a kilo of ghee bought outright and twenty on ghee bought by installment. She understood that interest charges are forbidden in Islam and justified her higher price for the "installment plan" as "payment for my patience since I wait for the money."

She explained that only because she can read and write had she been able to act as merchant. "How could I remember all the money I collected if I didn't write it down in front of the customer, and again mark it in front of them when they pay off the entire bill?" She added,

> I was the only girl in our family who went to school. I wore a long blue apron and a scarf around my head. My oldest sister, our first-born, was taught to sew at my father's tailor shop. Our second-born sister was taught to help our mother at home. The third child, a boy, was not clever in school. The teachers used to tell him: "Make an effort, you idiot." He would snatch my scarf and knot it all up because he envied my bright performance at school. He told me: "Make yourself dumb like I am in school."

> I graduated to the next grade every year. When I passed sixth grade and needed to change to school in the next town, my father refused to let me go alone. After that I learned nothing—not even sewing. I sat at home. After a couple of years my husband came and asked for me. Then I was married, and stayed two years before getting pregnant.

One day Zainab showed me her ledger, a school notebook with lines of writing that looked nothing like accounts to me. Zainab had learned to write names and numbers in school, and had developed her own method to organize accounts. When I asked her how many customers she had, she counted the names: "I have 110 names in my book." When I noted that some names were repeated, Zainab explained: "I tallied the same name twice when it stood for more than one person. For example, Um Shahid buys for several relatives, but I always write her name because I know it. After her name, I write the name of the person. On the next line I write the number of kilos they bought. On the next line I write the price. Every time they pay I write it down."

When I had first looked at Zainab's accounts I could not determine what the figures represented. When she explained her system, I began to understand. For instance, she wrote "5"—meaning five kilos of ghee bought; then "625"—the price, in piasters; then "100" or sometimes just "1"—marking every time the customer paid off 100 piasters or 1 pound. Zainab sometimes wrote the number of the balance due on the bottom line, and "the rest" next to it. But not all entries showed a balance due. When I asked

Zainab about her outstanding bills, she estimated them at one hundred pounds. Her son disputed this, saying they were closer to four hundred pounds.

As I glanced through the names of Zainab's customers, I asked about some recurring names to obtain a sense of her buyer networks and contacts. Some clients came to her because a friend or neighbor had told them about the fresh produce; some because they had met her as she collected her accounts. When I asked about the name Um Jabr, Zainab told me that Um Jabr was her landlady and also her point of contact for several of Um Jabr's relatives who lusted after fresh country ghee: "When I go to collect money from my customers, they hold on to me." It was clear that the limit on Zainab's business was not customers but rather the weight her back could bear. She explained to me one cold day that she had been able to bring back from the village only fourteen kilos of ghee in a tin can; she usually brought at least nineteen, but on that day the ghee was so hard that it did not pack well.

Zainab's business and her social life are inextricable: "My neighbor across the hall is an old customer of mine from Adawiyya. When she came here to apply for the apartment, the landlord said no, and the woman told him, 'Ask Zainab about me.' I told the landlord: 'She is my customer; she's all right.' But, horrors of horrors, she turned out to be a rotten woman who curses her children all the time and who shouts and carries on. Now the landlord wants to get rid of her; I didn't have to tell the landlord anything [to give her a recommendation] and now it is all coming on my head."

Zainab's trade is based both on her product's reputation and on her ability to provide friendly financing in an area where revolving credit does not exist. The amounts may seem small, but they are more than the average baladi woman can spend at one time. Zainab's capital for her ghee business was her humble nest egg earned selling bean sandwiches in her home village. She used some early ghee trade profits to finance her son's trip to Saudi Arabia to get a high-paying job. When her son returned from Saudi Arabia to find his mother ill, he contributed little to her medical bills. Zainab then rued the day she had trusted him, and she began to stash all her profits away to use for her medical expenses. A model of informal credit such as Zainab's must encompass both the financial and the social.

Case 4. Zakiyya, Peasant Grocer: Cattle for Capital

Zakiyya was the elder of two daughters-in-law who lived in a rural extended family in Menoufiyya in northern Egypt. Her household received cash from a son who was an army officer and, temporarily, from Zakiyya's husband when he traveled to Saudi Arabia to drive trucks. The family also gained some cash from a small grocery that Zakiyya and her husband operated from a cupboard in the front sitting room. The rest of the family cash came from selling household produce such as corn, pigeons, chickens, and cheese. Zakiyya's account, told to a group of women as we sifted flour, mingles loyalty to natal family with loyalty to conjugal family:

> My brother was angry because the family did not delay my marriage until he returned from the army. . . . He bought a gold necklace with seven strands of gold beads for me. [Here Zakiyya launched into a long story about her nuptial night.] My brother possesses many things. He owns six *feddan* of land [one feddan equals approximately one acre], forty [nanny] goats, and two male goats. He raises cattle for other people; if a man wants to invest money, he gives it to my brother to buy a water buffalo. That is why my brother could afford to give me such a nice wedding present. When my father-in-law, Gharib, needed money to buy the corner lot next to his property, he asked me either to sell my necklace or to borrow money from my father. My father had no money so I sold the necklace for thirty-three pounds. When Gharib repaid me, my husband and I and a relative bought a water buffalo for one hundred pounds, and every year we sold a calf from the water buffalo. . . . Finally we sold our animals and put the money into a small grocery.

In addition to selling livestock, women such as Zakiyya take a sack of corn, some eggs, and a few pigeons with them to sell on the market periphery to waiting middlewomen merchants. Women use that money to buy sugar, lentils, and tea up the road at the local market. Zakiyya buys dry goods for the home grocery at the local market using money from selling eggs and pigeons. Her husband sometimes buys rice and tea in Cairo at government cooperatives. Home grocery profits are small; for example, tea, bought at five piasters a packet, sells for six. Nevertheless the grocery venture supplements income.

Zakiyya's father-in-law recently seeded a grape arbor next to their house "because he knew people in a nearby town who had grown grapes and so decided to try it." He sold the 1976 harvest of two-thirds of a feddan for 450 pounds. Tending the arbor requires little work except irrigation and tying vines on sticks. A young nephew is hired to scare away birds looking to devour the harvest. Zakiyya remains on the look-out for ways to improve her family's economic status. As we strolled one evening at sunset by the irrigation canal, she pointed to family land: "That land past the grape arbor used to be a garden, but now it lies unused, as does the old stable for our water buffalo. We should try to rent it to make a little money." At other times, Zakiyya says that she wants to sell her silver footlets to buy a calf but that her husband will not let her.

The extended household shares cooking and common expenses with the salaried son who contributes money and the peasant son who contributes labor. Both daughters-in-law feel loyalty divided between their conjugal and natal families, and conflicts over family resources sometimes emerge. Zakiyya whispered that her sister-in-law, Aysha, had deposited with her natal family the money earned selling pigeons. Both Zakiyya and her mother-in-law criticized Aysha for spending so much time with her natal family. At the same time, Zakiyya depends on her brothers, and she often says that were she in trouble, she would seek refuge with them. Muslim women who give up their right to family inheritance to avoid fragmenting family landholdings expect, and receive, support from their brothers.

Zakiyya knows that her life as a peasant is different from that of urban women. One day she mused, with a faraway look in her eye, about the *binat al-bandar* (women of the town), who had "seen the world." What did she, a mere peasant, know? Zakiyya's thoughts often turn to family obligations and to her personal experiences of business, the small-scale investments in jewelry and livestock. But at the same time, Zakiyya is linked to the international marketplace by her husband, who now drives trucks in Saudi Arabia.

Conclusion

This chapter has suggested the contribution of the qualitative case study approach to construction of models of the invisible baladi economic sector. In all four cases here, baladi women plumb a multitude of social and material resources to enhance their position. This is not a crude strategy of a marginally economic, desperate group. Rather, the four cases demonstrate a flexible investment of multiple resources that is orchestrated to the cadence of changing social and economic trends. The "invisible" economic activity of a baladi quarter in Cairo is by definition complex and supple, for it simultaneously unfolds in multiple arenas: the government bureaucracy, the marketplace, the family, and the community. This richness of informal economic activity provides a window on baladi work culture and by extension baladi society. It also demands a complex model of intertwined material and nonmaterial resource maximization.

Notes

1. Judith Gran, "The Impact of the World Market on Egyptian Women," *Middle East Research and Information Projects Reports* 58 (1977): 3–77; Judith Tucker, *Women in Nineteenth Century Egypt* (Cambridge: Cambridge University Press, 1985).

2. Tucker, *Women in Nineteenth Century Egypt,* 101.

3. Ibid., 81–82.

4. Evelyn A. Early, *Baladi Women of Cairo: Playing with an Egg and a Stone* (Boulder, Colo.: Lynne Rienner Press, 1993), 139.

5. Sawsan El-Messiri, "Self-Images of Traditional Urban Women in Cairo," in Lois Beck and Nikki Keddie, eds., *Women in Muslim Society* (Cambridge: Harvard University Press, 1978).

7

Women, Work, and the Informal Economy in Rural Egypt

Barbara K. Larson

Since the 1970s, there has been a growing awareness that women's contributions to the economy are frequently overlooked, underestimated, and undervalued. Nowhere is this more true than in the Middle East and North Africa, where women's official participation in the economy is one of the lowest in the world: At the start of the 1990s, women's share in the labor force for the Middle East and North Africa was 27 percent, and only 16 percent of North African women and 21 percent of Middle Eastern women were considered economically active.[1] The corresponding figure for Egypt in 1986 is 5.9 percent.[2] The reasons for this official blindness are several: women's work is frequently concentrated in the domestic or family sphere, where tasks such as housework and child care go unrecognized and unpaid; women's productive activities in agriculture, crafts, and services are often performed as part of a family enterprise where women's contributions are not separately recognized or remunerated. Even when women engage in independent income-producing activities, such activities are frequently part of the informal or "invisible" economy, where they may escape official tallying and recognition, or they are seen as an extension of women's "domestic responsibilities" and hence are not culturally recognized as "work." As others in this book show, even a casual glance finds many women actively engaged in productive work. Lack of recognition of their efforts distorts the picture of the local, regional, and national economy.

What kinds of work, then, are open to women? How does women's economic participation compare with that of men? How does it articulate with both the formal and informal sectors of the economy? This chapter

examines these questions in the context of women in the Egyptian governorate of Beni Suef, where I carried out anthropological research on rural
markets and marketing in 1981–82 and again in 1984–85. The account
here first focuses on the nature of women's work and economic participation in rural Beni Suef. It then examines how their work fits into the Egyptian economy as a whole, and how it is relevant to debates about the formal
and informal sectors of the economy in general and the case of Egypt in
particular.

The Case of Beni Suef

Beni Suef is a predominantly rural governorate (74.9 percent rural; 25.1
percent urban)[3] about two hours' drive south of Cairo. This part of Egypt
represents a bridge between the relatively more urbanized, "sophisticated"
Egyptian Delta and the more conservative areas of Upper Egypt. The major
crops are fruits, vegetables, cotton, and grain that are grown on land irri-
gated by the Nile, which is highly productive and capable of producing
three crops a year. Though farmers consume part of what they produce, the
bulk of their production is commercial and geared for the local market, and
much of what they produce and market is heavily regulated by the government through agricultural cooperatives, which every farmer must join.
Though many people make a living partly from agriculture, the size of
landholdings is generally small. Many households are forced to supplement agricultural income through other sources, such as livestock and
poultry, commerce, government jobs, and so on.[4] Hence, even in rural areas, the local and household economies may be highly diversified, and
women's labor is essential in making such diversification possible.

Agriculture employs the vast majority (73.6 percent) of the economically active rural population, and services and construction jobs run a distant second and third (12.2 percent and 3.8 percent, respectively).[5] However, the employment profiles for women and for men differ somewhat, in
two respects. One is that women work somewhat less in agriculture and
somewhat more in services and commerce than do men.[6] The other difference is that women's employment is severely undercounted. According to
the 1986 census figures, only 1.8 percent of rural women in Beni Suef are
economically active, as compared with 39.6 percent of the men.[7] However,
simple observation easily demonstrates that that percentage for women is
nowhere near the truth.

What are the kinds of work that women in fact do? Why is women's
work undercounted? In rural Beni Suef, women's work falls into five cat-

egories: housework and child care, agricultural work (including dairy and poultry activities), crafts production, commerce, and more recently, for a handful of younger women with secondary school diplomas, government employment.

Housework and Child Care

As in most other societies, Egyptian women have primary responsibility for housework and child care. They are the ones who clean, cook, bake, launder, fetch water, process food for home consumption, and so on. These activities, of course, are not considered "work" in the formal sense, and nowhere in the world are they incorporated into government statistics. They are nevertheless time-consuming tasks that are essential to the maintenance, reproduction, and well-being of the family.[8] Given the conditions under which many villagers live—dirt floors, livestock in the house, dusty streets, few machines or labor-saving devices, and erratically supplied water and electricity—cleaning and laundry require much work. Similarly, food preparation, so essential to Egyptian hospitality and perceived well-being, requires a major commitment of time because food products must usually be cleaned and processed by hand. For example, chickens must be slaughtered and plucked, rice is picked over to remove pebbles and debris, and so on.

In such ways, women make a major contribution to the biological and social reproduction of the household. Additionally, women may engage in income-producing activity as part of their household duties. Rural women work on the family farm or in the family business; they raise poultry and livestock and process dairy products for sale; they may market agricultural products or crafts and sew clothes for kin and neighbors. Yet, although these activities make a direct contribution to family income and may even yield income entirely under a woman's control, as long as they are carried out in the home or on the family farm, they are not culturally coded as formal work but are seen instead as an extension of the role of housewife.

Agriculture

Agricultural work, too, is ubiquitous and multifaceted. Poorer women may hire out as agricultural day laborers, for £E5 (in 1985, approximately $5) per day. This is the kind of agricultural labor that is likely to find its way into official statistics. But the bulk of agricultural labor performed by women is as partners in their family farms, where women are entrusted primarily with the tasks of managing and caring for livestock, raising poultry, assisting in the harvest, and processing plant and animal products for consumption, home utilization, or sale. Marketing of the products may be done by either sex. In general, women market poultry and dairy products and small quantities of grain; men market livestock, large quantities of grain, and export crops; fruit and vegetable production may be marketed by either sex.

These kinds of agricultural labor and marketing services are not recorded in formal government statistics, yet they make a significant contribution to family income. Other studies in the Egyptian Delta have shown that income generated from livestock, poultry, and dairy products (for which women are primarily responsible) can contribute as much as 40 percent of the family's cash income on an average-size farm of 1.3 *feddans*,[9] and in some cases may bring in more than the wages of a son in nonagricultural employment. For example, one man said his wife's earnings from poultry were twice those of his son who was working in a tailor shop.[10] Furthermore, the income generated from poultry and dairying activities, or from livestock owned by women, is generally under the woman's control, though she invariably uses it to help meet family needs.

Agricultural work is not confined to fellahin (farmers) alone. Even nonfellahin families in the village raise poultry for home consumption and for occasional sale, and nonfellahin may own livestock as well—buying and fattening a few goats or sheep or even cattle or buffalo calves for resale, at a profit, in the village markets.

Crafts Production

Crafts production in the villages is also often a family affair.[11] While the male head of the family may be the one formally recorded or recognized as the craftsman, in many kinds of crafts production women work alongside men, and they frequently take part in marketing as well. In my base research village of nine thousand people,[12] the following local crafts were represented, each by one or two or a handful of families at most: makers of donkey saddles, pottery, and palm crates and paddles, as well as wool spinners, rug weavers, tailors, and carpenters.[13] In making a donkey saddle (*barada*), the wife sewed together cotton sacks, which the husband stuffed with straw and quilted to hold the straw in place; both went to the markets to sell their products. Women also washed, combed, carded, and spun wool. Men did the weaving of rugs; the women's job was winding the wool onto spools. As for making palm stem paddles and crates, the paddle maker said that his wife and daughters did not help in the process, while the crate maker reported that the whole family helped make the crates, which his wife sold in the suq.

Tailoring in the village is specialized by sex. Male tailors make *gallabiyyat* (sing., *gallabiyya*) for men.[14] Their wives may help during the busy seasons by holding the cloth to facilitate the cutting or doing some of the touch-up work on buttonholes and the like, but in general these are not women's regular tasks. Sewing for women is done by seamstresses, who are not usually full-time garment workers but housewives or fellahin who sew in their spare time to bring in a little extra money to the household. Male tailoring, recognized as a full-time specialization, is recorded in the occupational censuses, whereas women's activities as seamstresses, regarded as part-time and nonprofessional, themselves go unrecorded in official employment statistics. Indeed, many women deny that they are seamstresses, saying that they sew only for the family. But in reality "family" is usually extended to include neighbors and relatives beyond the immediate household (family in the larger sense), and transactions with family outside the immediate household are usually carried out in cash.

On the other hand, some crafts activities are exclusively male. They include carpentry and blacksmithing, as well as crafts not represented in the village but observed in rural markets, such as making sieves and *taqiyyat* (wool hats; sing., *taqiyya*), though occasionally a woman can be found making the hats. Commercial basketry was not represented in the village; however, some women made straw trays for use in their homes, and one old man made plaited palm baskets. Pottery making in this village was a male occupation except for the employment of one woman, who did the same kind of work as the men.

Few women are represented in crafts production other than sewing, which many women take up independently and say they learn on their own. In fact the overall number of crafts producers in the village—men or women—is small, and craft specialties tend to be inherited from generation to generation. Women engaged in crafts take up the work as the daughters or wives of male craftsmen. They then perform this work as part of a family production center rather than as an independent occupation. There is, then, no tradition of specifically female crafts production on an independent basis.

Commerce

Commerce, which offers more opportunity for independent income-generating activity, is the primary resource and refuge of women who seek to generate or supplement income from nonagricultural sources.[15] Again, women's participation in commerce is not accurately reflected in the statistics, for only full-time women traders, whose identity cards state their occupation as traders, are likely to be formally registered. Yet rural women's participation in commerce tends to be much greater than recorded. Particularly noteworthy is their presence in the weekly markets (*aswaq*; sing., *suq*).

Sellers in Rural Weekly Markets in Beni Suef

As noted, the weekly market, or suq, is the major marketing outlet for women's production of poultry and dairy products, as well as some grain. Most of the women either sell to traders upon their arrival at the suq, or wait to sell directly to consumers in order to keep for themselves the broker's fee. But women also carry their own weight among the full- and part-time traders in the weekly markets.

In general, on the basis of counts made in seventeen of the fifty weekly markets in Beni Suef, women sellers slightly outnumber men, 51.4 percent to 48.6 percent. That count excludes sellers of livestock, who are almost entirely men, but it also excludes the large number of women selling poultry or dairy products, so the numbers of men and women omitted from the count more or less balance each other out. However, though women and men are present in roughly equal numbers, they tend to specialize in selling different things (see table 5).

From this table, it is evident that women tend to specialize in selling agricultural and food products, particularly fruits and vegetables (almost two-thirds female, one-third male), whereas men predominate in sales of crafts and of manufactures and services (just the reverse: approximately one-third female, two-thirds male).

Another way of looking at this is to ask what percentage of all female sellers in the suq were involved in selling what kinds of products, and then ask the same for males. This way of looking at the data results in the percentages calculated in table 6.

The specific kinds of goods in which men and women predominate are detailed in table 7.

Besides some differences in the types of products sold by each sex, other characteristics differ as well. Women in general tend to go to fewer markets per week than do men, and they travel less far. Among the fruit and vegetable traders I have interviewed, men on average go to four markets per week, women to three. Among the fellahin selling fruits and vegetables, men go to three markets per week, women to two. However, among sellers

Table 5. Vendor Specialization by Product and Gender

Product	(N)	Females	Males
Fruits and vegetables	2,359	62.1%	37.9%
Grain and seeds	532	72.6	27.4
Meat, fish, poultry, dairy*	374	40.4	59.6
Services: food and drink	270	29.3	70.7
Subtotals	3,535	58.9	41.1
Services: nonfood	65	7.7	92.3
Raw materials	57	40.4	59.6
Crafts and manufactures	202	36.7	63.3
Subtotals	324	35.7	64.3
Totals	3,859	51.4%	48.6%

*These figures exclude sellers of butter, cheese, and *kishk,* as well fellahin selling poultry and sellers of livestock.

Table 6. Vendor Specialization by Gender

Kind of Product Sold	Females		Males	
	(N)	Percentage	(N)	Percentage
Fruits and vegetables	1,466	54.5%	893	35.1%
Grain and seeds	386	14.4	146	5.7
Meat, fish, poultry, dairy*	151	5.6	223	8.8
Services: food and drink	79	2.9	191	7.5
Subtotals	2,082	77.5	1,453	57.1
Services: nonfood	5	.2	60	2.4
Raw materials	23	.9	34	1.3
Crafts and manufactures	578	21.5	999	39.2
Subtotals	606	22.5	1,093	42.9
Totals	2,688	100.0%	2,546	100.0%

*These figures exclude sellers of butter, cheese, and *kishk,* as well fellahin selling poultry and sellers of livestock.

Table 7. Vendors of Products, by Gender

Females as % of Sellers	Product: Foodstuffs (FS) or Crafts, Manufactures, and Services (CM)	Males as % of Sellers
80–100%	FS: Dairy products, *kishk* (dried yoghurt and grain balls), *mulukhiyya* (spinach-like green) garlic, dates, bran, poultry.	0–19%
60–79%	FS: Salt, grain, greens, green *ful* (beans), fresh fish, spices, honey cones, mint syrup, potatoes, tomatoes, onions. CM: Skins.	20–39%
40–59%	FS: Dried beans, carrots, melons and other fruit, salt fish, summer vegetables (eggplant, peppers, etc.), innards and fat, poultry (traders), citrus. CM: Brooms, plastic shoes, notions, crates, baskets, and paddles; iron goods.	40–59%
20–39%	FS: Seeds, *bersim* (clover), turnips, *ta'miyya* (fried bean cakes), sweets, ice cream, and *turmus* (lupine). CM: Cigarettes, household goods, palm fiber products, clothes, rope and rubber buckets, pottery, saddles, aluminum, used clothes, wool hats (*taqiyyat*), raw wool.	60–79%
0–19%	FS: Cabbage, cauliflower, coffee and tea, sugar cane, meat, chicks. CM: Wood handles, stakes, palm fiber, primus repair, gold, tables, cloth, mats, rugs and blankets, leather shoe repair, shoeshines, donkey barbering, knife sharpening, plastic shoe repair, canes, locks, cassettes, sieves.	80–100%

of crafts and manufactures, the difference disappears: Both men and women average four markets per week.

Another gender difference is the degree to which market selling is a hereditary occupation. Approximately two-thirds (68.4 percent) of male sellers have inherited their trade, while only one-third (31.7 percent) of the women have done so, though another 17.1 percent have a husband or aunt or uncle engaged in the trade. A further breakdown shows that the chief differences are in the area of the fruit and vegetable trade, where 60.9 percent of the men have inherited their profession, versus only 16.7 percent of the women. By contrast, among sellers of crafts and services, the majority of both sexes have inherited their trade, and the differences between men and women are less: 69.2 percent of the men versus 57.1 percent of the women. In addition, more women than men work alone among the fruit and vegetable sellers (58.3 percent vs. 42.5 percent); the reverse is true for sellers of other kinds of goods: 55.8 percent of the men working alone vs. 38.1 percent of the women.

The reasons lie in the somewhat different work circumstances of women and men. In rural Egyptian society in general, men are considered the breadwinners. They for the most part continue in their fathers' occupations; the exceptions occur when through education a man gets a better-paying and more prestigious job, or when circumstances make it difficult or impossible to continue in the family business. Such is the case, for example, of agriculturalists who lose access to land.

However, for women it is a sign of status not to have to work outside the home, unless in an easy, clean, proper, and prestigious job as a civil servant in a government office. Hence, aside from the relatively small number of village women who have entered government employment, most village women who work outside the home do so because they are forced by poverty, divorce, widowhood, or the absence or illness of a husband to assume all or part of the responsibility for producing family income. In this case, selling in the suq offers one of the more accessible means of earning a livelihood.

In general, such women have two choices. If they are the daughters or wives of specialized craftsmen or traders, they may augment the family income by selling the specialized goods side by side with their menfolk in the local suq, or they may assume major responsibility for selling crafts while their husbands do the bulk of the manufacturing. If they are without husbands or other male family members, the women may carry on in their stead. Few women, and for that matter relatively few men, independently take up sales of specialized goods (iron, wool, aluminum, gold, or large-scale poultry wholesaling); most learn the trade from a family member.

If such specialized skills are lacking, the most likely avenue of trade is selling fruits and vegetables. Hence the fruit and vegetable trade tends to be less specialized (in the sense of being handed down from generation to generation) than other kinds of trade. It also requires little capital, for most goods are bought on credit from local wholesalers (whereas crafts goods, for example, often are bought in Cairo), and even a small stock of fresh produce is enough to start. Furthermore, women who want to deal in fruits and vegetables have extensive knowledge of pricing and quality, gleaned from their other responsibilities as housewives, and can thus draw on a certain amount of expertise. (The same is true for women dealing, for example, in small-scale poultry trading.) The other attraction of selling in the suq is its flexibility in fitting in with other responsibilities. Selling in the suq can be done full- or part-time; it can be fit in around the demands of child care, and older children can help with the trading as well. For all these reasons, then, trading in fruits and vegetables tends to be the kind of selling that attracts newcomers, particularly women, as reflected previously in the statistics on gender and inherited occupations.

The final aspect we might consider is the size and scale of commerce engaged in by male and female vendors. Although men and women tend to participate in the suq in nearly equal numbers, men tend to be disproportionately represented in the more lucrative and more capital-intensive kinds of business. The most expensive item in the suq is livestock—almost exclusively the domain of male traders. Men also monopolize most sales of cloth, gold, and aluminum. For native products like eggs and poultry, women generally are involved in the lower echelons of the trade, buying directly from the fellahin and reselling to a higher-level merchant. But the large wholesalers and those who export poultry to Cairo are predominantly men. Similarly, while many women display vegetable stock ample enough to rival the bigger male sellers, most women selling at the market have only a small basket of greens or tomatoes to offer. Thus many more women than men appear to be involved at the pettiest levels of commerce, while the reverse is true at the top. (I have, however, no exact counts.)

Other Kinds of Female Commercial Activity

Participation in the suq is only the most obvious kind of female involvement in commerce. Some women peddle tomatoes or fruit in the streets of most villages more or less regularly. Frequently these are older women who find going to the weekly markets too exhausting. In addition, there are many women, particularly older women existing on inadequate pensions of £E12 per month, who make a few piasters each day by selling biscuits and candy or other petty grocery items from their homes or from a temporary stand in front of their houses.

Yet other women work in grocery stores along with their husbands. In many cases, the stores are recorded in the woman's name, to get around the strictures preventing government employees from having a second job. Often the wife works in the store during the mornings, the husband in the evenings or afternoons. Many stores are open irregularly, but a customer who finds the shop closed may go to the house and make the purchases from either husband or wife. For other items also, such as poultry or gold, selling takes place from the house as well as from the shop or suq. The wife almost always has sufficient expertise to take over for her husband, and hence these are in some sense joint ventures. Yet other groceries are run by women, who carry on the family business after their husbands have died.

Government, Professional, and White-Collar Employment

For a few women, the availability and accessibility of free education through the college level has opened up prospects of government or professional employment. However, most village girls cannot take advantage of these opportunities for a variety of reasons—lack of confidence, lack of money for books and tutors, or their families' dependence on the daughters' labor.

Analysis and Theory

How does rural women's work fit into the general economy of Egypt, and what role does it play in the nature, functions, utility, and articulation of the formal and informal sectors of the economy?

Most of the economic activities discussed here fall into what is known as the informal sector of the economy. That is, they are small-scale enterprises of the self-employed; they require relatively little capital and usually generate low levels of profit; work is frequently occasional, seasonal, or part-time; there are few entry-level barriers (formal credentials or licensing mechanisms). The activities are not closely monitored or controlled by government tracking methods, though the extent of surveillance and monitoring varies somewhat by activity. Abdel Fadil describes the informal urban economy of Egypt as consisting of small-scale manufacturing and handicraft work, itinerant and jobbing artisans, personal services, and petty services and retailing activities. This serves as a pretty good summary of the informal sector of the rural economy as well.[16]

Both women and men are heavily involved in informal-sector activities for a variety of reasons. There are few entry-level barriers. Most rural Egyptians lack the education or capital to qualify for more formal kinds of employment or to launch larger-scale entrepreneurial activity. Furthermore, Egypt has a difficult time providing formal private-sector or public-sector jobs for its ever-burgeoning population, despite its official policy (since curtailed) of providing jobs for all college graduates if necessary. Because public-sector wages are too low to support a family adequately, most public-sector employees supplement wages with small-scale commercial, agricultural, or service activities on the side.

Participation in the informal economy is especially important for women, who, compared with men, do not have comparable access to the formal sector. Rural women are less educated than men, and most lack access to significant capital. Acceptance of careers for women, particularly in rural areas, is not yet part of the local culture, nor are there many opportunities. Though government has employed growing numbers of women in recent years, overall rates of formal employment for women remain low. Culturally, women's primary roles are those of mothers and housewives, and whatever work they do to bring in income must be combined with other domestic responsibilities. For all these reasons, women's economic participation is largely confined to the informal sector.

Activities in the informal sector are divided between those done for payment (the usual definition of the informal sector) and those that are unpaid but nevertheless make real contributions to family well-being. In general, such unpaid activities would be remunerated if performed outside the family circle, although at low rates of compensation. Such traditionally female tasks include the maintenance and social reproduction of the family unit (through housework and child care) and a contribution to family enterprises (particularly agriculture and crafts), in which the income produced gets formally attributed to the male head of household. At present there is no way of accounting for the worth of this labor, aside from some occasional time-budget studies that document for a small sample the relative contributions of women and men. Yet such activities are a vital part of the invisible or informal economy that should be monitored in some way. Fortunately work is underway by organizations such as the United Nations to formulate a better method for estimating their contribution to the economy.[17]

Another area worth consideration, though difficult to study, is the degree of informal, nonmonetary exchange that goes on within families. For many Egyptian households, family diversification of economic activities is the key to survival, and the goods and services exchanged among extended family members greatly contribute to the viability of all. At the same time, household-level exchange may also act as a leveling device both within and among households. Of particular importance are labor exchanges (including of children to help with housework and child care); exchanges of rural agricultural products for access to or information about urban services and jobs; and provision of urban lodgings for rural relatives coming to the city for school or work. Indeed, Egyptians from all walks of life and all income levels regularly invest in social relations as an economically worthwhile activity.

How the Informal Economy Is Linked with the Formal in Egypt

Discussion of the articulation between formal and informal economy generally follows one of three lines. Some theorists focus on the informal as a complement to the formal sector. Others, particularly those of a Marxist bent, concentrate on the extent to which the informal sector is conserved and ultimately exploited by the capitalist sector in order to maximize the profits of the latter. Still other theorists focus on the degree to which the informal sector is or is not controlled, regulated, or protected by the state, and the extent to which it is unrecognized by—or even acts in opposition to—the state.[18] The situation of Egypt is somewhat complicated in this regard, at least for the areas I know best.

On the one hand, though the activities of sellers and farmers fit the descriptions of small-scale entrepreneurs generally assigned to the informal-sector category, they are not entirely independent of the state. Despite the government's move from a state-planned, socialist economy in the 1960s, to a form of state capitalism with a degree of privatization in the 1980s,[19] it continued to regulate, protect, and exploit farmers and market sellers in several ways. Small farmers operated in a climate of extensive regulation through the 1980s. The government subsidized seed, fertilizer, and technical advice, dictated what to plant, and required the farmers to sell a certain portion of crops to the government at prices below the world market. It also regulated tenancy contracts and rent. Only the wealthier farmers could afford to buy their way out of these controls. Most observers[20] have argued that these policies, on balance, represented a net tax on agriculture. This was used to subsidize the consumer needs of urban areas and the investment needs of the state, which privileged industrial development over agricultural development.

Regulation of markets was somewhat similar. Although sellers were nominally independent small entrepreneurs, the government requires licenses for vendors, though only the larger-scale vendors are actually monitored. The government requires health certificates for dealing in foodstuffs, sends inspectors to check on health and sanitary conditions, levies fines for selling rotten or contaminated produce, and regulates prices of foodstuffs sold in the local markets. The latter, in particular, was seen as part of the government's overall strategy of keeping food prices low to prevent popular discontent, while at the same time using the agricultural sector to subsidize urban growth and industrial development. This strategy worked to the benefit of the state but did nothing to promote or sustain the growth of agriculture, on which the economy depends. In addition, the state "taxes" public markets by auctioning to the high bidder the rights to collect market fees. This "owner" of the market then charges the sellers set fees, according to the size of their operations, and pockets the difference between the fees collected and the auction price.

At the same time, the market sellers themselves are regulated to only a minimal degree. Provided they have their licenses and health certificates where necessary, pay their relatively minimal fees to the "owner" of the suq, and are not caught trying to evade price or sanitary controls, there is little further monitoring or accounting of their activity, though the sellers of foodstuffs are of course greatly affected by the system of price controls.

Hence it is quite clear that the small-scale private sector in agriculture and marketing by and large works to the benefit of the state and the consumer, but not necessarily to the benefit of the farmers or the sellers. Therefore one can make the quasi-Marxist argument that these areas of the informal sector enable the formal sector (or rather in this case, the public sector) to increase its profits at the expense of the producers and sellers. Hence the informal sector activities complement rather than undermine the interests of the state, and very much work to its benefit. In this regard it is significant that the governnment never tried to do away with small-scale commerce in the way that the Tunisian government did in the 1960s, despite occasional press campaigns in the 1980s which lashed out at price-gouging by merchants. (The targets were primarily the large-scale merchants in Rawda al-Faraj who control most of the wholesale produce market in Egypt, rather than smaller informal sector operators).[21]

At the same time, the informal sector also benefits the poorer segments of the populace by providing low cost goods to help them weather the dislocations of the strained economy and the growing income gap between rich and poor which resulted from the political and economic crises and policies of the last three decades. In 1952, when the revolutionary government under Gamal Abdel Nasser's leadership overthrew King Farouk, economic conditions in the countryside were at an all time low. Egypt's socialist policies during the 1960s generally resulted in improved living conditions for the rural populace during the first half of the decade. But in the second half of the decade the Egyptian economy declined once again as a result of the diversion of Egypt's attention and resources to military concerns (against Israel and in Yemen) and growing corruption and mismanagement at home. During the 1970s, President Sadat's "Open Door Policy" sought to turn the economy around through privatization and reduced government control over certain areas of the economy in order to attract foreign investment. The decade of the 1970s was also a period of increased revenues from oil and remittances from abroad as more than a million Egyptians went to Iraq, Syria, Jordan and the Gulf states to meet the demand for labor.[22] President Mubarak continued Sadat's liberalization policies in the 1980s, under increasing pressure from international donor agencies such as the World Bank and the International Monetary Fund to adopt structural adjustment policies and privatize.

The results of these policies and developments were inflation and a growing gap between rich and poor. People who already had some capital, or who possessed the skills to go abroad or assume the positions being vacated by departing migrants, were able to benefit from the new opportunities and even acquire new capital to invest in small-scale ventures. In the rural areas, poultry projects and taxi services were especially popular, and some women benefited as well as men. For example, Saunders and Mehenna report that a number of village women in the Delta were able to invest in livestock and poultry projects which greatly augmented their incomes and their control over economic resources.[23]

But those who were not in a position to take advantage of the new opportunities suffered from stagnant incomes coupled with rising inflation and thus were left behind. Many were obliged to take up supplementary employment as laborers or in petty commerce to help make ends meet. Here the informal economy provided some relief. By providing everyday goods and services to consumers more cheaply than larger or more formal enterprises and establishments, and by providing employment opportunities (however small-scale and petty) even to people without extensive capital or skills, the informal sector helped ordinary citizens make ends meet.

The informal sector thus provided a resource and opportunity for people at both ends of the spectrum. That is, it provided cheap goods and subsistence-level employment to those adversely affected by the deterioration of the domestic economy, while also offering real and profitable entrepreneurial opportunities to those with enough capital to invest in producing or selling the kinds of consumer goods and services which were now in high demand.

In summary and conclusion, then, we would have to reiterate the following points: The informal sector is alive and well in Egypt. It operates in and around the interstices of the formal economy, which is still heavily dominated by the public sector. Informal sector activities by and large complement the formal economy, and work to the benefit of the state and the consumer, rather than to producers and sellers. Though women are barely present in the formal statistics on labor participation, many are economically active—mostly in the informal sector. Their activities in the informal sector take many forms, but in rural areas they are most visible in agriculture and commerce, and to a lesser extent in craft activities. Most of these activities are carried out within the context of a family enterprise, and hence often go unnoticed and unrecorded both statistically and in village perceptions: That is, these activities are seen as extensions of the housewife role, and hence are not formally perceived or registered as "work" or "employment." Yet women's economic activities (both their productive activities and their activities in social reproduction) are vital both to the economy and to the well-being of their households, and as such deserve better documentation and recognition in any assessments of either the roles of women or the nature of the economy in Egypt.

Notes

This chapter is a revision of a paper published as "Women's Work and Status in Egypt," *NWSA Journal* 3, no. 1 (Winter 1991): 38–52. Portions of that article are reprinted here with permission from Ablex Publishing Corporation. The research on which it is based was supported by a fellowship (funded by the U.S. National Endowment for the Humanities and the International Communication Agency) from the American Research Center in Cairo in 1981–82 and a Fulbright Islamic Civilization Research Grant in 1984–85.

1. This compares with female economic activity rates of 59 percent for eastern

Asia; 50 percent for North America; 47 percent for Southeast Asia; 46 percent for sub-Saharan Africa; 45 percent for Australia, Europe, Japan, and New Zealand; 40 percent for Oceania; and 32 percent for Latin America and the Caribbean. Only southern Asia had a comparably low female labor force participation rate: of 24 percent. *The World's Women 1970–1990: Trends and Statistics* (New York: United Nations, 1991), 82.

2. *Census of Population, Housing and Establishments, 1986,* vol. 2: *Final Results, Total Republic* (in Arabic) (Cairo: Central Agency for Public Mobilisation and Statistics [CAPMAS], Arab Republic of Egypt, 1991), 40, table 7.

3. *1986 Census: Total Republic,* 4, table 1.

4. By 1977 only 50 percent of total rural household income in Egypt came from agriculture. Yahya Sadowski, *Political Vegetables? Businessman and Bureaucrat in the Development of Egyptian Agriculture* (Washington, D.C.: Brookings Institution, 1991), 87.

5. *1986 Census: Total Republic,* 37, table 7. (The entire table covers pages 34–40. It provides only raw numbers; I calculated the percentages.)

6. For women, the figures are 42.2 percent in agriculture, 39.0 percent in services (community, social, and personal), and 5.9 percent in commerce; for men, 74.6 percent in agriculture, 11.4 percent in services, 3.9 percent in construction, 3.2 percent in manufacturing, and 2.5 percent in commerce. *1986 Census: Total Republic,* 37, table 7.

7. Ibid.

8. See Sonja Zimmerman, *The Women of Kafr Al Bahr: A Research into the Working Conditions of Women in an Egyptian Village, and the Cheese Makers of Kafr Al Bahr* (Cairo/Leiden: Research Centre for Women and Development, State University of Leiden, 1982).

9. Zimmerman, *Women of Kafr al Bahr,* 45–46. A feddan is equivalent to approximately 1.1 acres.

10. Lucie Wood Saunders and Sohair Mehenna, "Unseen Hands: Women's Farm Work in an Egyptian Village," *Anthropological Quarterly* 59 (July 1986): 105–14, 112.

11. For an excellent detailed discussion of women's participation and skills in more specialized crafts production, see Patricia Lynch, with Hoda Fahmy, *Craftswomen in Kerdassa, Egypt* (Geneva: International Labor Office, 1984).

12. Officially 8,860 people, according to the *1986 Census: Final Results, Governorate of Beni Suef,* 19, table 1.

13. Out of a total of 1,679 households in the village (author's rough count), there were 12 households of carpenters, 7 crate or paddle makers, 2 makers of reed mats, 2 makers of straw trays or baskets, 2 blacksmiths, 5 potters, 7 saddle makers, one rug weaver, 7 wool processors, 11 tailors, and an unknown number of seamstresses.

14. A gallabiyya is a long, free-flowing gown that is the traditional dress for men.

15. Though only 0.1 percent of all rural females over the age of six in Beni Suef governorate were engaged in commerce in 1986, according to the 1986 census, 5.9 percent of the women who were economically active were so engaged, making commerce the second largest employer of women after agriculture. *1986 Census: Total Republic,* 37.

16. Abdel Fadil, working with a 1967 census of industrial production, found that roughly one-third of the establishments employing fewer than ten persons were located in the rural areas of Egypt. Mahmoud Abdel-Fadil, *Informal Sector Employment in Egypt* (Geneva: International Labour Office, 1983), 6.

17. For a discussion of the difficulties of measuring women's work and the efforts to better incorporate it into official statistics, see United Nations, *World's Women,* 81, 85.

18. For an overview of definitions of and theoretical perspectives on the informal sector, see Norman Long and Paul Richardson, "Informal Sector, Petty Commodity Production, and the Social Relations of Small-scale Enterprise," in John Clammer, ed., *The New Economic Anthropology* (New York: St. Martin's Press, 1978): 176–209; Gracia Clark, introduction, *Traders Versus the State: Anthropological Approaches to Unofficial Economies* (Boulder, Colo.: Westview Press, 1988); M. Estellie Smith, "The Informal Economy," in Stuart Plattner, ed., *Economic Anthropology* (Stanford: Stanford University Press, 1989): 276–82.

19. See Alan Richards and John Waterbury, *A Political Economy of the Middle East: State, Class and Economic Development* (Boulder, Colo.: Westview Press, 1990): 215.

20. Karima Korayem, "The Agricultural Pricing Policy and the Implicit Taxation of Agricultural Income" (paper presented at Princeton-Egyptian Income Distribution Research Project Conference, Lisbon, 31 October–4 November 1979); William Cuddihy, *Agricultural Price Management in Egypt* (Washington D.C.: World Bank, 1980); Khalid Ikram, *Egypt: Economic Management in a Period of Transition* (Baltimore: Johns Hopkins University Press, 1980). See also Sadowski, *Political Vegetables?* chap. 5, for a more nuanced view of the winners and losers of these policies.

21. See Sadowski, *Political Vegetables?* chap. 5.

22. Saad Eddin Ibrahim, "Oil, Migration and the New Arab Social Order," in Malcolm Kerr and El Sayed Yassin, eds., *Rich and Poor States in the Middle East* (Boulder, Colo.: Westview Press, 1982), 17–70.

23. Saunders and Mehenna, "Unseen Hands."

8

Women and Home-Based Microenterprises

Marie Butler

The role of Egyptian women in rural agriculture as household producers is well known.[1] Although women's contribution to the rural labor force is undercounted and officially unenumerated,[2] women have traditionally generated income for families living at or near subsistence level. What is increasingly controversial is the undocumented role of women in the informal, or "invisible," sector of the economy who produce goods and services for production that is surplus to family survival.

Recent innovations in technical assistance include foreign capital investment that goes to small farmers who have not previously qualified for credit from indigenous sources. Traditional methods of production targeted for improvements include enterprises in which surpluses produced in the past have been sold to local markets, such as dairy products, vegetables, and poultry. Technical assistance addresses small-scale agribusiness through improved methods, new seed varieties, and systematic care and feeding of caged birds.

This case study focuses on an upgraded chicken battery of ninety-six birds, three or four birds per cage, which is based on credit to small farmers under government and foreign assistance sponsorship. The study points out women's level of contribution to the household income. The evidence suggests that this cooperative venture differs from urban petty commodity production as a result of direct foreign aid intervention for rural agricultural households. This chapter, which explores the sociocultural context of the household organization of female labor, suggests that the nature of the enterprise and the availability of inputs fit naturally with laboring responsibilities of women.

The evidence also suggests that the subsidized supports have the potential for altering the structural dimensions of the household division of labor, while encouraging women's participation in the informal sector. In implementing the specialized assistance, there is an absence of regard for the character of the household division of labor in rural Egypt. Given this absence, there is room for speculation on the long-term viability of similar supports to diversify and unify household strategies in poor countries. The chapter discusses whether women's duties have been changed through the specialized assistance and whether anticipated changes in women's status and role in the household division of labor may result from their increasing economic role.

Theory and Concepts

The concept of the informal, or "invisible," economic sector applies to the economic context for egg-laying battery production. Portes[3] leads in criticizing the dominant definitions of informal sector as being segmented, incomplete, and containing ahistorical contradictions about the variety of relationships of production that coexist and coalesce. According to Portes,[4] the concept of informality is "defined as the sum total of income-producing activities in which members of a household engage, excluding income from contractual and legally regulated employment." For many rural women in Egypt, wage employment is not socially possible because of the competition between mobility and reproduction, thus keeping women's income-generating possibilities in or near the home. Employment outside the household or village is limited by cultural constraints, by lack of education and skills, and by familial laboring responsibilities.

Options for enterprising and lucrative occupations for women, particularly young married women, are restricted by lack of economic resources and by community cultures that encourage formalized labor for men and an elevated social status for women who remain homebound. (For restrictions on labor force participation rates in nonagricultural occupations, see Youssef.)[5]

Boserup[6] argues that, because of capitalist domination of markets and commodity production, increased technology tends to erode traditional enterprises, especially those held by women in rural areas. But informal-sector enterprises often exist alongside, and are often created by, formal-sector activities; household strategies are usually diversified even in predominantly wage-based modes of production. Both institutional and cultural practices act either to restrict or to encourage women's formal labor force participation as economies are thrust from production for consumption to production for larger markets. Given that childbearing adds to their status in most Third World countries today, women's participation is often limited to traditional subsistence occupations. During periods of labor scarcity, women are regarded as reserve labor suppliers in formal occupations. The sociocultural basis for the household division of labor persists long after the economic basis for either formalized or informalized labor exchange has been altered by a capitalist mode of production.

Although the chicken battery described here is itself modernized and upgraded within the cultural context (that is, more systematized than the wandering flock), the labor arrangement remains much the same. This may not be inconsequential. Peasant families concerned with survival are aware of the multiplicity of family labor arrangements. The allowance of female labor spent in the enterprise may be viewed as one way to circumvent the rising pressures of the modern economy. The preservation of informal enterprise is both an economic necessity and a sociocultural strategy that protects women's role and status. This latter aspect casts a shadow over the success of foreign capital in assisting small farmers. Portes's position[7] that the informal, invisible sector consists of heterogeneous components that function by virtue of their relation to the dominant economic arrangement of the state is supported in the research on the chicken battery production project, but with cultural specifications.

Smith,[8] attempting to bridge the definitional gap between nonwage work in general and housework as nonwage work, is critical of the absence of this distinction in the work of Portes and Walton,[9] who she adds "have little regard for women's special role in the informal sectors." Using the household mode of production framework, it is more accurate to report on the competitive advantage of the informal over the formal sector for women, as reflected in the absence of opportunity for female labor elsewhere, challenging the current limits of the concept of informal sector.

Methodology

In this case study of a rural income-generating activity, female owners and operators of egg-laying batteries were interviewed in the village of Aghour, approximately one hour northwest of Cairo in Kalyubia governorate. The Aghour Village Bank has lent funds for 350 batteries now operating (each family averaging two batteries). Data on production levels, household activities, and marketing were gathered through a questionnaire presented to village women producers. The research was conducted in three phases: interviews with Egyptian agricultural extension agents and financial analyst at the village bank; informal discussions with U.S. project personnel and with participants; and structured interviews with a randomly selected number of participating women owners of egg-laying batteries in Aghour between November 1983 and August 1984.

The Study Area: The Peasant Household in Rural Egypt

The fellahin are the smallholder peasants of rural Egypt who derive most but not all of their income from the land, from family labor, and from related small-scale family enterprises. Following the 1952 revolution, land reform created a preponderance of family-owned holdings of fewer than five *feddans* (a feddan is slightly more than one acre). Generally, these family operations include a male head of household and, depending on the number of sons, usually at least one son occupied in a wage-sector job. Subdivision of family land as inheritance for sons is often problematic, since the small parcels, once divided, cannot sustain a household.

Crop prices in Egypt are kept low to avoid an inflationary spiral in urban areas that would drive up the cost of labor. Although small farmers pay no taxes per se, there is de facto taxation via policies that depress crop prices, such as extraction of capital for industrial development, state intervention in costs and allocations of inputs, regulation of imports-exports when designating crops to be grown, and an official purchase price that is set below market value.[10] Farmers obtain subsidized inputs through the Ministry of Agriculture cooperative; in the past, small farmers on marginal plots often failed to qualify for the credit necessary to purchase required inputs.

Peasant strategies can follow either a production or consumption route.[11] The fellahin kin-based household intersects with the wage-based economy in order to diversify its economic base and to supply domestic consumption items not produced by the family or to meet external demands for direct or indirect taxes. Peasants increase household production or reduce consumption of such items rather than purchasing from outside vendors. Peasants employ either strategy when demanding external pressures of change threaten their traditional way of life.

Although variation persists even within a kin-ordered mode of production described by Wolf,[12] women often form the pivotal core of the family workforce in pursuing survival strategies. Egyptian rural domestic relations function under a patriarchal system of work relations. With the male head being the primary cultivator, the sexual division of labor is enforced on both religious and social grounds. Given woman's primary role as producer of the family labor, there is extreme family pressure on young people to remain in the village. Even after extended periods of employment overseas, young men return to live in the family village. Often, wife and children remain behind with the husband's kin.

The share of agricultural investment in Egypt's development policy declined from the all-time high during the Nasser era to a low in 1978; investment in technology rose, based on revenues from Suez Canal traffic, foreign aid, tourism, and foreign capital. By 1980, however, plans to invest in agriculture were made a top priority. The Small Farmer Production Project (SFPP) began with an initial $25 million grant from the U.S. Agency for International Development (AID) to the Egyptian government; the purpose was to coordinate loans to small farmers while providing agricultural technical assistance. Services were provided through the Ministry of Agriculture, the Principal Bank for Development and Agricultural Credit (PBDAC, known as the Village Bank), and cooperative institutions at the local level. Recipients were farmers holding five feddans of land or less who previously had been denied credit because of an absence of collateral or standing in the community.

How Women Generate Income in Rural Egypt

Women's contributions to rural household incomes in Egypt account for a greater portion of labor than is often recognized. According to current estimates from the Egyptian Central Agency for Public Mobilization and Statistics (CAPMAS), women's overall share in the labor force is around 4 percent, although official undercounts exist. Rural women's contribution spans both agricultural and nonagricultural activities. Survey data from the Small Farmer Production Project[13] (see table 8) indicate that a significant percentage of vegetables and dairy products are marketed locally by cooperating female farmers. The extent of unregulated income generation for rural women is difficult to estimate; it includes all unpaid household labor and unremunerated, traditional tasks performed in lieu of hired labor. Most family-based operations surveyed, made up of one or two workers, revealed that their production levels and incomes went unrecorded.

El Seoud and Estira[14] report that, in general, the female economic role in rural Egypt has traditionally emphasized poultry raising, milking, transporting crops, and reaping. These activities are the basis for involvement by women in food processing and small-scale industries,[15] especially dairy processing and textiles.

Table 8. Outlets and Percentages of Product Marketed

(Cooperating Female Farmers, N = 60)

| | % of Marketing Outlets | | | | | | % of Total Product Marketed | | | | |
Commodity	Village Bank*	Market	Friends, Relat.	Nearest Vill./City	Comb.**	Middle-men	1–25	26–50	51–75	76–100
Eggs	0	17	17	0	9	0	58	0	34	8	58
Crops	71	6	6	6	0	6	9	2	12	24	62
Veget.	4	34	4	4	46	-	9	0	12	17	71
Fruits	0	0	0	11	22	11	56	0	0	0	100
Dairy	0	9	50	17	0	9	17	48	24	23	5
Meat	5	42	0	11	0	0	42	11	10	5	74

*Village Bank is the name for the local cooperative.
**Combination category represents multiple responses.
Source: SFPP Survey Raw Data, 1983.

New evidence for the underenumeration of women in key small-scale rural enterprises is found in phase 1 results of the Michigan State University survey of small-scale enterprises and, to a somewhat lesser degree, in the Small Farmer Production Project Assessment of Participation of Women in Project Activities, completed in 1983. Both surveys were conducted in Kalyubia governorate. These data correct previous undercounts of female workers found in national censuses. According to the most recent Census of Industrial Production (1966–67), for example, "females account for only 7.4 percent of the entire artisanal labor force."[16] The artisanal sector includes enterprises with fewer than ten employees and accounts for only a portion of the total income-generating activity within the rural areas where family-based operations of one or two workers predominate.

In operations where family members predominate, production data and profits are easily concealed. In contrast, the Michigan State data suggest a heavy concentration of women in small-scale rural enterprises—for example, women make up 99 percent of the food products subsection (primarily dairy production), the largest single industry. Of greater significance, however, is that women own and operate 43 percent of all the small-scale enterprises (excluding dairy farming) studied in the survey (including hat making, textile production, and basket making)—a fact overlooked by the official census.[17]

Generally, women's work in the rural economy is an essential component of household (and individual) income-generating strategies, yet it remains unrecognized because of data collection discrepancies. The extent of women's production for markets and their localized operations are largely unknown, given their limited mobility and status.[18] Concern with the household's disposable income remains a central responsibility of the woman. Egyptian women in all social classes are governed after marriage by social norms of family patriarchal arrangements. In most rural areas, the control is tightened to include seclusion of women and strong objections to their working or traveling outside the village of residence.

Small-scale home-based economic enterprises thus fit well with the physical setting of the household, as well as the social relations of production for married women. Employment figures show significantly lower labor force participation by married women than by those who are single or divorced,[19] notwithstanding the underenumeration of unpaid family labor. Married women's work as a function of the family life cycle is undercounted for the following reasons during censuses: the census enumerators are generally male and speak only to male heads of households; the household males do not view women's income-generating activities as work and they see the profits as negligible, therefore not subject to taxation; and, given the traditional view that women are to be provided for by the husband, revealing information to the contrary would bring shame upon the male of the household. Hammam[20] points out that the benefits inherent in home production, such as the possible combination of child-rearing and productive activities, allow the exchange of commodities with others in the village, enhance the buying power of the family's cash income, and imply an overall household strategy to reduce dependence on market goods.

Marginal household production brings in small cash earnings that are valued as disposable income and are usually spent on basic family needs. In the invisible sector, the absence of regulation eases both entry and exit of a marginal producer. Income generation opportunities increase for married women in their reproductive years.

Small Farmer Project Data

In the village of Aghour in May 1984, 173 new project loans were extended, totaling £E83,203 (one Egyptian pound equals U.S.$1.17).[21] Roughly 83 percent of these loans went for egg-laying chickens, feed, supplies and poultry equipment. Generally, the number of feddans owned directly related to the need for outside employment and for income generation by women in the household. The farmers in this sample overwhelmingly reported land ownership of one to three feddans.

Although the goals of government aid to small farmers did not specify female household producers, women generally heard about the project through their husbands or sons. Since the egg production operation was totally supervised by the women and was located within the household (either in a vacated bedroom or on the second story), women were automatic customers for credit.

As table 9 indicates, loans to female borrowers in the Kalyubia governorate outnumber those to other governorates in the project, and 15 percent of the loans were for purchases of poultry and livestock, a traditional source of income for rural women. In this enterprise, women "continue to control a significant portion of the income generated."[22] In a sample survey of 60 female borrowers from the Kalyubia governorate (table 10), respondents tended to be illiterate, married or widowed, more than 30 years of age, and living in households of five or more persons. Most households have at least four children under the age of 16, and any grown children typically live in the same village.[23]

According to additional SFPP survey data, a comparison of cooperating and noncooperating households in the Small Farmer Production Project (meaning farmers receiving loans) revealed that only one woman in ten in either sample was employed outside the household in agricultural or non-agricultural occupations. Table 11 indicates that about half of participating and nonparticipating women spent time each day milking animals, and more than 80 percent fed the animals. Not surprisingly, the participating women spent more time tending batteries and gathering and marketing eggs than did the nonparticipating women; they were also more likely to

Table 9. Number of SFPP Loans by Region (Cumulative 1980–84)

	Kalyubia	Sharkia	Assiut
Total project loans	9,019	4,738	8,801
Loans to:			
Women	813	318	N/A
Men	8,206	4,420	8,801
Percentage to women	9	7	N/A
Loans for:			
Poultry	385	310	13
Buffalo	870	718	847
Cows-livestock	63	98	213
Percentage for poultry-livestock	15	24	12
Other loans	7,701	3,604	7,741

Source: Small Farmer Production Project, as reported by Self et al., 1984.

Table 10. SFPP Profile of Cooperating Farmers (N = 60)

Percentages of Female Borrowers, Kalyubia Governorate, Egypt

Marital Status		Education		Age	
Married	70%	Illiterate	78%	20–29 years	18%
Widowed	28	Primary	12	30–39 "	38
Never married	2	Above primary	10	40–49 "	15
Divorced	0			50+ "	28

Household Size		Number of Household Members under 16 Years of Age		Residence of Grown Children	
1–4 Persons	13%	0 Persons	13%	Village	48%
5–9 "	62	1–4 "	58	City	5
10–19 "	18	5–8 "	28	Combination	13
20+	7			None grown	25
				Abroad	8

Source: SFPP Survey Raw Data, 1983.

spend time marketing crops (other than those produced for sale to the village cooperative). There was little difference between the two groups in the time spent on housework, however, suggesting that women borrowers on average worked longer hours per day than nonborrowers in directly productive and household activities combined. The skills of poultry raising are intrinsic for most household women and children, who usually tend to such duties. Since women were already involved in flock tending, animal fattening, vegetable production, and other small home-based production enterprises, the transfer of their labor to more organized, systematic care and feeding of caged birds was viewed as part of their household responsibilities. Women could continue other household duties since the upgraded chicken-raising operation was easily monitored.

The location of the battery operation within the family home was not culturally limiting for females' roles in giving birth and tending children, and it allowed indigenous production for consumption. Some fellahin who have a profitable income, after loan repayment and input purchase, now abstain from field work in favor of battery operation, hiring field labor when necessary.

The volume of cash exchanged and controlled by female small farmers amounted to £E100–200 per month, depending upon the number of sur-

Table 11. SFPP Time-Distribution of Cooperating Farmers vs. Nonborrowers, Kalyubia Governorate, Egypt

Agricultural Activities: Cooperating Female Farmers (N = 60)
(Percentage of Time Spent)

Woman-Hours/Day	Livestock Feeding	Milking	Egg Gathering	Battery	Marketing Own Produce	Marketing Crops	Household Activity
0–1	10	27	45	28	27	8	0
1–3	75	23	7	7	13	8	33
3–5	3	0	2	3	5	3	43
5+	2	0	0	0	7	3	15
Work not done	8	48	43	54	38	18	9
Men did work	2	2	3	8	10	60	0
Total	100	100	100	100	100	100	100

Agricultural Activities: Noncooperating Female Farmers (N = 60)
(Percentage of Time Spent)

Woman-Hours/Day	Livestock Feeding	Milking	Egg Gathering	Battery	Marketing Own Produce	Marketing Crops	Household Activity
0–1	38	27	23	5	2	3	0
1–3	42	17	3	3	1	3	22
3–5	2	0	0	0	0	3	54
5+	0	0	0	8	0	5	20
Work not done	16	54	72	79	97	53	2
Men did work	2	2	2	5	0	33	2
Total	100	100	100	100	100	100	100

Source: SFPP Survey Raw Data, 1983.

viving and producing chicks. The amount of money realized from chicken batteries was far greater than that from either animal fattening or farm produce sales. Feed for chickens was less expensive than for livestock and the cost of the feed was readily available through the Village Bank cooperative, an advantage not overlooked by fellahin when considering the merits of the enterprise and the profits possible. Mature hens in a battery produce an estimated sixty eggs per day, which sell for about eight piasters (eight cents) each. The profit margin, after payback and medicine, amounts to approximately four to five piasters (five cents) for each egg produced and sold. Some farmers have sold their livestock so as to invest in the more profitable poultry enterprises. The scale of the upgraded battery shifts flock raising from a subsistence level to egg production primarily for marketing.[24]

Inputs such as baby chicks, cages, inoculations, and feed are provided to battery borrowers by extension and bank (cooperative) personnel. They coordinate the need for new pullets through a loan program to large producers in the village, where day-old chicks are raised for sixteen weeks in a rearing farm unit. Arrangements for transfer to the home-based batteries are easily accomplished. The large rearing units receive batches of 3,000 day-old chicks of high-product strains (L.S.L. breed) from the General Poultry Company of Egypt. After a rearing cycle of 112 days (three cycles per year), the large producers ship chicks to the home-based batteries. The dependence of participating women on such input from private enterprise was critical to the operation of the batteries. Besides the Village Bank supervision of chicks, feed, and inoculations, veterinary supervision, essential to survival and production capacity of the birds, is provided through the Ministry of Agriculture.

The poultry microenterprise has standardized and upgraded the traditional flocks. Inputs are based on a "putting out" system coordinated by local authorities who oversee supply and demand and the administration of assistance to small farmers. Although home-based, the chicken battery resembled a small factory model, unregulated by government authority. The improved technology offered higher returns on labor, through a higher scale of production easily handled in the home setting, while requiring no records of production and profits for scrutiny by authorities.

The loans for chicken batteries allowed informal enterprise to begin on a scale that few fellahin had witnessed. Women without husbands had often been forced to sell vegetables and dairy products or other small items on a regular basis in distant markets. Before the loans for batteries, however, married women, whose job it was to maintain household subsistence, had not generally taken part in markets outside the nearest village, although they had raised and sold chickens locally. There was no way to extend and diversify the household economy through a family enterprise supervised by women in the household. The microenterprises, however, have a hybrid quality that combines standardized basic supplies and technical inputs with a mix of independent, informal marketing, largely through women's individual efforts or through enterprising middlewomen who collect eggs and market them in the city.

Informal marketing mechanisms have indirectly encouraged the expansion of the invisible economy and the marketing avenues for household-based production. Unlike crops, however, which are marketed largely through the Village Bank cooperative, eggs are marketed through middlewomen, friends and relatives, in village markets, and direct sales in the nearest city. In the SFPP survey of women borrowers, all women sold at least one-quarter of their eggs and over half marketed more than 75 percent.

While government support subsidizes supplies of raw materials, there is no full-fledged marketing system. The Village Bank cooperative may institute a sell-back arrangement under which local producers deposit eggs, and price supports are agreed upon. Meanwhile, in marketing eggs on an infor-

Egyptian egg seller. Photo: Marie Butler.

mal basis, women seek the best possible price through middlewomen and middlemen. They sell directly to middlemen who have trucks available for transporting to markets having the best price per unit. Middlewomen generally do not have the resources or community acceptance to meet increasing market demands.

Women's Traditional Roles in Household Survival

Peasant household survival strategies in Egypt often include the contribution of family members through labor exchange in both the formal and informal sectors of the economy. Women's special role in egg production from chicken batteries is a unique contribution to household strategies of diversification. Primarily through formalized governmental inputs, a traditional female income-generating activity has been expanded and upgraded without noticeably altering the woman's role in the sexual division of labor within the family.

One unique feature of this development program was the way in which women were indirectly encouraged to participate in the informal marketing of eggs. Control over their profits both enhanced the role and status of women producers in the household and reordered the laboring responsibilities. In most instances, large surpluses intended for distant markets are handled by men.

The loans for chicken batteries allowed informal enterprise to begin on a scale that few fellahin had witnessed. In the past, women without husbands often had to sell vegetables and dairy products or other small items on a regular basis in distant markets. However, married women, whose job it was to maintain the household subsistence, had not generally been involved to any great extent in markets outside the nearest village, although they had raised and sold locally. The government program made it possible to extend and diversify the household economy, combining productive and consumption strategies in a single family enterprise supervised by women.

In specifying the conditions under which women's informal activity is classified, the overriding effect on women's role originates with the household. Within the Egyptian context, it is argued here that not only does the elasticity of industrializing policies affect the predominance of informal enterprises, but also that the various modes of labor utilization bring adjustments in household strategies, cultural constraints on female mobility. Depending on pressures that operate in determining overall resource accumulation, household strategies have an elastic quality with respect to dominant forms of labor exchange. Female household members in family-

Egyptian women and their chicken battery. Photo: Marie Butler.

oriented modes of production often act creatively in self-contained production arrangements necessitated by cultural networks and practices that promote and protect families.

Although home-based, the chicken batteries qualify as a microenterprise rather than an indigenous enterprise, primarily because they require substantially higher capital investment (credit) and more complex skills than the traditional household enterprise, namely, the flock-raising approach to egg production.[25] Marketing of eggs, however, remains informal, primarily because women distribute their products to local middlewomen or market the eggs themselves, and the amount of total profits is largely undetected. The sociocultural context of household organization of labor and the women's participation in local markets are conducive to the transformation and upgrading of the chicken battery. It was the informal household work that women perform unnoticed, including chicken raising, that led to the success of this particular small-farmer project.

Before the battery funding, women were producing eggs for sale from roaming flocks of chickens. While the concept of tiered cages and a stationary location for birds was new to both the foreign donors and the small farmers of this area, the tradition of women rearing chickens was not. The liberalized lending policy, a form of financial assistance to peasant families, meant higher production and increased work for women supervising the care and feeding of this new configuration of birds, although men (husbands) generally received credit inputs and training.

The question remains whether women, with no clear-cut marketing guidelines or arrangements forthcoming from donors of battery assistance, will eventually lose control over profits as levels of production increase. It is not surprising, then, to find certain deceptive practices by women associated with chicken battery operation—specifically, mental rather than written accounting of profits and production, modesty in revealing to husbands and neighbors the number of eggs produced and sold—despite the women's agreement that the batteries were a good idea. Women continually said they were not yet gaining any advantage in terms of monetary rewards above the payback level of the loan, so no profits were admitted from the operation. Higher profits might be considered accessible by males.

The failure of project personnel to attach much importance to an organized, formal marketing outlet for the eggs is puzzling. Perhaps, in failing to plan for marketing outlets it was assumed that traditional marketing strategies would be in effect: specifically, that men would stake claim to this domain if production levels warranted it. The inaction indicates a lack of support from financial institutions for women's income-generation activities.

Knowing that economies of scale generally demarcate male and female responsibilities in consumption or marketing channels,[26] the likelihood of continued control by women provides an interesting case study. The lucrative nature of the batteries apparently has not provoked male intervention, and women continue to supervise all aspects of the operation. This particular enterprise appears well within the realm of what is considered women's work. Given that foreign aid is generally aimed at development according to a capital-intensive production strategy carried out by male rather than female entrepreneurs, encouragement of female commodity production with a possible alteration or conflict in the household division of labor would appear to be an unintended consequence of a common oversight: disregard for the invaluable contribution of women who are relegated to the status of unremunerated household labor.

In the event of centralized marketing and control, women's place in this traditional occupation may be lost, at a cost to the household unit in terms of foregone income and well-being. Since women's income is spent primarily for household subsistence and men's generally for personal consumption and household consumer durables, the implications for child welfare and nutrition are thus obvious.[27] Women's income maintains relations of equilibrium between household production and consumption strategies. There is evidence on both fronts for this speculation. The relationship between household income and well-being and the quality of life for families would be affected by women's loss of income from the informal economy. Women who assumed effective control over their chicken batteries tended not to talk freely about incomes or levels of production from the egg-rearing units. This may be a tactic for drawing less attention from both husbands and technicians to the personal leverage women gained from the profits of the lucrative enterprises. Women's interest in maintaining control is a response to patriarchal family arrangements and a safeguard against male domination.

Since the informal use of labor is a continuation of an existing practice, legitimate use of this form of labor reserve is widely accepted and re-emerges as legislation and regulation of wage labor by the state proves disadvantageous to employers.[28] A more flexible labor supply makes use of informal-sector workers. Possible evidence may be found in rural women's "invisible" work activities. Women tend to protect their niche by defending the home-based operation and the use of family labor in order for women to dominate in the domestic sphere. Chicken raising and livestock fattening are areas where female labor and enterprise are expected but are not yet regulated or accounted for by husbands or the government.

Although Portes[29] speaks of a general category of unregulated labor that is pushed and pulled by the demands of regulated economic forces, he does not explicitly discuss the cultural constraints to which both men and women are subject. These cultural forces are precapitalist phenomena that guide women's involvement in informal household enterprise. Since these factors predated capitalist encroachment, this case study looks at the ways in which income generation for household workers has been modified, altered, or made compatible through the current government intervention.

Conclusion

Women's work in the upgraded rural enterprise of modernized poultry and egg production retains women's traditional role in household labor. The transitional nature of the chicken batteries is not yet clear, since small-scale enterprise for women has usually changed hands, going to their male counterparts in the household as economies of scale dictate production for larger markets. Similarly, this particular microenterprise relies on initial capital investment from family members or credit institutions in order to purchase inputs. The maintenance of these credit inputs is uncertain since foreign donorship for this project is limited by government approval. Flock upgrading is a direct result of government intervention in rural community life, a form of intervention that is unusual for women in development. Women (and men) qualified for loans primarily because they were small rural poultry producers.

In this particular approach of development assistance to small farmer-cultivators, an increasingly liberal lending policy provided credit, supplies, equipment, stock, and technical assistance that upgraded the organization of egg production. Through these formal inputs, the prevailing form of subsistence, low-technical, low-capital production for consumption was converted into a middle-technical, middle-range capitalized investment for the purpose of marketing a small commodity.

The immediate consequence of this transformation was to add to the incomes of rural households and to diversify the contributions made by female members, thereby augmenting their control over the income. The upgrading of traditional flock raising provided substantial returns to female labor. Long-range implications for family diversification strategies and the household division of labor are less obvious. The form that women's income generation took was in line with the elements of tradition, a good fit between informal enterprises and reproductive responsibilities.

While male members of the household may provide substantial earnings, the economic participation of women remains an expected, necessary contribution to household well-being. Participation by women is viable as long as reproductive responsibilities are constant, since the need for many children encourages women to continue household income-generating activities. "Invisible," noncapitalist forms of labor exchange are needed by the family for female reproduction and should be viewed as neither transitional nor traditional but as cultural responses. Male members of a rural Egyptian household are in the position (socially, politically, and economically) to compete in both formal and informally based economies, while rural women are limited.

Notes

1. Nadia Youssef, "Women and Agricultural Production in Muslim Societies," *Studies in Comparative International Development* 12 (Spring 1977): 41–58; D. DeTreville, *Food Processing and Distribution Systems in Rural Egypt: Grain, Bread and Dairy Products* (Cairo: Ford Foundation, 1983); M. Badr et. al., "Small-Scale Enterprises in Egypt: Fayoum and Kalyubia Governorates (Phase I Survey Results)," Working Paper no. 23 (Michigan State University Rural Development Series, 1982); I. Harik, "Socio-Economic Profile of Rural Egypt," Cornell University Rural Development Committee Report (Cairo: U.S. Agency for International Development, 1978).

2. R. Dixon, "Women in Agriculture: Counting the Labor Force in Developing Countries," *Population and Development Review* 8 (September 1982): 539–66.

3. Alejandro Portes, "The Informal Sector Definition, Controversy and Relations to National Development" (paper prepared for the Third Seminar of the Working Group on Latin American Urbanization, Tepoztlan, Mexico, August 1982).

4. Portes, "Informal Sector Definition," 10.

5. Nadia Youssef, *Women and Work in Developing Societies,* Population Monograph Series no. 15 (Berkeley: University of California, 1974).

6. Ester Boserup, *Women's Role in Economic Development* (New York: St. Martin's Press, 1970).

7. Portes, "Informal Sector Definition."

8. Joan Smith, "Nonwage Labor and Subsistence," in J. Smith, I. Wallerstein, and H. D. Evers, eds., *Households and the Third World-Economy* (Beverly Hills: Sage Publications, 1984), 64–89.

9. Alejandro Portes and John Walton, *Labor, Class and the International System* (New York: Academic Press, 1981).

10. Marvin G. Weinbaum, *Food, Development and Politics in the Middle East* (Boulder, Colo.: Westview Press, 1982).

11. Eric R. Wolf, *Peasants* (Englewood Cliffs, N.J.: Prentice-Hall, 1966), 15.

12. Eric R. Wolf, *Europe and the People without History* (Berkeley: University of California Press, 1982).

13. Howard Merriam, "Women's Participation in the Small Farmer Production Project in Kalyubia Governorate" (unpublished summary of survey, Small Farmer Production Project, Cairo, 1983).

14. Abou K. El Seoud and F. Estira, "A Study of the Role of Women and Youth in Rural Development with an Emphasis on Production and Consumption of Nutritive Elements," Food and Agriculture Organization (FAO)/Middle East (1977).

15. Badr et al., "Small-Scale Enterprises."

16. Ibid., 34–36.

17. S. Davies et al., "Small Enterprises in Egypt: A Study of Two Governorates," International Development Working Paper no. 16 (Michigan State University, 1984).

18. Youssef, *Women and Work,* 94–100.

19. Ibid., 64.

20. Mona Hammam, "Trip Report Review of U.S.A.I.D. WID Strategy and Portfolio of Projects: Findings, Considerations and Recommendations" (internal document, U.S. Agency for International Development, Cairo, March 1981).

21. M. Butler, "Rural Women in the Informal Sector: The Case of Egypt," *MERA Forum* 7, no. 2 (Fall 1983).

22. Janet Self et al., "Women's Access to Productive Resources: Recommendations for an AID Program Strategy" (report to U.S. AID Mission in Egypt, International Center for Research on Women, Washington, D.C., September 1984).

23. Personal interviews by author, 1983.

24. Author's interviews with project personnel, 1983.

25. Davies et al., "Small Enterprises in Egypt," 86–87.

26. Boserup, *Women's Role;* DeTreville, *Food Processing.*

27. Hammam, "Trip Report Review."

28. Portes and Walton, *Labor, Class,* 86.

29. Portes and Walton, *Labor, Class.*

III

Methods and Measures: The Invisible Economy of Tunisia

Much of the problem of studying the invisible economy comes down to definitions of who is included or excluded and how to count those who are part of it. This problem is tackled by the Tunisian sociologist Sophie Ferchiou, who explores the situation of Tunisian women who work at home or who are family helpers within the context of patriarchal society. The dimensions of the feminization of work and rural/urban differences are also seen as confounding.

Focusing on the same area of the francophone world, much overlooked by anglophone researchers, Richard A. Lobban, Jr., works—within the limitations of male researchers, excluded from private spaces—to explain why the invisible economy has been so neglected in the first place. His study underscores why household-level, in-depth interviews will go a long way to correct these problems.

The study by geographer Isabelle Berry-Chikhaoui also views the presence of women in public space. Her street-by-street, case-by-case inventory of informal activities gives sharp definition to the spatial distribution of urban and suburban income generation. From these three studies it is easy to see why the female half of the population of Tunisia is "invisible" while still playing a critical role in domestic production and wage-earning.

9

"Invisible" Work, Work at Home: The Condition of Tunisian Women

Sophie Ferchiou

Many anthropological and sociological studies have shown that in all societies, including the most modern, prevailing standards differentiate more or less clearly between roles to be played by women and by men. In Arab-Muslim societies, this dichotomy takes on an extreme form: hierarchical sexual differentiation, a patrilineal inflection of kinship, and patriarchal and patrilocal organization for the family.

In fact, the sexual order of Arab societies is in no way specifically Muslim but belongs to a social structure extending far beyond the Islamic geocultural sphere. What distinguishes these societies is that the standards of hierarchical sexual differentiation are sanctioned by religious texts. The Quran says, "Men have priority over women because of the preference God has given them over women and because of the expense they incur to support them."[1]

Of all Arab countries, Tunisia has certainly made the most efforts to improve the condition of women. However, based on an Islamic postulate of economic expense, the marginality of women is perceptible in several domains of social life, particularly in the sphere of work. Economic activity places women at the junction of two contradictory forces: development-driven modernism and identity-based traditionalism.

The problem is how relations of continuity/discontinuity articulate between (1) the traditional work process, conceived as a specifically female task performed within the family framework, and (2) the salaried work process, which is part of a capitalist mode of development or movement toward capitalist intervention.

Methodological Options

In view of the uncertainty characteristic of official surveys on the work of women, the methodological option chosen for this chapter focuses less on statistics relative to women's work and its evolution, and more on the work process and its repercussions on the conditions of women. Since the 1960s, the Tunisian economy has undergone profound changes marked by the widespread creation of jobs for women, notably in the textile industry, in tourism, and in the food processing industry. Social and economic restructuring also gave women access to noncommercial service jobs in the tertiary sector.

Having opted for an economic and social system of a capitalist type, the new Tunisian independent state promptly took measures to encourage "the entry of women into the production process." In fact, Tunisian women had traditionally participated in family-based production, whether agricultural or crafts, but in Tunisia production was understood in terms of a monetary economy implying salaried work, most often performed outside the home.

The arrival of women in the public job market was promoted not only by a modernist policy but also by vacancies created by the massive departure of the French, especially from administrations, schools, and hospitals. Work for women was stimulated by the economic needs of city-dwelling families deeply impoverished by the colonial system. Once the process was underway, the percentage of working women rose from 5.5 percent in 1966 to 21.8 percent in 1984. The sudden appearance of women in the formal job market, especially in the urban centers, doubtlessly constitutes the most important event in the social transformation of Tunisia since the beginning of the century.

During the first decade of independence, the growth of the tertiary sector was accompanied by a rapid increase in the number of women undertaking a salaried activity, but very soon this movement stagnated and even experienced a marked decline. Today however, job creation is rare and the obstacles to the employment of women are increasingly high because, in filling a vacancy, employers demand greater skills from women than those they demand from men. This discrimination is apparent in all sectors and at all levels of the professional hierarchy.

Certainly the increase in salaried jobs for women introduced a new factor into Tunisian society. But whatever its novelty and importance, the participation of women in the work force remains substantially low both in comparison with that of men and in relation to the potential of women of working age. According to the latest surveys, the percentage of working women is no more than 21 percent, whereas it reaches 78.6 percent for men. On the whole women's socioprofessional condition remains very poor, particularly in industry where efforts toward modernization have been the greatest.

At first this situation seems paradoxical in view of the bold measures taken in favor of women. However, it is linked to the persistent cultural constraints and to the economic choices implied in the mode of dependent development. The hypothesis of this chapter is that in production the combined effect of these modern/traditional paradigms places the work of women in a hybrid process, dominated by the model of "invisible work," that is, work performed within the framework of women's traditional roles, most frequently in the home.

Development Policy and the Socioprofessional Status of Women

Of course, the official line is that the salaried work of women is "an important factor of modernity" and an "essential component of development," but at the same time it refers to a system in which women remain defined by their domestic roles. "Women should make no mistake as to the proper meaning of their emancipation," stated Tunisian President Habib Bourguiba. "They must not demonstrate excessive independence. . . . Women have access to schooling because they will thus be better equipped to carry out the twofold tasks expected of them . . . they will be better housewives and better able to educate their children."[2] The Tunisian code of obligations and contracts requires prior authorization by the husband if a woman is to work, and he may withhold authorization for a "serious reason posing a threat to the life of the couple."[3] Women must be made aware, said Bourguiba, "that their role in public life, must, in their minds, be secondary compared to their family responsibilities as mothers and housewives."[4]

This official definition of women's work, which refers to their traditional role and their economic dependence on men, helped slow down their penetration of the job market and kept their salaries at the lowest level. The offshoot of the secondary character attributed to women's work is the notion of the "complementary" salary, which serves as justification for all forms of discrimination in employment of which women are victims. Women's work thus lies at the very heart of the contradictions of a developing society grappling with the problems of identity. In the sphere of work, the condition of women is problematic because of the opposition between the two ideologies of the models: development-driven modernism versus an identity based on traditionalism.

What is the reaction of women to this opposition? Where does their work fit in with respect to development structures? This chapter analyzes women's work in the context of two types of society, rural and urban, and both are featured in the implementation of many development projects. The aim of this chapter is to see how the "invisibility" of women's work is linked to the patriarchal structures of the traditional economy, and how such underpinnings connect with the capitalist structures of a modern economy, such as those in national and international development plans.

The Work of Women in a Rural Environment

Despite profound changes in rural areas, family structures remain largely unchanged. The economic dependence of women on men is virtually *total;* he owns the land and is solely responsible for managing the family budget. Thus, despite the fact that they play a leading role in agriculture, rural working women whose work is unpaid have long been ignored by official surveys. Today, their participation in agricultural work is confirmed on the quantitative level, but it is depreciated on the qualitative level.

Family Helpers

Of 95,000 women surveyed,[5] 65,700, or 70 percent, were considered "family helpers." The term applies to a woman who lives under the roof of the household head and owner of the farm and who works for him at no charge. Generally she is the wife, a daughter, the mother, or a sister of the male family head.

These auxiliaries, permanent or temporary (during seasonal work), are totally marginal to the socioprofessional status of farmers. They are considered neither female farmers (*fellahat*) of the land nor female farmhands (*khammasat*); they do not constitute a professional category, their identity refers exclusively to a family framework of a patriarchal type, and their work is relegated to nonremunerated domestic tasks. Even when women's agricultural duties are performed outside the family farm (such as work for a state-run agroindustrial company or on a private farm), their work is not remunerated on an individual basis. The family group as a whole is hired, including women and children; payment for collective work and per task goes to the head of the family.[6]

Besides such agricultural labor, female forms of work within the agricultural sphere are apparently very simple tasks such as cleaning and packing vegetables and fruit before sending them to market. While this is a crucial step in the process of commercial production, nevertheless it is not counted as productive labor.

In the sexual division of labor, the harvesting of carrots and turnips, for example, is a mixed agricultural activity. Women pull up the root vegetables, and men then tie them up in bunches and pile them on top of each other. The work is then regarded as done. However, before being sent to market, the vegetables again pass through the hands of women. Every day, the women bend over the nearest water pipe (as at a rural borehole) for hours on end, their clothes wet to the waistline, while they wash and rewash carrots and turnips—in ice water during the months of January and February. This task, relegated to women, is not considered proper agricultural work, but simply domestic work included in the process of agricultural production.

Similarly, women pull weeds every day during all growing seasons while they are returning from work in the field; weeding, too, is not considered proper work but a "natural gesture" that women perform to clean up the plots to avoid returning home empty-handed. While they weed, they collect grass for animal fodder. They also pick wild plants (such as *khubeza* and *harra*) used in stews and couscous without meat. Such inexpensive dishes are widely eaten in the Tunisian countryside. Certainly not all the "natural" agricultural and household tasks performed by women are taken into account in calculating the profitability of family production.

Moreover, each family has its flock of sheep and goats, sometimes only a few, but an essential complement to the family budget; women and children are almost always responsible for domestic animal husbandry. Despite the income it provides, this work is not considered productive, simply another part of women's domestic work.

The weaving that women do is also an important source of income for all families, particularly young households. However, the activity is generally considered a pastime rather than productive work. In rural areas, rarely do women sit idle; when they meet to chat or whenever they have a free moment, they weave as an integral part of their daily lives.[7]

Intensive Production and the Patriarchal Family

Clearly the situation of rural women has been aggravated by development plans in which the process of modernization has primarily concerned production factors and agricultural techniques outside the family. The process did nothing to alter relationships of production inside the family. Indeed, with the modernization of techniques and financial assistance from national and international development plans, the family farm moved from a system of subsistence economy to a commercial economic system. The *combination* of production-oriented development and the patriarchal family organization has now resulted in a distortion between economic growth of the family production unit and deterioration in the professional status of women.

In fact, the rural development strategy has conformed to the standards of industrial countries. The goal of building up family capital necessarily pushes toward intensive agricultural production. Under the increasing pressure to produce, the head of the family adds to the *unpaid* workload of women of working age and calls more upon young female labor to fill the ranks of "family helpers." This category thus rose from 45 percent in 1975 to 62.1 percent in 1989. Recruitment usually takes place among young girls, who are often taken out of school after only two or three years or who never go to school at all.[8]

Hence, by linking the capitalist system to a traditional patriarchal system, the productionist drive of development has caused further erosion in the condition of women. While the heads of families take on the roles of bosses, the women, whose workloads are heavier and more generalized—though unpaid and brokered—take on the subproletarian status of family helpers.

Feminization of Agriculture

Statisticians often interpret the rising numbers of family helpers over the last decades as a feminization of agricultural work. Besides the negative effect of the productionist drive of development and its ties to patriarchal family forms, the depreciation of female work was further aggravated by the rural exodus of men. Between 1975 and 1984, agriculture was progressively abandoned by men who emigrated. Given the shortage of male labor, farmers resorted to female labor, which increased by 39 percent. However, after 1984, when the migratory movement slackened, the shortage of male labor became less acute in the rural areas, and its availability relegated the agricultural work of women to the background, without really reducing it. Thus, when men return, women step aside and return to being simply family helpers. This explains the considerable drop in the number of "self-employed" women farmers, which dropped from 22,700 in 1984 to 9,500 in 1989.

The relative segmentation of male and female jobs shows how socioprofessional status is linked not to the nature of the job performed, nor to the role played by production, but to the sex of the person undertaking the work. Even when women take the place of men on the farm, their work is depreciated and considered transitory. Their function as a labor reserve is totally reversible. When men are present on the farm, women become family helpers or are simply considered inactive. Once assimilated into the domestic tasks for which they are "naturally" responsible, their work again becomes "invisible."

The Work of Women in an Urban Context

Segmentation of Employment and Dependent Development

The phenomenon of false "feminization" of employment is clearer in the urban context, where in the sphere of cheap labor women are paid salaries that would be unacceptable to men.[9] Certainly, the adoption of specific industry-dominated modes of development has contributed to multiplying jobs for women. But, as a consequence of the international division of work and capitalist economic competition, some of those industries most concerned with minimizing operating costs are manufacturers that have established themselves in Tunisia, particularly in the textile and clothing sectors. According to surveys by the National Institute of Statistics, the range of jobs filled by women in cities reveals a strong concentration in the textile branch where, in 1984, they represented 82 percent of the sector's labor force.

This massive concentration is directly associated with the 1972 law enacted within the framework of a development policy. This legislation encouraged foreign investment by granting special advantages to companies producing exclusively for export. However, in an economic system that exists in a relationship between the developed and underdeveloped nations the interest shifts to fiscal and financial advantages; thus, foreign investors are highly interested in female labor. Such labor is not only less expensive but also has a predisposition for certain types of manual work that carry a strong tradition of craftsmanship, which has been passed down for generations.

Although they have received little professional training outside the home, women are generally hired because they are known to have skills that manufacturing industries require. Such skills, however, are not taken into account by the system of values prevailing in modern economies. They are not recognized as "proper" qualifications but are seen as inherent to the female condition in Tunisia. If massive female labor is sought, the sole reason is that it is considered unqualified and therefore can be underpaid.

Hence the "natural" dexterity of women, in contrast to their lack of "technicity" (in the industrial sense of the term), both determines their widespread recruitment by the manufacturing industries and justifies their low pay, and it keeps them on the lowest level of the socioprofessional hierarchy. Thus, the textile industry employs almost solely women workers, but such feminization certainly does not entail truly equal employment. Although integrated into the market economy, women's work remains depreciated and affords them no possibility of social promotion; it merely serves the implementation of a capitalist economic project seeking to replace qualified workers by those unqualified, or by badly paid women.

Female Work and the International Economic Context

Textile firms that employ women are largely export-oriented and thus, depending on the fluctuations of the international market, may close factories and unlawfully sack employees. Hence the nature of female work in this branch of Tunisian industry is precarious and unstable. During 1966–75, when the Tunisian textile industry developed rapidly, the temptation to reduce payroll costs led to a substantial demand for female labor. But unqualified female workers found themselves poorly paid, at the bottom of the socioprofessional scale.[10]

In the 1980s, the international capitalist environment became less favorable, and women textile workers were either fired or were laid off for indefinite periods. Today most jobs offered to women are floating (casual) in nature, and even a job considered permanent is available no more than eight to ten months per year. Moreover, apprenticeship is excessively long and work is interrupted by successive layoffs and rehiring. The result is the mobility and the youth of the labor force in this sector, where 44 percent are under the age of twenty-five, although they make up only 27 percent of the global active population. Such "flexible" management policy finds justification in the traditional conception of woman's role, seeing factory work as a extension of domestic work and salaries as a simple addition to the family budget.

The textile and clothing sectors are a pertinent illustration of problems in the relationship between traditional work processes and the modern salaried work process. Clearly firms resort, for the purpose of modern economic rationality, to cultural traditions of feminine activities that will make available to them apprentices, unqualified workers, those who work at home, and self-employed producers.

"Invisible" Work in the Textile Branch

Remarkably, the major part of the workforce employed by the textile and clothing industry works not in the factory but at home. The majority of women attracted to the industry sector work at home—a mass of marginalized women categorized as either self-employed or family helpers.

Work in the home is a very ancient form of female activity in Tunisia in the form of arts and crafts, particularly weaving, embroidery, and sewing. Women have long made *chechias* (red woolen caps commonly worn by men from North Africa and several other Muslim nations), and both rural and village women make a substantial contribution to the family budget.[11]

Throughout Tunisia, the loom is part of a woman's world. In each region, each ethnic group has its own type of weave or embroidery, which distinguishes it on technical and functional levels as well as on aesthetic and creative merits. The product of this domestic craft is theoretically intended for family use and for building a girl's trousseau. But in fact, most women's products (carpets, blankets, and *bournous*) are sold by men in the suqs of large cities and in weekly country markets.

This domestic, invisible work by women was traditionally integrated into the family production system. But in the context of the Tunisian development process, the ancient mode of production has been placed at the service of modern economic structures. Almost a quarter of the jobs in the textile and clothing sectors are, in fact, held by women working at home.[12]

In general, these women are former salaried workers who after marriage continue to work at home as part-time salaried workers for large firms or as self-employed producers. Very often their status is determined by national and international economic fluctuations. They work to order, directly for a retailer in the case of tourist attractions such as carpets or kaftans, or for a microindustry controlled by a large wholesaler. At times, there may be demand for these "invisible" women as pieceworkers, hired for a task on a casual basis.

Qualified workers who are in a position to obtain state or private financing are tempted by the prospects of setting up a small workshop or business operation in the home, equipped with a few looms or sewing or knitting machines. According to official statistics, 80 percent of women belonging to the nonstructured sector participate in such small-scale production, for which tax controls are very difficult or impossible. Work in the home, outside official scrutiny, is profitable for women with a low level of education, who are part of the invisible category. There are few men in this sector, and it is perfectly compatible with women's traditional status.

However, the conditions of the majority of women in at-home workshops are poor: low salary or none at all for apprentices, absence of social security, and job instability. In their attempt to make the most of meager capital, the women in charge often resort to methods of the traditional work process such as the use of *san'at,* very young apprentices who have not reached working age, or who are age-undeclared and, thus, underpaid workers. Work at home is thus an extension of an ancient work process, renewed and reinvented according to the new circumstances of the Tunisian economy, but this type of work does not ensure improvement in the condition of all women taking part in it.

The woman self-employed at home is perceived as the expression of a new type of economic behavior, which paves the way for an industrial process that is becoming more important in the modern Tunisian economy. As heads of businesses, these women are playing an avant-garde role as agents in the change of their own status and environment. At the same time, however, they are contributing to a *hybrid work process* in which the mass of women workers experience the poorest of conditions.

Conclusion

For centuries Tunisian and North African women in general have been considered a homogeneous and marginal group within society. Although subject to similar ideological pressures, women are not a uniform social group but one in evolution, in the process of transformation and diversification. As for the impact of development policies, their working situations differ according to social environment and to the national and international socioeconomic circumstances.

In a rural environment, where patriarchal family structures prevail and where development aims at moving from subsistence to commercial agriculture and the accumulation of capital, invisible work is generalized and the status of family helper incorporates greater numbers of ever younger women.

In an urban environment, where the feminist state policy is starting to take effect and where export-oriented industrialization has priority, the invisible work of women takes on atypical forms, of varying impacts. While self-employed women are moving toward a real female entrepreneurship fitting into the modern industrial process, the exploited, unqualified workers are a growing part of an urban subproletariat.

Notes

Appreciation for the translation of this chapter is gratefully accorded to Dr. Ghislaine Geloin, French Department, Rhode Island College.

1. *Holy Quran,* "Women's Surah" (in French), trans. R. Blahere (Paris: Maison Neuve, 1996).

2. Habib Bourguiba, president of Tunisia, in speech to the Congrès de l'Union Nationale des Femmes en Tunisie (UNFT), Monastir, Tunisia, 13 August 1976.

3. Legal Code of Obligations and Contracts, article 831.

4. Bourguiba, 13 August 1976.

5. *National Population Employment Survey* (National Institute of Statistics, Ministry of Planning and Regional Development, Tunisia, 1989).

6. Sophie Ferchiou, *Women in Tunisian Agriculture* (Aix en Provence: Edisud, 1985).

7. Sophie Ferchiou, "The Place of Women's Domestic Production in the South Tunisian Family Economy," *Revue du Tiers Monde* 19, no. 76 (October–December 1978); Ferchiou, "Women's Work and Production Relationships within the Traditional Tunisian Family," *Questions Feministes* (Paris) 2 (1977); Ferchiou, "Food Preserves and the Role of Tunisian Women in the Family Economy," in *Techniques de Conservation des Grains à Long Term*, ed. F. Sigot (Marseille: CNRS Publication, 1979).

8. Dora Mahfoudh, "Young Women and Work," *Cahiers du CERES*, Série Soliologique No. 4, Tunis, 1980.

9. Fatima Mernissi, *Divided Women* (Casablanca: Fennec, 1988).

10. André Michel, *Women and Multi-nationals* (Paris: Karthala, 1981).

11. Sophie Ferchiou, *Technique and Society, the Example of Chechia Production in Tunisia* (Paris: Institute of Ethnology, Musée de l'Homme, 1977).

12. Monique Gadant, *Women from the Maghreb in the Present* (Marseille: CNRS, 1990).

Women in the Invisible Economy in Tunis

Richard A. Lobban, Jr.

This chapter turns to the theoretical and empirical aspects of the women's presence, or absence, in the economy of the greater metropolitan area of Tunis. It takes off from an earlier work[1] that focused on the informal economy in Tunis in general. However, this study is guided by the assumption that there is an integrated and unitary economy overall.

While the overt public economic presence of women is not great in Tunis, this study of the invisible economy requires a model that articulates the role for both men and women. As described in the introduction, this research recognizes the fundamental, dependent, and necessary connections of the invisible economy to the wider economic system. Although this invisible sector is peripheral to the sources of finance capital, it is essential for the grassroots provision and distribution of goods and services in the wider economy.[2] Moreover, the logic of all capital-based systems, which seeks to maximize earnings and minimize costs, is followed by *both* the "visible" (formal) and "invisible" (informal) sectors.

The street-level methodology of this chapter shows what can be done on this level. But as a male, I am aware of how much is missed if household surveys and observations made by female researchers are not also incorporated. Fortunately this book provides field data generated almost exclusively by female researchers, who have investigated the issue at the neighborhood and household level.

Definitions and Dimensions of the Tunisian Invisible Economy

As noted elsewhere in this book, the invisible economy has gone by many other names, such as the *nonstructured sector,* the *traditional economy,* the *informal economy,* and the *spontaneous economy,* but each term has various drawbacks as well as advantages. It is often difficult for differing disciplines to apply such concepts consistently.

The possibilities for confusion expand given the related aspects of the invisible economy, including squatter housing and popular transport, not to mention the gray and black (illegal) economies. They operate quietly or clandestinely outside conventional administrative structures and with very little record keeping. Social and economic transactions in these spheres are deliberately ephemeral and obscure.

Decades ago, a study in Cairo noted the ruralization of its population, notably based in the informal sector.[3] In fact, the rural origins of urbanites keep the intimate connections between city and countryside. Even formal-sector employment can be at such low levels that the term *underemployment* is more apt, and many formal-sector workers may have important income supplements in the informal sector. With these points in mind, it is clear that even the empirical investigation of the informal sector is filled with contradictions and difficulties in measurement.

Literature on the informal sector in Tunisia includes the work of Charmes,[4] which has created a solid quantitative base by which to measure the scale of the informal ("non-structured") economy in Tunisia. Other Tunisian research on the informal sector has investigated "spontaneous" housing (*bidonvilles, gourbivilles*);[5] the history;[6] income and employment;[7] urban demography;[8] construction and manufacturing;[9] and transport and commerce.[10]

According to current multidisciplinary inquiry,[11] the "constitutional coup" of Ben Ali in 1987 has brought notable economic reform, but the government has also inherited grave economic problems. Not least of these is the very high level of Tunisian youthful unemployment. According to official figures,[12] the rates of unemployment grew from 1984 to 1989, and in 1989, 48.4 percent of the unemployed were between the ages of 18 and 24 years. Of the Tunisian population of 7 million in 1986, 53 percent was urban, and of the 1.6 million people in the Governorate of Tunis, 49 percent were younger than 24. Of the working residents of Tunis, almost 55 percent were in the service or manufacturing area, and a great many of them were employed in the informal sector.

Data from research by Charmes[13] on the scale of the nonagricultural informal sector in Tunis are presented in table 12. Clearly great numbers of people do such work. Note that the categories include a wide range of small-scale enterprises that, in many cases, operate from permanent locations, unlike the subjects of my own research, who performed work only in public space.

Table 12. Approximate Size of Tunisian Informal Sector

Type of Activity	Informal Workforce	
	Number	Percentage
Foods	8,900	2.4
Construction materials	13,500	3.6
Metals and electricity	8,500	2.3
Textiles-clothing	106,500	28.5
Wood, printing	22,300	6.0
Construction	42,000	11.2
Transport	8,600	2.3
Hotels	12,900	3.4
Repairs	24,200	6.5
Other services	36,200	9.7

Source: Institut National de la Statistique, 1980, Table ACT 58.

Concurrent with other economic problems in Tunis, Tunisian workers' option of traveling to Europe to search for work was recently made substantially more difficult. As a consequence, there has been a rise in such conditions as marginalization, individualization, social segregation, frustration, and even violence.[14] Such is the case particularly among poorer male youths in urban Tunisia. Many commentators consider that these conditions have contributed to the rise of Islamic extremism and subsequent state controls on human rights and democratic expression.

Because of those struggling to survive the burden of urban poverty, there appears to be an absolute and relative increase in the scale of the invisible urban economy. Either explicitly or implicitly, a large portion of the studies cited above attribute the growth of this part of the economy to some or all of the following factors: (1) gender differentiation and sexism, (2) urban poverty and unemployment, (3) expansion of the cash economy and capital accumulation, (4) growth of wage labor and cash crops in rural agriculture, (5) rural-to-urban migration, (6) restricted access to jobs in Europe and the Arab world, and (7) overall postcolonial class formation in Tunisia.

My research in Tunisia discovered a vast array of activities such as street vending, squatter markets, begging, labor pools, seasonal work, car washing, and informal transport. Although women are found in such activities, they are especially concentrated in the hidden, or invisible, economy of household production and domestic services, as well other categories outside formally registered and structured urban life. The illegal area of the invisible economy includes the drug trade, smuggling, theft, tax evasion, and prostitution outside the legally permitted form.

Within the informal street economy, the breakdown of participants in commercial activities, who in Tunis are overwhelmingly male, is estimated as follows: sellers of merchandise, 35 percent; food sellers, 30 percent; shoe shiners, 15 percent; sellers of journals and books, 10 percent; beggars, 5 percent; unemployed journeymen and porters, 5 percent.

There are also substantial numbers of unseen wholesalers, transporters, artisans, seamstresses, agricultural workers, and food preparers. The items supplied by such vendors include tobacco and cigarettes; fruits and vegetables; chicken, meat, and eggs; and *fripperie*, used clothing that is imported in bulk.

The scale of commercial activity varies in terms of costs and profit. Some merchants have little inventory—only fifteen to twenty bananas or six potatoes and one bunch of carrots. Others might have as few as twenty pieces of homemade chewing gum. The very few butchers selling meat on the street are probably among the least poor and are virtually all men. They usually sell either sheep and beef, or chickens, not usually together. In weekly peripheral markets, women sell live chickens and rabbits.

Informal-sector inventories vary considerably in terms of capital investment. Often the total value of goods would be 50 Tunisian dinars, sometimes 100 DT, rarely 1,000 DT.[15] Often the total inventories are small. For example, 8 kites at 1 DT each; 3–4 kilos of potatoes at 200–400 millemes, depending upon quality; 20 pairs of socks at 600 mms each; 5 liter-bottles of rose water at 2 DT; 15 balls of gum at 100 mms each. Street selling of flowers is rare except in the affluent communities like Carthage, or in Place de l'Indépendence.

Refinement and clarity in studies of the informal sector require definitions that aim toward cross-cultural comparison; work on structural issues such as the dualistic or unitary nature of the urban economy; and empirical field studies that give a concrete expression of taxonomic, structural, and functional dimensions of the informal sector.

The urban informal commercial sector exists within both capitalist and state-planned economies. It functions as a survival mechanism that serves the economic interests of poor and low-income merchants and consumers. These functions are maintained by generally small-scale investment and inventory and low and negotiable prices. Service functions of the informal sector are especially difficult to observe and describe, but they form a large part of informal economic activities, especially for women.

The commercial portions of the informal sector are located largely in public space and at transportation nodes with high-density pedestrian traffic. Service portions are usually hidden from public view, especially those in the marginal, illegal, and female-based portions of the informal sector. Gender dimensions within the informal sector have generally been underestimated and unappreciated.

When there is policing, licensing, and administrative supervision, and when realistic alternatives are lacking, the informal sector is incorporated within or tolerated by the larger urban economy; when this is not the case, there may be active state repression. Given these facts, the definition of the term *informal sector* should indicate that the informal sector is more likely a special economic niche within a unitary but structurally diverse economic system, rather than a set of parallel or dual systems.

The informal sector is notably diverse in terms of services and commodities offered, scale of activity, official legitimacy, labor resources, and location. Direct participants in the informal sector follow highly patterned internal organization and regulation; it is not a spontaneous or unstructured activity, despite terminology suggesting the opposite. Historical research on the urban Middle East also suggests that it is not at all a new phenomenon.

In this chapter, the invisible economy of greater Tunis is hesitatingly defined as activity that exists on a temporary basis, occupies public space, and leaves little permanent or official evidence of its presence.

Toward a Taxonomy of Informal Commerce in Tunis

Direct field observations of 4,012 individuals (154 of whom were females) in the public, commercial portion of the informal sector in Tunis are the basis of table 13, a condensed taxonomy of the job categories for females; the taxonomy for males is part of an earlier report.[16] The inductive and empirical approach yields a number that is an absolute minimum; the actual number is assumed to be considerably larger. Within the taxonomy, data on the legal sector of the informal economy were gathered by direct observation and enumeration; the marginal and illegal sectors were reconstructed by interviews, observations, estimates, and published sources, as possible. The information on these sectors is less accurate, given the nature of what is described. A recent journalistic series[17] about the extent of sexual services in modern Tunisia suggests that the illegal economy is quite large.

The full census of 4,012 individuals included only street merchants in the legal or marginal sections who were not directly associated with estab-

Table 13. Taxonomy of Tunisian Women in Informal Sector

I. The Legal Sector: Female Work
   A. Domestic Services
      1. House cleaners, launderers
      2. Maids
      3. Water delivery
   B. Household Production
      1. Clothing and rug making (*bernous, cashabea*)
      2. Food preparation for sale (*tabuna, houbs, tajine*)
      3. Artisans and light manufacture (pottery)
   C. Street Beggars
      1. Impoverished:
         a. women with children
         b. elderly
      2. Mentally ill
   D. Street Sellers (bread, eggs, sandwiches)
   E. Private Tutors, Translators, Language Services

II. The Marginal Sector:
   A. Tourist Sector: (Rare, selected places) makers of "ancient" lamps
   B. Nontourist Sector: Rue Zarkoun legal prostitution

III. Illegal Sector:
   A. Illegal Prostitution
      1. Solicitation in hotels, parks and forests of Carthage, and in other tourist areas
      2. Upper-class call girls
   B. Petty Domestic Theft
   C. Masseuses
   D. Sorciere (*tagaza*), fortune tellers

Note: The roles for males in the informal economy may be found in Lobban (1997).

lished stalls and shops. If all petty merchants were included, this number would be increased, conservatively, eight to ten times, or to about 30,000 to 40,000 petty merchants and service providers. This study does not adequately consider women whose supporting roles were not enumerated in the visible, public sphere of my research and those in the illegal sectors. Additional research should also seek to estimate the numbers of women in domestic service and the many day laborers in construction and transport. These members of the informal sector require special techniques for more precise identification.

Ethnography of the Informal Economy in Tunis

Areas of Low-Level Activity

In areas of light manufacture and production such as carpentry, baking, leather work, shoes, marble work, glass and mirrors, informal-sector activities of males and females on the street are virtually nonexistent. Informal street commerce activities are very few in areas of low pedestrian traffic; they are seldom found in the "formal" zones of food markets and the Old Medina of Tunis, where confined streets and established formal space will not permit them.

Even in a poor area, Mellasine, where substantial numbers of street sellers might be expected, it was decidedly quiet. I saw only five sellers after walking on all sides and down the middle service road, thus viewing every public roadway, but a number of old, yet serviceable, vending carts were noted. I assumed that they were parked at the homes of sellers, but the carts were not in use.

On the Sebkhet Sejoumi side of Mellasine are large dumping grounds for garbage and trash of all sorts. Artisanal firing of pottery in Mellasine causes a disagreeable thick black smoke. Stored on the roofs are large collections of broken objects and salvaged spare parts. There are surprising numbers of livestock for an urban area: about twenty cows, hundreds of chickens, scores of sheep and goats, all within walking distance of downtown Tunis. This is thus an impoverished area where survival skills are at a premium, but there is little pedestrian traffic, and consequently there is little informal commerce in the area.

The rue Kasbah in the medina has a greater level of street merchant activity, in clothes, shoes, and light merchandise. Informal-sector merchants at the rue Kasbah were on the street, not associated with stores. They were almost entirely young men, but they were not serving the tourist market, as would be the case at the rue Zeitoun, also in the medina.

Areas of High-Level Activity

The highest concentration of informal commercial activities in Tunis takes place in open spaces and on the peripheries of larger markets. There is a greater diversity of goods and services and much greater numbers of potential customers. The area around the medina supports the highest daily level of informal-sector activities. At the peripheries of the urban area of Tunis, such as in Kram West or Hammam Lif, informal markets can only be achieved on a weekly basis, but in these places the greatest numbers of women are present.

Within the medina is also the lively, quite poor, but extremely crowded Marché aux Puces (flea market). For the 195 vendors my study enumerated in this location, there were thousands of customers, including scores of women. The distribution of goods sold at this informal market was about 50 percent clothes (70 percent old; 30 percent new); 40 percent electrical, metal, and hardware parts, all used; and about 10 percent foods, mostly fruits. The adjacent rue Marr, a main axis road, has many small-scale activities in shops discussed in more detail by Berry in this volume.[18]

In the area of the medina around the Place Halfaouine mosque, the buildings indicate poorer economic conditions, but there is very high pedestrian traffic and very little vehicular traffic. Thus there is for sale a very wide array of fruits, vegetables, and new manufactured items. The 119 informal street vendors enumerated there included 5 women selling old clothes (especially in front of the mosque at Place Halfaouine), 7 fish vendors, and 3 vendors of meat cutlets. Meat is rarely sold on the street outside a fixed-location butcher shop. In short, informal street commerce was confirmed as regularly high in areas at the peripheries of the medina and *aswaq* (markets), especially in zones of much pedestrian traffic.

At the popular location for street commerce at rue Zarkoun, the merchants offer mainly small-scale services and small items with a high rate of turnover that require little warehousing or capital investment. The rue Zarkoun merchants handle more high-tech items than at any other place; it is rumored that some of the merchandise is stolen.

Tunisian Women in the Invisible Economy

For purposes of studying women in the informal sector, I had to go beyond unlicensed street merchants occupying public space and having impermanent facilities for storage of their merchandise or provision of their services. Typically the numbers of women were low in these circumstances, which account for only one part of the much bigger informal sector. As other chapters in this book show, women at home often produce goods that men sell on the streets, and the women in domestic service, illegal activities, and prostitution are extremely difficult to enumerate, although there appears to be an unprecedented growth in the role of women in the informal sector in recent decades.

In order to study the invisible role of women in the Tunisian economy, the work in this chapter relied on informants, unobtrusive measures, and data derived from a general survey of the informal sector, in which men were overwhelmingly dominant in the public arena. Nonetheless the taxonomy in table 13 provides a focus for public positions of women. What may be most useful in this case is to contrast my observations with studies of men or with the numerous studies of women by the women authors of other chapters in this book. In either case, the neglect or minimization of the role of women as a subject of research will lead to false conclusions. Even in the public activities listed in the following section, it requires effort to discover female activities.

Overwhelmingly, public informal street commerce in Tunis is built upon young men, although fruit sellers and shoe repairers may be a bit older. Even in the case of highly concentrated informal activity at Place Barcelone, there were only four women among the hundreds of informal-sector merchants, and these four occupied a peripheral location on the west side. The women, who occupied this spot on a regular basis, sold only eggs and wafer bread with peppers. Similarly, in the highly concentrated informal commerce at the Marche Aux Puces, where 195 men were selling, only two women were vendors; one sold old clothes, and the other sold spices.

At the weekly markets such as Kram West and Hammam Lif, the numbers of women vendors were greater but still very small, located at peripheral areas and selling either foods or old clothes. One informant said that used clothes are brought into the port city of Monastir in bulk from Europe and America, then sold around Tunisia. Some are reexported widely within Africa after being sorted. The bulk bags of clothes are to be seen widely, but they have no mark as to origin. One *frippe* vendor confirmed that the used clothes come from all over the world; he buys them in bulk by kilo, then sorts and markets the clothing throughout the country.

The main street of legal female prostitution in the medina, the rue Sidi Abdallah Gueche, just off the rue Zarkoun, is an impasse with a T-shaped branch. The twenty-six prostitutes enumerated there were soliciting about 150 customers waiting in lines around doors. There were a total of some 100 closed doors, as well as street doors opening onto five or six private rooms inside, the basis for an estimate of the prostitute population at 150. Within this area, there was a solitary male street merchant with his cart located strategically at the T-juncture, selling peanuts and paper handkerchiefs to his customers.

Beggars in the Informal Sector

The mass media often project that many people in the informal sector are beggars. In fact the presence of beggars in the areas of informal commercial activities is almost negligible. For example, within the broadest scope of the Central Business District (CBD) there were fewer than one hundred during an extensive walking survey of about six hours. Most of them were men, but there are more women in this subsector than in any other single public informal activity involving women.

Interspersed within a group of twenty-seven street sellers in the rue Kasbah in the medina were five women beggars, not far from the Zeitoun mosque. These women were poor or elderly, or both, but had no visible handicaps.

Areas around important mosques such as the Zeitoun were often locations for women beggars, typically very poor and often accompanied by children. I have also observed informal, nonstate harassment of women beggars with children; some pedestrians try to shame them. Women beggars are the worst off, for sure. Beggars at the TGM Metro station range from one to four, established next to the ticket office to beg for small change from Metro riders.

A smaller proportion of the beggars were very poor and likely homeless. Some also appeared emotionally distressed or mentally ill. Most of the men had a variety of physical handicaps such as amputations, crippled limbs, or blindness, yet many of them were well shaven, had wheelchairs, and wore decent clothes and shoes. The locations for begging activity were remarkably constant over a period of many months.

Transport in the Informal Sector

Informal-sector transport within the CBD (medina and adjoining neighborhoods) involves an estimated three hundred small handcarts that can reach areas otherwise inaccessible by cars or trucks. Rental fees for motorized or man-powered carts are determined by the distance and difficulty of the job. There are two main places near the medina for three-wheeled vehicles; in the north at Bab al Khadra and in the east in front of the CERES building on rue d'Espagne next to the medina. The handcarts, either small-sized or large, reached inner areas of the medina. Of the hundreds of these handcarts, some are owner-used, and others are for hire. The three-wheeled vehicles probably number fifty at the very least. No pushcart operators were women. Taxi drivers either have their own cars or work for a company as drivers. Only once in six months was a woman taxi driver observed; they are a great rarity although there are no legal constraints against them.

Women and Low-Density Informal Commerce

The Case of Hai Et Taddaman

Hai Et Taddaman is a new and expanding area plunging into the countryside to the west of Tunis, up to old olive orchards. In its informal economy the majority are small cart merchants and merchants displaying their wares on fences, walls, and cardboard sheets. Lots of fruits and vegetables are for sale, especially in the smallish vegetable suq (market). There were a few butchers, but none were women.

Many small shops in this area sell manufactured items or furnishings. Among the street merchants three were cobblers. There were no beggars. Only one woman was seen on the street in a mercantile role. She was trying to sell four old coats; she was very poor, and there was little interest in her old clothing. Unlike middle-class areas, the National Guard office in Hai Et Taddaman has officers alert and armed with standard automatic rifles. Aside from roadside stalls to serve a passing clientele, there was little informal street commerce in general.

The Kabaria Market

The Kabaria market stop on the Ben Arous tram, halfway between Place Barcelone and Ben Arous, was the site of market activity not to be seen at any of the other intermediate stops. While there were six small butcher shops, no livestock was visible in this decent working-class residential area. The Kabaria area was said to supply many workers to France. The street sellers worked from carts, tables, and canvases. They lined the road giving access to the small central market.

Of the 102 street vendors enumerated at Kabaria, 5 were women, who were selling food and old clothes. In the established municipal market there were 7 women, who sold beans and other vegetables. All women wore traditional (rural) costumes and jewelry. There were more women counted in Kabaria than in most other places visited, except for large weekly markets. In the cases of Ben Arous and Ariana there were few pedestrians and virtually no informal street merchants of either gender in such areas.

High-Density Weekly Markets in the Tunis Urban Area

The weekly markets have a very high level of informal-sector activities. There are at least four and perhaps six of these weekly markets in the urban agglomeration of Carthage-Tunis. In the Tunis urban area, my research surveyed the Sunday markets at Kram West and Hammam. According to Michalak, in Hai Et Taddaman and Ariana there are also untaxed Friday markets and municipal markets at Galaat Andaleuss on Wednesdays and at Sidi Thabet on Saturdays.[19]

The vendors sell the usual array of merchandise, but hundreds of merchants are concentrated in a single location, many more than in a more central urban area of the typical informal-sector activities. Assuming that there are only four weekly markets in the wider urban agglomeration of Tunis, and 500 vendors at each, the total number is 2,000 active members of the invisible economy. Whether they sold at other locations during the week I could not easily determine, but I presume that they were primarily focused on the weekly, rather than daily, market as I noticed no major decline elsewhere in other markets on Sundays, only on Fridays.

The Kram West Weekly Market

The Kram Sunday market, in a vast open space in westernmost Kram on a football field, was the second-largest single site of informal commercial activity in this study. The total of enumerated merchants was 683, including 26 women, mainly in vegetable and food sales but a few in other areas as well. Thus women accounted for 3.8 percent of the vendors. As with the Kabaria market, the women were often in traditional (rural) dress. There were vast arrays of goods—fruits, vegetables, ten flocks of sheep totaling two hundred or so animals, a variety of foods, new clothes, new and used hardware, furniture, used appliances, pots and pans, cassette tapes, fish and octopuses, snails, and eggs. No meat was sold. Three beggars were observed; all were women. In the used clothing trade, about three-fourths of the customers were women, but men were the sellers. Used clothes represented about one-third of the total area.

The Hammam Lif Weekly Market

Hammam Lif, a huge Sunday market, was even bigger than Kram West. The informal-sector merchants enumerated there totaled 708, of which 25 were women, or 3.5 percent of the total. Most women were selling food and clothing. Three women were selling small manufactured items such as toys, and two were selling rabbits and chickens. There were four women beggars, one with two children and one with one child. Two other women beggars seemed simply to be very poor. There were no male and no handicapped beggars.

The Hammam Lif Sunday market is at the easternmost extension of the suburbs of Tunis, lining the rue Mendes France all the way to the beach. The street gives the market a long narrow axis; cars are parked everywhere at the periphery, and only pedestrian traffic is allowed in the market area. In a remote corner of the market near the beach was the fripperie, where I counted 95 vendors of used clothing, all men. Among their customers, women were highly represented.

The census data here, primary documentation from the research, may

Table 14. Informal Economy by Location and Gender in Tunis

General Area	Males	Females	Totals
1. Outside the Medina	878	6	884
2. Inside the Medina	1,081	62	1,143
3. Urban Periphery	1,899	86	1,985
Totals	3,858	154	4,012

Note: The relatively high number of women inside the medina is accounted for by the number of prostitutes on one street.

help to create a baseline for future study of the gender composition of the informal economy in Tunis.

Observations and Discussion

If judgments about the economic role of Tunisian women were based solely on observations in the public sphere such as I have reported, a very false conclusion could be reached. In general, informal-sector activities for men or women on the street were virtually zero in the areas of light manufacture and production such as carpentry, baking, and leather work. On the other hand, informal economic activity rose at the gateways and peripheries of the medina and aswaq; it was low in the formal zones of food markets and in the medina, where there are confined streets and established commercial space.

The marginal public position of women was very apparent, and the proportion of women beggars (often with children) pointed to a serious deficiency in social services. No instance was found of women selling higher-value items such as flowers, dates, fruits, meat, or coffee. Since police harassment of male sellers may be intense in certain areas, one might anticipate equally severe measures against women. The few women in the street economy are often associated with food sales, but not a single woman operator was observed among the hundreds of sellers from pushcarts, who may occupy the same locations over long periods of time. At the weekly markets, however, where carts are less common, women were more commonly observed selling food and clothing. In another case, four women frequently sold eggs and wafer bread with peppers from the same spot, on the periphery of the high-traffic railroad-metro nexus at Place Barcelone.

Women might be expected to play a significant role in the huge fripperie and junk market at Mellasine, just west of a major highway intersection. While women were heavily represented among the customers, the 55 sellers were all men. In an adjacent complex there were an additional 115 male vendors of various building materials, furniture, appliances, and other new and used materials of all sorts. It was only at the entrance area that five food sellers were present, and only one was a woman, selling eggs.

An exception to the limited economic role of Tunisian women was the Kabaria market, where they sold beans, other vegetables, and old clothes. Kabaria is a residential location for recent rural-to-urban migrants and thus may be considered under relatively traditional social control. The Kabaria area has also produced a high number of migrant laborers, who may have left their wives with limited income.

In Kram and Hammam Lif, both centers of redevelopment and rapid urbanization, the weekly markets offer considerable informal economic opportunities for women, and the greatest number of women vendors is found there. Even though they make up only 3–4 percent of the total vendors, some sixty to eighty women gain additional income at such sites. In the relatively poor areas of Tunis, the numbers of women sellers are very few. However, women are quite numerous among the customers, especially for used clothing.

Conclusion

This chapter has focused on the sales and services available to the public in public areas in the urban agglomeration of Tunis. While the data and details describe this portion of the informal economy, this research does not adequately inventory informal manufacture or production, domestic or household services, construction labor, and illegal activities. If these were included, the numbers of people directly involved would be considerably increased.

That the informal sector is a response or survival mechanism for the urban poor is without question. With a few important exceptions, the largest number of merchants and clients are the poor. Operating at relatively low cost in merchandise and overhead, informal-sector merchants make additional income and serve others. In data from the National Institute of Statistics not presented here, I ranked nineteen neighborhoods of Tunis by the proportion that owned the following items: television, refrigerator, car, telephone, and five or more rooms. For the wealthiest there was almost no informal street merchandising except for tourist items. The next wealthiest had some limited informal-sector activity and participated in weekly markets. The poorer areas had the highest levels of informal-sector activity. The very poorest neighborhoods had very slight informal street sales. This circumstantial evidence supports the conclusion that the street sellers in the informal sector were of the struggling poor and were selling to people of their own social stratum or only somewhat above.

The idea that the informal sector is small-scale is refuted by the fact that central wholesalers use the informal sector for the break-in-bulk of manufactured products and agricultural goods. The international network and very large volume of used clothing is anything but small-scale or simple.

To describe the informal economy as unstructured or spontaneous is also far from the mark. To the contrary, the participants in the informal economy have regular locations or regular days for selling an established range of goods and services. The judgments they make about high or low density and frequency of markets and clients also demonstrate sophisticated economic choices to maximize profit.

The gender relations in Tunisian society are preserved in the informal sector in Tunis. The widespread exclusion of women from public areas continues to be the main practice in the informal economy. The exceptions to this are women sellers or buyers of food and clothing, considered to be gender-specific. The few cases of women beggars are highly stigmatized.

The informal sector serves as an economic survival mechanism for the urban poor of Tunis. It is well organized and structured by internal and external forces. It is connected to the global economy and it follows, on a small scale, a wider economic logic. The irony is that "invisible" working men and women among the urban poor of Tunis cannot live well on the proceeds of their informal economy, but they would probably live even worse without it. As a matter of development policy and of the empower- ment of women, one might propose marketing cooperatives through which women could participate more directly in selling foods and clothing, rather than being primarily customers.

This study of women in the economy must thereby be considered incomplete, since the involvement of women in agricultural production, clothing manufacture, and animal husbandry is substantial, as the research of Dammak and Ferchiou[20] has illustrated. As Dammak noted, the seasonal, rural, and household locus of women's work adds to its "invisibility." Ferchiou notes that as much as half of rural agricultural production is based on women's labor, yet it is often not remunerated. The relatively high level of illiteracy for women compounds their relative marginality to the formal economy, yet the goods contributed by women appear in both formal and informal markets. Accounting for women's labor is not only an empirical problem. As Ferchiou has noted, it is also an ideological issue: recognition of women's rights to the fruits of their labor. This study also shows the necessity of having female researchers centrally involved in investigations of this sort. Even when highly motivated male researchers attack this problem, the data are not easily accessible, and many male researchers could say that women workers and producers were not visible when their presence was, in fact, everywhere, but just out of view.

Notes

1. Richard A. Lobban, "Responding to Middle East Urban Poverty: The Informal Economy in Tunis," in Michael Bonine, ed., *Population, Poverty and Politics in the Middle East* (Gainesville: University Press of Florida, 1997).

2. D. W. Drakis-Smith, "Socio-economic Problems—the Role of the Informal Sector," in G. W. Blake and R. I. Lawless, eds., *The Changing Middle Eastern City* (New York: Barnes and Noble, 1980), 92–119. Helen Safa, ed., *Toward a Political Economy of Third World Urbanization* (New Delhi: Oxford University Press, 1982).

3. Janet Abu-Lughod, "Migrant Adjustment to City Life: The Egyptian Case," *American Journal of Sociology* 67 (1967): 22–32.

4. Jacques Charmes, "Méthodes et résultats d'une meilleure évaluation des ressources humaines dans le secteur non structuré d'une économie en voie de développement" (Institute National de la Statistique de Tunisie [INS] and Office de la Recherche Scientifique et Technique Outre-Mer [ORSTOM], 1983); Jacques Charmes, "Employment and Income in the Informal Sector of the Maghreb and Mashreq Countries," *Cairo Papers in Social Sciences* 14, no. 4 (1992): 21–45.

5. Rachid Bellalouna, "L'habitat spontané dans le district de Tunis: étude d'identification, les quartiers, donnés de base" (Tunis: Ministère de l'Intérieur, 1972); Morched Chabbi, "Une nouvelle forme d'urbanisation à Tunis: L'habitat spontané peri-urbain" (Ph.D. dissertation, Université de Paris, Val de Marne [n.d.]); Liz Dunn, "A Case Study of Spontaneous Settlement in Southern Sousse, Tunisia," *The Journal* 15 (1977); Tayachi Hassen, "Les cités 'populaires' programmes solution à l'habitat spontané à Tunis?" (3rd-year thesis, Université de Tunis, 1982).

6. James Allman, *Social Mobility, Education and Development in Tunisia* (Leiden: Brill, 1979); Nicholas S. Hopkins, "The Emergence of Class in a Tunisian Town," *International Journal of Middle Eastern Studies* 8 (1977): 453–91; Lilia B. Salem, "Hypothèses à propos des hiérarchies sociales qui caractérisent la société Tunisienne," *Les Cahiers de Tunisie* 32, no. 129–30 (1984): 5–29.

7. J. J. Cauche, "Sur quelques aspects de Gourbiville du Kram-Ouest, Séminaire du CERES," *Bulletin d'Information Géographique* (Université de Tunis) (April 1972): 34–40; J. J. Cauche, "Habitat spontané, emploi, revenu: L'exemple du Kram-Ouest (banlieue nord de Tunis)" (paper presented at IIIème Colloque du Géographie Maghrebine, Rabat, 3–13 September 1973).

8. H. Attia, "L'urbanisation de la Tunisie" (paper presented at IIème Colloque de Géographie Maghrebine, Alger, September 1970); A. Baouendi, "Croissance urbaine à Tunis de 1956 à nos jours," in C. Coquery-Vidrovitch, *Le processus*

d'urbanisation en Afrique (Paris: L'Harmattan, 1988); Charmes, "Méthodes et résultats"; Ellen C. Micaud, "Urbanization, Urbanism and the Medina of Tunis," *International Journal of Middle East Studies* 9 (1978): 431–47.

9. Moncef Bouchrara, "Rampant Industrialization in Tunisia," *Economie et Humanisme* (Paris) (1987); Bouchrara, "Seven Million Entrepreneurs," *Dialogue* (Tunis), 9 February 1987; Oum Kalthoum Dammak, "A main-d'oeuvre féminine dans l'industrie de l'habillement à Tunis" (Ph.D. dissertation, Université de Lyon, 1976).

10. Isabelle Berry, "Le secteur non-structuré dans la rue El Marr, Tunis" (master's thesis, Université Paul Valéry, 1986); Berry, "Le faubourg sud de la Medina de Tunis: Etude de géographie urbaine" (Ph.D. dissertation, Université François Rabelais, 1988); H. Djmassi, "La crise économique en Tunisie: Une crise de régulation," *Maghreb-Machrek*, no. 103 (1984); Rejeb Hajji, "L'économie Souterraine: Mythe ou réalité?" *Revue Tunisien*, nos. 82–83 (1985).

11. Dirk Vandewalle, *Ben Ali's New Tunisia*, Field Staff Reports, no. 8 (Indianapolis: University Field Staff International, 1989); I. William Zartman, *Tunisia: The Political Economy of Reform* (Boulder, Colo.: Lynne Reinner, 1991).

12. INS (Institut National de la Statistique), *Enquête Population-Emploi, 1980. Recensement Général de la Population et d'Habitat* (Ministère du Plan et des Finances, République Tunisienne, 1984); Abdel Majid Taktak, "Urbanisation et criminalité," *Revue Tunisienne de Sciences Sociales* 66 (1985): 11–19; "Caractéristiques de la Population en Chômage," *La Presse* (Tunis) (23 March 1990).

13. Charmes, "Méthodes et resultats."

14. Ridha Boukraa, "Espaces urbains, culture et violence, de la ville et émergence de la violence," *Les cahiers de Tunisie* 34, nos. 137–38 (1986): 349–60; Abdel Majid Taktak, "L'emploi en Tunisie, 1976–1986," *Revue Tunisienne de sciences sociales* 65 (1981): 101–28; Taktak, "Urbanisation et criminalité."

15. The Tunisian dinar (DT) was worth $0.85 U.S. in 1990. One thousand millemes equal 1 DT.

16. Lobban, "Responding to Middle East Urban Poverty."

17. Mouldi Mbarek and Ahmed Krifa, series on "Beznessa," *Le Temps* (Tunis), "Ce doux métier de Bezness," 21 August 1992; "L'argent n'a pas de sexe," 22 August 1992; "Gigolos, mais prévoyants," 23 August 1992.

18. Berry, "Le secteur"; Berry, "Le faubourg."

19. Laurence Otis Michalak, "The Changing Weekly Markets of Tunisia: A Regional Analysis" (Ph.D. dissertation, University of California, Berkeley, 1983), 35, 37, 112.

20. Dammak, "A main-d'oeuvre féminine"; Sophie Ferchiou, "Place de la production domestique féminine dans l'économie familiale du Tunisien," *Tier Monde* 19, no. 76 (1978): 831–44.2.

11

The Invisible Economy at the Edges of the Medina of Tunis

Isabelle Berry-Chikhaoui

The informal economic sector of Tunis, as an object of research, may be understood in different ways. The first studies conducted by the National Institute of Statistics (INS) adopted a macroeconomic point of view, that is, they evaluated the informal economy as a sector of activities within the national economy. Notable features of this research included the economic characteristics of the informal sector, its possibilities for promotion, its contribution to general employment, and its role in the GNP.[1] Such investigations then extended into studies of the relationship of the informal sector with the official production network.[2] Researchers on the Maghreb were especially interested in the medinas[3] in terms of the dynamism of informal activities, concentrated in traditional domains but having influences far beyond the local level.

The INS study was led off by the Group of Eight in 1977, which examined the tertiary activities of the urban center.[4] Although the study is old, it is a baseline reference document, including a definition that can be applied more broadly than in just the city center. Localized artisans in the suqs of the Old Medina of Tunis were also taken into account.[5] However, the great majority of commerce and its neighboring services (small workshops, light manufacturing, and repair) operate in other quarters of the medina and are hidden in the suburbs. The central region of the old city (with the exception of the East-West Axis stretching from the Porte of France to the Qasba), is peripheral to the Central Business District, or hypercenter.

The closest informal activities are located in the southern section of the Old Medina of Tunis, that is, the Rbat Bab al-Jazira.[6] A 1988 compilation showed 1,396 businesses and 261 street merchants,[7] the great majority of whom can be described as working in the male informal sector. Their activities reveal a remarkable vitality and centrality in urban social and economic life. Often underevaluated in urban statistics is the presence of women in the urban informal sector, as well as in all central districts of Tunis. Women disappear into the textile sector and small shops and into household production. Being barely visible in the urban environment, these activities are difficult to account for in a simple survey of establishments. In the census of 1984, on which I worked, it was very difficult to evaluate or account for the importance of women's domestic work despite the fact that such workers appeared to be numerous in these suburbs of Bab al-Jazira. Their role is certainly as important as their numbers in this quarter, yet it is not adequately recognized. The problem in defining and describing the informal sector in the Bab-al-Jazira district lies in distinguishing this sector of activities from the modern sector of the economy. The problem seems almost insoluble even today, since the several definitions of the informal sector include a variable range of activities.

Defining the Invisible or Informal Sector

In our research on the Bab al-Jazira district, we opted for the broadest definition of the informal sector. We included most of the retail businesses (sales and services), crafts, and street merchants. What these activities have in common is that they compensate partly for the inadequacies of the modern sector and they alleviate the harmful effects of rapid economic growth by allowing the workforce to feed and clothe itself. They also permit groups of people to become consumers who would have been excluded had they not turned to informal activities. This judgment may seem arbitrary, but it is a fact that the businesses and the street merchants established in the urban periphery constitute a striking and cohesive cluster of activities that contribute to the vitality of the urban periphery. We are more interested in analyzing the socioeconomic and spatial complements between these activities than in studying their economic functioning from within, although we acknowledge that the latter remains a fundamental line of research.

In spite of our choice of a broad definition of the informal sector, the division of activities between this sector and the modern sector is not always obvious. If we accept that small-scale handicrafts concerns with fewer than ten employees belong to the informal sector, we cannot so systematically include shops and services, unless these are carried out in the streets.

Several factors make it difficult to classify these activities. The same goods, or similar goods, can be sold by an activity which is related to the modern sector or to the informal sector. If we had been able to conduct thorough surveys of every shopkeeper of the urban periphery, we could have added another category to our classification. This category would have included activities that at the time of their creation belonged to the informal sector and during our study belonged to the modern sector of the economy. In accordance with our definition of the informal sector, out of the 1,657 businesses and street merchants established in the urban periphery, 1,342 belong to this sector of activities, that is, 81 percent.

The proportions of men and women exercising informal activities in these suburbs, as well as the nature of the female activities, tend to reproduce sexual segregation and a public/private dichotomy. Of sixty-five independent workers established on one of the major streets of the Rbat in 1988, only two were women. One was a dressmaker, the other repaired clothing and did some knitting. This commercial activity had been established early in this district as almost exclusively male.[8] It is at home that most women work. "Women's work" is represented in thirty-two hair styling salons for women, as female staff in ten *hammam*s (public baths) for women, and as seamstresses (of whom seven work on the street), workers in candy and clothing workshops, cooks, and cleaning women. Work with food and clothing are the most represented among domestic activities of women. Table 15 presents the full inventory of informal activities for men and women in this district.

Classification of Suburban Informal Activities

Within the invisible economy, the diverse activities have been classified according to their economic vitality and the needs that they meet. First of all is the need to reproduce the labor force by limiting costs. This is certainly one of the reasons for the expansion of this sector, since a certain number of activities provide a specific and immediate answer to poverty by allowing the most underprivileged sections of the population to enter the labor market, albeit in a precarious way. In addition, the informal sector opens the way to consumerism, not only for the poorest but also for the masses and the middle class. For the last two groups, resorting to the informal sector is a means of saving that allows them to buy items fabricated, sold, and purchased in the modern sector.

The well-to-do turn to purchases in the informal sector in order to acquire a product that does not have its counterpart in the "modern" sector. For instance, the informal economy provides Arabic furniture for a sitting

Table 15. Summary of Activities of Informal Street Sellers in Bab al-Jazira in 1988

A. Survival Response to Poverty (flea markets; street sellers of diverse, small quantity goods: foods, used clothes, cigarettes, candies, bread)	272
B. Response to Traditions and Food Needs (small-scale food production, bakeries, pastries; seamstresses; public baths; hairdressers; small- scale metal work, textiles, and leather; artisanal crafts; potters; scribes; street food sales)	745
C. Response to Modern Aspirations (modern sector services; small-scale manufacture; repair and recovery services; furniture; carpentry, small-scale mass production metal and stone work; electrical supplies; transport; repair of modern goods; garages and car repair; photo studios; book stores; glaziers; plumbers; tourist items)	325
Total	1,342

Source: Field Data, May–June 1988; note that this table includes both women and men. In each category, women are a minority, but they are most represented in category B.

room built by local carpenter craftsmen and carved by local woodcarvers. The informal activities are well adapted to such demands, which also factor into its expansion, because they cleverly address a varied and complex range of needs. These needs reflect a complex society, a result of Tunisia's entry into the global economic system and of the confrontation of local values with the new values of the Western world.

For the sake of our classification, we have separated the desire for modernity from the traditional needs. However, this rigorous division does not take into account the complexity of the needs of people that cannot be confined to ambivalent concepts of modernity and tradition. Nor does it allow an understanding of the large variety of products offered by some shops. Nevertheless we chose these terms because they are convenient. The classification was based on a complete list of businesses and street merchants of the urban area and also on surveys conducted with shopkeepers, craftsmen, and neighborhood street merchants; women were relatively numerous in work in boutiques and workshops or on the sidewalks of the neighborhood. We interviewed about sixty shopkeepers, craftsmen, and street merchants of Al-Marr Street to find out how they operate their businesses and how their activity changed after 1986, when this survey began.

We interviewed a few other shopkeepers, craftsmen, and street merchants settled in the urban periphery, using the same questions, in 1990. During this investigation we likewise interviewed a dozen female household heads and young women who worked at home on the subject of their activities at home, as well as those of their neighbors. In an additional study we conducted during the summer of 1992, we surveyed fifty-seven other economic participants established in the various neighborhoods of the urban periphery. This study focused more particularly on the customers' characteristics and motives for visiting the shop surveyed; it was completed with a straightforward interview with the customers. The study supplied additional data about how some businesses function economically.

Classifying the businesses and street merchants within the informal sector posed a certain number of problems. Subsistence activities are certainly more numerous than indicated by the counts in table 16. This category included only the activities for which sufficient data were available, collected throughout our research on Al-Marr Street and in the Bab al-Jazira urban periphery. The mere appearance of an activity was not considered sufficient for listing it. For instance, most of the fruit and vegetable vendors found on Al-Marr and Bab al-Falla streets, whose locale is precarious, do not belong to this sector. They often draw hefty incomes from their activities because they sell large quantities of merchandise and make huge profits, not being subject to price control. Elsewhere, the economic vitality of an activity can be observed only at the end of a survey on its operation and its possible modification from the date of its inception to that of the study. Therefore, if our surveys allowed us to distinguish a number of activities likely to experience growth from others that remained steady,[9] the same information is not available for every offshoot of these activities. Shoe manufacturers are an example of classification that was a problem to us. Using the work of Charmes[10] as a starting point, we listed them among the activities that remain steady. In the leather and textile sector, the market is dominated by the capitalist industry, and the illicit squatter workshops do not grow. In order to survive, they lower their prices and compete with the legal workshops. The process is reversed in the wood and the mechanical engineering sectors, where the squatter workshops "strike upward" because of growing demand and because there is no competition from big industry. This process is ongoing.[11]

Bab al-Jazira: Adaptation of a Socially Diverse Clientele

One of the main characteristics of the informal sector is its diverse range of activities. The activities surveyed progressively filter into a market that

Table 16. Typology of Nonstructured Activities in Bab al-Jazira

Economic Dynamism of the Activity	Level of Disposable Income		
	High	Medium	Low
STEADY (N = 1,270)	Response to poverty (N = 272)		Survival activities; "market chasers"; personal services
	Response to food needs; traditional (N = 732)	Various commerce and services; small-scale production; blacksmith and mechanics	Various commerce and services; small-scale production; blacksmith and mechanics
	Small-scale food production	Small-scale food production	Small-scale food production
	Response to modern aspirations	COMMERCE/SERVICES IN MODERN SECTOR GOODS	COMMERCE/SERVICES IN MODERN SECTOR GOODS
	COMMERCE/SERVICES IN MODERN SECTOR GOODS		
	(N = 266)	Recycling activities REPAIRING ACTIVITIES	Recycling activities REPAIRING ACTIVITIES
	REPAIRING ACTIVITIES		
	Response to traditional needs (N = 13)	Handicrafts Traditional art objects	Handicrafts Traditional use needs
	Handicrafts Traditional art objects		
INCREASING (N = 72)	Response to modern aspirations (N = 59)	CARPENTRY AND FURNITURE METAL WORKING WORKSHOPS FOR SMALL-SCALE MASS PRODUCTION	METAL WORKING WORKSHOPS FOR SMALL-SCALE MASS PRODUCTION
	CARPENTRY AND FURNITURE METAL WORKING WORKSHOPS FOR SMALL-SCALE MASS PRODUCTION		

UPPERCASE LETTERS = Developed in Tunisia
Lowercase letters = Underdeveloped in Tunisia
(data as of May–June 1988)

embraces a variety of social classes, from destitute households to affluent customers.

Subsistence activities are foremost among those that meet the needs of underprivileged populations. The urban periphery incorporates 141 of them. These activities respond so well to consumer demands that their number and the products they offer vary from one season to another. Ramadan and other religious festivals are times particularly propitious for the expansion of the invisible economy. Vendors of grill pans, knives, and *canouns* (pottery heaters) display their wares on the sidewalks of the busy streets of the urban periphery at the time of Eid al-Kbir; vendors of clothes and toys during Eid al-Sghir; of candies and pine seeds during Moulad; eggs, *brik* leaves, *tajin* or *tabouna* bread, and dates during Ramadan. The brik leaves and the bread are produced *diari,* that is to say, produced by women at home. The district of Melassine is especially known for this seasonal activity. The women themselves or their children return to Bab al-Jadid or Bab al-Jazira to sell these goods.

The subsistence activities allow the underprivileged to fit into the labor force, even if they do so in a precarious way, because they require only small capital at the outset and only small working capital for their operation. Thus these activities allow the poor to reach the subsistence level.

One example is a woman who, after being widowed, found herself obliged to work to support her family, who lived in Ain Draham in northwestern Tunisia. This woman continued to rent the nine-square-meter locale (for 15 dinars [$13 U.S.] a month in 1986) on Al-Marr Street where her husband since 1969 had repaired cycles. She took advantage of the sewing and knitting machines that he had bought secondhand in 1978 and in 1979 to do alteration and knitting jobs.

In addition she continued to sell a few spare parts for cycles. She and her youngest daughter (three years old in 1986) live in Tunis in their shop and go back every other month for two weeks to Ain Draham. In another locale on Al-Marr Street is a man who does on-site plumbing jobs to support his family. Seated in front of an old table in a four-square-meter space, this man has as working tools only one old soldering iron and two pairs of pliers. At one time he had sold spices in the same location, but buying his foodstuffs on credit, he had sometimes been unable to pay back the wholesaler. The plumbing jobs he did at the time of the survey in 1986, required very little working capital. The spare parts used for repairs were inexpensive scrap materials or paid for with the customer's deposit.

Most of the subsistence activities are adapted to the purchasing power of the least solvent—small repair services, shoemaking set up on the sidewalk, or sales of lesser-quality goods. For instance, the clothing vendors (including a few women) set up on the sidewalks of Al-Marr and Bab al-Falla streets of the urban periphery offer clothing of very poor quality, therefore at a very low price. Some among them get their wares from the unsold items of secondhand clothes dealers in commercial places of the urban periphery. Vendors can be found selling all sorts of items: second-hand spare parts, rags, old shoes, scrap mirrors made of fragments of glass, and old umbrellas. But only men sell such items. As the previous chapter noted, the presence of women working or begging on the street is often a sign of extreme social precariousness. Such was the case in 1992 of a wid-owed female household head who lived with four children in tiny board-inghouse (*oukala*) accommodations in the medina. Each day she came to the rue El-Marr to sell old clothes on the sidewalk. Subsistence vendors sometimes offer new goods, sold singly, to accommodate small budgets: cigarettes, combs, hairpins, glasses, and plates. Their activities are often short-lived, given circumstances such as an invasion on the Tunisian mar-ket of imported products from Libya, tea, "Vache qui Rit" cheese, and razor blades.

Among the subsistence activities are some that also meet the needs of solvent customers. This is the case of bread vendors of Bab al-Jazira. Their flexible schedule, late hours, and their clustering around a main crossroads leading to the north and south neighborhoods of the urban area make them attractive beyond the local scene to a great number of customers, however solvent. The Al-Asr suq (city market) at Mourkadh built its fame on un-beatable prices and unlimited choices of bargains. Here are gathered ven-dors of old clothes, old shoes, tools, and spare parts of all kinds, but also vendors who offer new goods, the provenance of which is not always cer-tain. One of them explains that residents of the working-class areas are not the only shoppers. Other shoppers arrive from the posh districts of Tunis, looking for spare parts such as burners or bottles of butane gas, and water taps that cannot be found or are excessively expensive in the stores.

The Undersellers

The working-class inhabitants of the first-generation *gourbivilles* (periph-eral suburbs) and worker districts in the west and the south are attracted to the numerous vendors on Rbat Street who offer foodstuffs, mainly fruit or vegetables. These vendors organize themselves into spontaneous markets, one on Al-Marr Street that comprises about forty vendors and the other on Bab al-Falla Street, having more than a hundred vendors. Such markets are better adjusted to customers' needs and purchasing power than the municipal markets and consequently they set themselves up as "undersellers." They are a challenge not only to the town markets in the west and south of the urban periphery but also to the two town markets of the Bab al-Jazira: the Al-Marr market and the Al-Jazira market established at the entrance of the Sabkha and Sidi al-Bachir streets, facing Al-Jazira street.

The Al-Marr market, which has seventy-three stalls, sheltered scarcely forty vendors in 1986; the Al-Jazira has fifty-two stalls, of which only seventeen were still occupied in 1988, and the vacancies are so great that the Department of Town Markets is considering a plan of relocation. Several vendors of the two markets adjusted to the crisis by setting up shops among the undersellers, while keeping their stalls in the market. The only female seller in the Al-Jazira market was displaced to Bab al-Falla, where she found some benefits. The woman sold in a municipal market but was fairly marginal in sidewalk sales. The rare women selling food products on the sidewalk are not readily able to associate with the bulk-quantity merchants who supply neighboring shops or boardinghouses (oukalas) and are thus deprived of the considerable benefit of dealing directly with producers.

The Board of Town Markets tried in 1990 to make the spontaneous market of Bab al-Falla official in order to clear the streets of congestion and to deal with alleged sanitary concerns, thus calling into question the operations that made the market so competitive.

The effects of the restrictions were not long in being felt. The owner of an eating place in the neighborhood said,

No one is happy, now that the goods are more expensive—even the farmers, they are not happy. The vendors of Bab al-Falla would buy directly from farmers, in Solimann, in Grombalia, in Mornag, in Mareur, in Bizerte, but now they must buy at the wholesale market. The farmers must sell at the wholesale market and come with their van; it is more expensive. The vendors of Bab al-Falla used to have a lot of goods—heaps of potatoes, of parsley—but now that they only get two or three meters of space [the length of the stall of the official market], they cannot display many goods, either by width or by height.

Before, they would come with their vans, they would park them everywhere. Those who had vans would buy from the farmer, early in the morning. They would come back to Tunis, would find men waiting, men who did not have a job. The van owners would propose to these men that they sell the goods for a flat sum agreed upon at the beginning, for example 20–25 dinars. If the vendor grossed 50-

dinars, he gave 25 dinars to the van owner and thus earned 25 dinars. Before, when the town officials came by, they would not take away everything. Now, they steal everything. The vendors cannot set up shop in the street. Even on Sabkha street, there is always a police truck at both ends of Bab al-Falla street. Even the other shopkeepers at Bab al-Falla are not happy. It is not as busy now. The people who work at Bab al-Falla are not tramps. They want to work, they work hard, twelve to fourteen hours a day. They do not go to the movies or to the sports stadium, they constantly work. If we take their job away from them, they are left on the streets. What are they going to do? They are going to hang around, steal.

The overall discontent and the laxity of the control by the town, however, foiled the attempt at making the Bab al-Falla market official.[12] The success of these vendors therefore rests on the prices they offer their customers. They can hold prices down by short-circuiting the wholesalers and buying rejects and unsold merchandise. Although lower in quality, it can be sold in small quantities that attract buyers looking for bargains, to meet daily needs for food, for example. Moreover, the vendor's profit margin can be improved to a certain degree by the limited need for warehousing. Less poor customers are attracted by the advantages the vendors offer: They work all day long, whereas the town markets close at 1:30 P.M. The well-to-do customers of the Central and Lafayette markets fall back on the vendors, and men and women who work downtown shop with them before returning to their residential district.

Responses to Traditional Needs

The activities that supply food and that meet traditional cultural needs are numerous. Indeed I enumerated 608 shops and various services; 39 workrooms of small food industry; 63 craftsmen in leather and textile; 22 rooms for working iron and other metals; 5 craftsmen of *tami*s, *sakhan*s, and *mida*s;[13] and 8 workrooms making traditional objets d'art for the suqs—in total, 745 activities representing 55.5 percent of the entire range of informal activities. Their customers are not only those with little money or the residents of the neighborhood. Their adjustment to traditional needs makes several of them attractive beyond the local area. It is in this sector that women are most numerous, thanks to the female work in textiles and domestic production.

The *hammam*s (public baths) at the urban periphery function not only for reasons of health but also for socializing of neighbors, friends, and relatives from various neighborhoods. They also play a powerful symbolic role in the purification by the water ritual. Several residents of the gour-bivilles or the worker districts in the west and the south of Rbat claim that they visit one of Rbat's baths instead of those in their new neighborhoods, linked by affection for their former neighborhood. Similarly the bath atten-dants at the hammam make up a socially egalitarian environment that serves women in the same way as the hair stylist salons. Other examples are the food shops, especially during Ramadan, when the vendors of *maqroudh*s, *baqlawa*s, and *zlabiya*s (Tunisian pastries) of Bab al-Jadid and Bab al-Jazira are particularly appreciated. These vendors are usually men. Adjusted to the demand, such activities usually bring in surplus income that supports the owner's family and, for some shops, allows the owner to hire one or more employees.

In other neighborhoods of the larger urban area the traders who sell tamis are retailers, and their prices are higher than those of the manufactur-ers on Al-Marr Street. A woman living in Ouardia, in the southern part of the urban area, came to this street for the sole purpose of buying a tamis sieve at a lower price. The fame of Al-Marr Street today is partly due to its sieve makers. They are very few, not only in the capital but also in the whole country, so their influence is felt all over northern Tunisia. Retailers indeed come from Beja, Jendouba, Kef, and central Tunisia to stock sup-plies of sieves from the manufacturers.

The wool vendors at Mourkadh in the urban periphery no longer attract many Tunisian women, only a few older ones. Their customers are retailers from various regions of Tunisia or women from small towns. One of the wool vendors managed to check the drop in the demand by manufacturing his own kilims (carpets), and he now owns eight workrooms in Cap Bon and Siliana. His activity not only attracts well-off Tunisian patrons who go directly to his Mourkadh shop, but he also reaches the tourists who shop in the boutiques of the luxury hotels at the Tunisian seaside resorts of Sousse and Hammamat. The weaving of rugs in workshops involves intensive fe-male labor, which includes carding, washing, and spinning the wool used for the carpets.

Among women who work inside the house in order to increase their income, some are self-employed; others work for shopkeepers or craftsmen situated in the urban periphery, as in the case of the wool vendor, or in the suqs of the medina. Some women rotate the two kinds of work at home, depending on demand. Work inside the house to supplement income is usually a part-time job. Women work at it when they finish their chores. Some take advantage of their daughters' help during vacation so that they can work full-time. Some young women are economically active at home during holidays so as to earn pocket money.

The most common home activities are in the textile sector, whether their practitioners are self-employed or wage earners. Among the self-employed, seamstresses are in all likelihood the most numerous. There is also demand for embroiderers who apply beads on evening or wedding dresses, *foutas*, *blousas*, gloves, and cushions used for the preparation of the bride during the henna ritual, especially in summer, when the number of weddings increases. Weavers of kilims and *battaniyyas* (blankets), knitters, and women who do crochet work also find employment. The wage earners may also do many kinds of jobs as requested by their bosses at various stages of clothing manufacture. Some cut out and sew aprons for schoolchildren, and attach pockets and buttons, while others sew together work overalls for men. Still others make shorts, embroider *babouches* with colored threads, make Tunisian fans, or knit woolen caps to make *chechias*, but this activity is increasingly rare. These women are paid either by the item or more often by sets of items.

Other income-adding work that women do at home is more seasonal in nature. The month of Ramadan is propitious for female production of food, including brik leaves, *malsouqa*, bread, and Tunisian pastries (baqlawas, *ka'ak*, or *rayba*), which all have symbolic importance during this religious holiday. Another seasonal time of domestic work is the 'Aoula festival during the month of August, when women prepare couscous and *mhamas* (a kind of big couscous grain). Since weddings take place mainly in the summertime, the *hennana* woman, who attends to the bride (applying decorative henna dye to her hands and feet), works mainly at that time, along with the *tabakha* woman, who helps in preparing the wedding meals, cooking pastries, or offering her services for Aid al-Sghir holiday. For other celebrations, some of the neighborhood women gather provisions and charge for this service, or the female household head may hire a local woman to assist in this task.

Some women also sell merchandise inside the house. For example, during a pilgrimage in Saudi Arabia, they may buy various kinds of Saudi products, as well as items from Turkey and Cyprus during plane stopovers: gold and silver jewelry, rolls of fabric, clothing, lingerie, leather goods, shampoo, toothpaste, cosmetics, sets of plates and dishes. Turkey has become a well-known place for shopping, and women go there to bring back goods much appreciated by Tunisian women, especially leather, gold, and fabric. Tunisian women also travel to Morocco to buy leather products at good prices. The purchased items are usually sold within the neighborhood; the news soon spreads that one of the residents is back from her trip and that she brought back a great deal of merchandise. Women visit her to do their shopping or wait until she visits them; they know they will be granted easy terms.

Informal economic activity within the home in a suburb is an outgrowth of the social network of female ties that breathes life into the neighborhoods. The customers are usually female neighbors or the neighbors' female friends. More often than not they themselves provide the raw materials—fabric, beads, fabric or wool scraps to make rugs and blankets. A young woman living in the urban periphery at Ras al-Darb embroiders evening gowns for the customers of the neighborhood and babouches for a craftsman of the al-Baghajiyya suq, a friend who is himself a shopkeeper. At the time of our survey (summer 1990), the young woman was working on embroidering a neighbor's outfit of fouta and blousa. It had been cut by a seamstress working at home in the same neighborhood. The seamstress asks 90 dinars for her work, and the embroiderer wants 50 dinars for her work on two puffed-up sleeves and the fouta (bouffant pants)—one and a half to two weeks of work.

The young woman surveyed learned her craft from a woman in the neighborhood over the period of a month during her summer vacation. Once her apprenticeship was over, she continued to work for the woman for 5 dinars a week. Then she set up her own business. She had a loom made for about 12 dinars by a carpenter whose workroom is set up in the street where she lives. She also owns a small round embroidery frame that she bought for about 1.5 dinars from a sieve merchant on Al-Marr Street. In babouche embroidery, the young woman earns 15 dinars a week for approximately thirty hours of work. In some cases, such work inside the house is real artisanship. Thus one woman living in the urban periphery employs several girls to make and embroider wedding dresses.

The Bab al-Jazira urban periphery includes 325 activities that take into account customers' desire for "modernity"; they represent 24.2 percent of all informal activities. Women are few in modern service activities, generally because they lack the required knowhow. The formal commercial sectors of their neighborhoods are monopolized by men.

Cohesion in Informal Neighborhood Activities

The presence of diversified economic activities within the neighborhood reinforces the vitality of each, for each benefits from the others' customers. Furthermore, every shopkeeper, artisan, and employee in the urban area, male or female, is a potential customer.

Distinct economic sectors that meet specific needs are noted inside the urban periphery. Fifty-four percent of trades and food services, "under-sellers," and other vendors of foodstuffs are grouped together on the two main commercial axes of the urban periphery: the Al-Marr Souk des Armes Street and the Al-Hajjamin Street axis in the northwest; the Bab al-Falla axis and the Bab al-Jazira intersection in the west.

Because of their bustling activity, these two axes are favorable areas for other street vendors to set up their wares (worn-out clothes, kitchen uten-sils, care products, sewers, and cleaners); 63.6 percent of them have settled there. They operate thanks to the customers of the other activities and especially to the under-sellers organized in spontaneous markets. The ex-ample of a male vendor of children's clothes and women's lingerie who settled amid the vegetable vendors of Bab al-Falla is particularly significant in this symbiotic operation. During the attempt to make the Bab al-Falla market official in 1990, this vendor was driven off the street. He was told to sell his wares at Hafsia in the medina, because that area specializes in the sale of clothes. But his departure to resettle in that area would have been commercial suicide; if he had left Bab al-Falla Street, he would have lost his main customers of the last fifteen years: the women of the market. So this vendor, refusing to lose his customers and his livelihood, continued as long as possible to sell in Bab al-Falla Street.

The miscellaneous activities established on Bab al-Falla Street can be contrasted with Al-Marr Street, where the activities have a strong inner structure. Production and repair activities are located in the north, the food trade and others in the south. The meeting point occurs at the town market where animation is at its peak due to the presence of the under-sellers. Restaurant activities are concentrated at both ends of the axis; at the north end, vendors of snacks cater to the civil servants from the ministries located at Qasba and in Government Square. At the south end, the restaurants target customers of both genders passing through, since this area is the meeting point between Bab al-Jadid Avenue, Bab Manara Boulevard, and Mourkadh.

Conclusion: The Invisible Economy Adapts to Urban Life

The informal economic activities of women in the urban neighborhoods of Tunis fall into two types. One type exists throughout the city to meet the needs of residents: public baths, hair salons, cafes, cosmetics and health products, dressmaking, and shoe repair. These functions activate the social life of the neighborhood and transform the street into a meeting place for discussion and information exchange. In the second type of female informal activities, large numbers of women work at home, where they have access to exclusively local, female clientele. Without gender-based research, these women may have escaped our attention completely.

Notes

1. Jacques Charmes, *Le secteur non-structuré en Tunisie: Son importance, ses caractéristiques et ses possibilités de promotion* (Tunis: INS, Ministère des Affaires Sociales, 1981); Jacques Charmes, "Méthodologie et resultats des enquêtes sur le secteur non-structuré en Tunisie," in J. Charmes, H. Domenach, and J-P. Guengant, *Etudes sur le emploi aux Antilles et en Tunisie*, Archives et Documents, no. 54. INSEE, August 1982.

2. Of interest in this respect is that small-scale or informal enterprises link the three districts of the old city of Tunis. These are the central Old Medina; the Bab al-Jazira urban periphery (*faubourg* in French), which is the subject of this chapter; and the Bab Souiqa urban periphery north of the medina.

3. The following are major studies of the economic activities of several medinas: Lagdim Soussi, "Le poids de l'artisanat dans la medina de Marrakech," in *Présent et avenir des medinas (de Marrakech à Alep)* (Tours: URBAMA, Université de Tours, 1982), 83–90; Lagdim Soussi, "Les activités artisanales à Marrakech et leurs retombées économiques" (third cycle doctoral dissertation, Université de Tours, 1984); M. Belfquih and A. Fadloullah, "Réorganisation spatiale et reclassement fonctionnel des medinas de Rabat-Salé," in *Présent et avenir des medinas de Marrakech à Alep* (Tours: URBAMA, Université de Tours, 1982), 147–98; F. Martin-Hilali, "Le centre de Tanger, bi- ou multipolarité?" (Ph.D. dissertation, Université de Tours, 1987); B. Pagand, "La medina de Constantine: de la cité traditionnelle au centre de l'agglomération contemporaine" (Ph.D. dissertation, Université de Poitiers, 1988); and M. Gdoura, "La medina de Sfax: la primauté de la fonction économique," in *Présent et avenir des medinas (de Marrakech à Alep)* (Tours: URBAMA, Université de Tours, 1982), 83–90. These studies have investigated informal activities in the peripheral neighborhoods, but one of the characteristics of the informal sector is its capacity to join together "pioneer fronts" in the process of urbanization.

4. Groupe Huit, *Etudes des activités tertiaires de centre de Tunis; Le centre et le sens de la capitale* (République Tunisienne, Ministère de l'Intérieur, District de Tunis, 1977).

5. Today this artisanal area is in the process of liquidation and is being replaced by commerce and resale of products manufactured elsewhere. See P. Signoles, "L'espace Tunisien: Capitale et état-région" (URBAMA Fasc. de Recherches no. 94, Université de Tours, 1985).

6. I. Berry, "Le secteur non-structuré dans la rue El Marr" (master's thesis, Université de Montpellier, 1986), 11.

7. The list of businesses and street merchants of Bab al-Jazira was drawn up in May–June 1988.

8. On the other hand, in Hai Et Taddaman, a spontaneous periurban community in the Tunis agglomeration, a great number of women are the heads of commercial microenterprises. This is undoubtedly explained by the economic investment in the newly formed quarters, which coincides with the economic crisis, especially for women; they face poverty and urban unemployment and have been led to invest in activities formerly reserved for men. Yara Abdelhamid is preparing a study on women of Hai Et Taddaman, "Coping Strategies for Low-Income Urban Women" (forthcoming).

9. J. M. Miossec, "De suq au supermarché à Tunis: Une évolution contrariée?" (paper presented at the Conference on Retail Environments in Developing Countries, Glasgow, September 1987).

10. J. Charmes, *Recueil d'interviews auprès de menuisiers et ébénistes de Tunis et de Sfax* (Tunis: INS, 1978); J. Charmes, "Les contradictions du développement du secteur non-structuré," *Revue Tiers-Monde* 21, no. 82 (April–June 1980): 321–35; J. Charmes, *Recueil d'interviews auprès de fabricants de chaussures de Tunis et de Sfax*, vol. 1 (Tunis: INS, 1981).

11. Charmes, 1978, 1980.

12. During our last stay in Tunis, in July 1992, the market had returned to its previous ways: The stalls in the market were no longer used, the vendors set up their wares on both sides of the street, and the evicted vendors had come back.

13. A tamis is a sieve to make couscous. A sakhan is a rack of wooden blades placed above the canoun, where clothing after being washed is hung and dried in winter. A mida is a low table.

IV

Locations and Linkages in the Invisible Economy

The ability of a woman to manipulate her circumstances favorably through the use of limited resources is one of the main purposes of the invisible economy. In the case of Marcel, described by Suad Joseph in chapter 12, a Lebanese woman worker gains mobility by means of her ambiguity in the socioeconomic order. The marked complexities of religion, politics, and ethnicity in Lebanon are the barriers that Marcel surmounts in her search for multiple supportive relations.

Homa Hoodfar in chapter 13 examines potential for cash earnings in a low-income neighborhood in Cairo. While intimately linked to the formal economy in many ways, women opt for local employment that gives them access to cash and a great deal of flexibility. The forces of Islam and patriarchy are not barriers to women working in pink-collar rather than blue-collar jobs. The rich details of the case studies and the women's own words show that, in preference to the formal sector, they are more comfortable and productive in using domestic and neighborhood resources.

In chapter 14, Diane Singerman engages us with the global and national connections of women's work in Egypt. The linkages she sees function as economic exchange and intertwine economics with politics for the popular *sha'bi* classes. She documents the intimate but generally unreported intersection between formal and informal segments of the economy. She investigates rotating credit and *gam'iyyaat* associations, parts of the informal economy that have empowering political associations. Such systems are a rational way to achieve coherent objectives, particularly for women.

12

Marcel

Straddling Visible and Invisible Lebanese Economies

Suad Joseph

Marcel is a woman who always had a story to tell, information to share, an interpretation of local or national events to press upon a guest. Exuberant, even in anger or anguish, she welcomed a stream of callers with an abundant sociability that kept them coming back to visit her. Adolescents, teenagers, young and older adults, and elder neighbors found warmth and engagement in her tidy apartment in the urban working-class Camp Trad neighborhood of Borj Hammoud, Lebanon. She had something to say to each in this highly heterogeneous, densely populated neighborhood, regardless of age, gender, religion, ethnicity, or nationality. Firm in her thoughts, she broke relationships (or others broke with her) less than one would have expected in a neighborhood in which intense social involvements often led to fragile friendships.

Marcel was not ambivalent in her opinions in the early 1970s, the period in which this chapter is set. Yet she, like many of her Camp Trad neighbors, was a complex mix of ambiguities in her actions. She was articulate in her views on her behavior, yet straddled multiple zones of identity and action. Both certainty and ambiguity characterized her work as well as her personal life. In this regard, Marcel was not unusual in Camp Trad. In the twenty-seven years I have known her, since 1971, she has displayed an unusual continuity despite basic tensions around her.

In the early 1970s Camp Trad was primarily an urban working-class municipality. Almost all of the ethnic groups and religious sects of Lebanon and the neighoring Arab countries were represented. About 40 percent of the population were Armenian (mostly Orthodox, but also Catholic and

Protestant). Forty percent were Lebanese Shi'a. About 20 percent were Maronite, Roman Catholic, Greek Orthodox, Greek Catholic, Arab Protestant, Syrian Orthodox, Syrian Catholic, Sunni, Druze, or 'Alawite. Borj Hammoud residents came from Lebanon, Syria, Palestine, Greece, Jordan, and Egypt. Camp Trad included members of all these communities.

Most of the families in Camp Trad were recent migrants to the area. Predominantly Lebanese Maronite at the turn of the century, the neighborhood mix transformed in the 1940s with the influx of Armenians. Palestinians entered in 1948. Other Christian and Muslim Lebanese and Syrians in large numbers moved into the area in the 1950s–70s. Few residents had lived there more than one generation. Most came from rural backgrounds and had maintained the ever-vital kin ties. Some residents had reconstituted parts of their extended families within Camp Trad or Borj Hammoud.

The Lebanese state in the early 1970s was deeply divided by factions organized around familial ties, reinforced by class, religious, ethnic, regional, and ideological alliances. Leaders and followers offered and obtained access to information, services, and protections by mobilizing networks grounded in proximity, the most central of which was kinship.[1] In this state, relationships lubricated the political machinery. What family you came from, who you knew, and what face-to-face networks you could mobilize were critical in achieving political ends.[2]

During the 1970s, gender, ethnic, religious, occupational, class, and national identities in Camp Trad were in flux and actively contested. Globally oriented movements competed for loyalties—ethnic or secular nationalism, pan-Arabism, socialism, Islamic fundamentalism, secular humanism. Camp Trad residents felt the pressures of the international economy, emotionally and materially, in their familial and work lives. They did not see the state as a protector from wars, economic instability, social insecurity, and political danger. They secured themselves instead through kin and idiomatic (acting as if someone were) kin relations.

Liminality also characterized many aspects of Marcel's life. Forty years old in 1971, when I first met her, she had been born in the predominately Shi'i southern Lebanese village of Nabatiyyi to a Lebanese Maronite father and a Palestinian-Lebanese Maronite mother. She was the third-oldest of ten children. Her parents had lived in Palestine at various times, including two years with Marcel, 1946–48. One sister had Israeli citizenship and lived in Israel with her Palestinian Catholic husband. All Marcel's other married siblings had Lebanese Maronite spouses.

Marcel had married a Lebanese Shi'i, however. Intersectarian marriages were neither common nor unusual in Camp Trad. Initially Marcel identified herself to me as a Shi'i even though she was divorced and attended the Maronite church. The contradictory religious identification may have been strategic, though. She wanted to maintain the Shi'i identity of her son so that he would inherit from his father.

Here also, Marcel was neither the norm nor marginal. Given the lack of civil marriage laws in Lebanon, all marriages were religious in nature. In intersectarian marriages, therefore, one of the partners had to convert to the religion of the spouse in whose church they married. In this patriarchal society women usually converted to the religion of their husbands. Often they initially identified themselves to me in formal interviews by the religion of their husbands. It was common for them to carry simultaneously the identity and the practices of the religion of their fathers.

Marcel lived alone with her son, Rafik, who was born in 1954, the year she left her husband. She stood out as the only divorced, Christian, single-parent woman living alone in my data set, which included more than a hundred families in a four-street neighborhood of Camp Trad. Most divorced women would have lived with their parents. She also stood out as one of the few working women household heads in the neighborhood. Most women were homemakers or, if unmarried, they lived with their families of origin. Marcel had struck out on her own when she left her husband. Given that her husband was Shi'i and that they were married under Shi'a family law, her husband could have taken custody of his son when he turned seven years old. The husband had not claimed the son, though. Marcel had chosen to work and support her son rather than return to her family when she left her husband. It was not clear whether she could in fact have returned.

Marcel also stood out as a worker who straddled visible and invisible sectors of the economy simultaneously. Many workers in the neighborhood had a career punctuated by frequent job turnovers. Their work often wove them into and out of different economic sectors. However, full-time workers, mainly men, tended to have only one job at a time. Most workers were in either the visible or invisible sector at any given time. Marcel had held two or more jobs during most of her working years, which straddled sectors.

Bridging Visible and Invisible Economic Sectors

Her work, like other aspects of her life, manifested aspects of stability while resisting unambiguous classification. In 1973 (the year in which most of the data for this paper was gathered), her work history stretched back to

1954. For two years, 1954–56, she had held three jobs lasting one to eight months each. She collected money for schools, cleaned rubber rings in a factory, and did sewing repairs for a tailor. In 1956 she began what remained her life-time work, cleaning for various businesses.

In a neighborhood in which job changes were common, Marcel displayed rather remarkable work stability. During 1955–72 she did cleaning work for a merchant in the port of Beirut. From 1956 to 1963 she also cleaned for a bank there. During 1958–67 she added a second merchant, and during 1958–73 she cleaned for a third merchant. From 1965 through 1973 she worked at a bank with the same man for whom she had formerly worked when he was a merchant (1955–72). When that man died, his nephew took over the bank, and Marcel continued working for him. All of her job changes, except one, were precipitated by the need for higher wages. In the single exception, the business had been expanded, and Marcel could not keep up with the workload.

For most of her work career, then, Marcel had held more than one job simultaneously. Her work in the banks placed her in the visible economy, with regularly scheduled wage increases, health insurance, paid vacations, and social security. When she worked for small merchants and factories, she was part of the invisible economy, with none of these benefits. Thus, for most of her adult life, she straddled visible and invisible economic sectors.

The bank where she worked in 1973 was owned by a Lebanese Maronite in partnership with Bulgarian businessmen. The merchant's business was owned by a Catholic Syrian. She had found the bank job through the bank owner, for whom she had worked previously. She found the job with the merchant through a former Jewish neighbor whom he had previously employed. In seeking work, Marcel had never read advertisements in the newspaper, nor applied at an employment office, nor asked a religious leader, a school director, or a political party leader for employment assistance. "Asking people you know is best because when you know someone, the employer is more secure," she said. "People find jobs for people. It's *wasta* [brokerage, contacts, networks]." Even in finding work for her Rafik, her son, they had mainly resorted to wasta. Rafik had looked at newspaper ads. Once he contemplated talking to a political leader to find a job but changed his mind. He mainly asked neighbors, friends, and relatives, including his mother.

In all of her jobs from 1956 through 1973, Marcel was paid monthly, an indication of stability. In 1973 she earned 565 LL (Lebanese liras) a month, about $174 then. At that time, male household heads in the neighborhood commonly earned 400–500 LL ($123–154). Of the 1973 monthly total,

Marcel earned 465 LL ($143) at the bank, having started at 150 LL ($46) a month in 1965, and 100 LL ($31) at the merchant's (where she started at 40 LL [$12] a month in 1958). Rafik, her son, painted cars for a living, making 300–400 LL ($92–123) a month. He gave his mother 200 LL ($62) a month for household expenses. Managing her money effectively, Marcel was able to save for retirement, and at times she lent money to neighbors and work friends.

In 1973 Marcel worked an average of 6.5 hours a day, 5 hours at the bank and 1.5 hours for the merchant. She usually worked six days a week at the bank and five days a week for the merchant. Although this amounted to 37.5 hours a week, Marcel calculated that she actually worked 40 hours per week (30 at the bank and 10 for the merchant). The work hours did not include travel time to and from home or between places of work. It usually took her only 10 minutes by bus to reach the bank, but travel to the merchant's shop took 30–60 minutes, via a Mercedes taxi that operated along specific routes like a bus. Marcel left home at 7:30 in the morning for work at the merchant's shop, coming home daily around 10:00 A.M. for a rest and lunch. She left at 12:30 for the bank, returning at 7:30 P.M. Since she worked at two places, she had no formal lunch hour or rest time on the job. She took a 15- to 30-minute break at the bank.

Unlike the cases of many workers in the neighborhood, neither her salary nor her wages fluctuated with seasons. She considered herself fortunate to work indoors in a place that was neither hot and humid in summer nor cold and damp in the winter. She reported that both places had plenty of windows, sunlight, fans or air conditioning, toilets, drinking water, and first aid equipment on hand. Additionally, she felt confident that she was not in contact with much hazardous material. She said she was comfortable in both places of work.

Like most workers in Camp Trad, Marcel did not have a formal contract with either of her employers. There were no savings plans in either place of work, although the bank did enroll her in a newly established social security system. She explained that the merchant refused to enroll her because he would have had to increase her wages. She felt that the government should check businesses to make sure that non-Lebanese were not employed. She also thought that foreigners should not be enrolled in the social security system. "They are getting everything and are still swearing at us," she complained. She made this assertion even though many of her close neighborhood friends were Syrians or Palestinians and her mother had been born in Palestine. At that time, in 1973, there were about 500,000 Syrians and

300,000 Palestinians living and working in Lebanon, a country with a population of only 3 million. The rights of foreign workers and the burdens they represented to the state were frequently debated.

At the bank, Marcel was covered by full medical and accidental injury insurance paid by the bank. She was not covered by the merchant. If she became ill there, she had to find a substitute cleaning person and pay that person her wages. Once she missed a month's work because of an illness. Both employers paid her wages, but she had to use the wages from the merchant to pay her replacement worker. If she became seriously ill, Marcel thought the bank would allow a year's sick leave at full pay and then half pay indefinitely. The bank increased her wages by 25 LL ($8) a month every two years. The merchant gave no regularly scheduled wage increase nor cost-of-living increase. From the bank, she had twenty-one days of paid vacation annually, but the merchant gave her none. Both employers gave paid leaves on the twenty national holidays. Marcel had Sunday off at the bank and both Sunday and Monday off at the merchant's. In neither place did she receive extra pay for overtime work.

Marcel believed that a 5–10 LL monthly raise every year from the merchant would be justified, or a 25 LL ($8) monthly raise every two years. "They have millions. They would not feel 25 LL," she claimed. She also wanted one month's bonus pay every year. She was in favor of the possibility of a union organization and an employment office for cleaning people. She believed that unions would protect workers and that employment offices would make it easier to find new work. When she had occasionally asked for advances on her wages from the merchant, she said, he had given them to her. She added that she would be willing to lend money to either of her employers if they needed it. They had never asked.

On the whole, Marcel thought the director of the bank treated the workers well. "He treats us like a family. He is good to us," she claimed. About the merchant, she said, "The only thing is that he is stingy. He does not increase wages for the cleaners. The big people [*kubar*], he gives them increases, but for us, no. Otherwise, he is good."

Worker's Consciousness

Lebanese labor law required employers to give workers severance pay if they were laid off. Marcel was confident that the bank would give her severance pay in one lump sum, equivalent to one month's pay for each year of her employment. The problem, she pointed out, was that it would take four to six months and lots of paperwork on her part to get her severance. She was doubtful that the merchant would pay any severance at all: "He's very stingy. Probably he won't give me severance without my making a case [in court] against him." She had pursued a lawsuit against a previous employer, who had finally given her 1,000 LL ($308) to silence her.

In the event that either employer exercised the right to fire her, Marcel said the bank was required to give her one month's notice and one month's severance pay, but the merchant could fire her without notice or severance pay. "They consider us nothing," she claimed. She was not concerned, however, that she was at risk of losing either job at that point. She had never been fired from any position, she claimed, but had always left of her own accord. In only one of these instances did she receive severance pay, the one in which she went to court. Even then, she did not receive her full severance. She felt a reciprocal responsibility to the bank, saying that she would give them one month's notice if she decided to leave her job. She felt no obligation to give any notice to the merchant. She had no intention of leaving the bank in the near future, but she hoped that her son's work would improve so that she could leave the merchant in the next year and a half.

Marcel's experience in bridging visible and invisible sectors of the economy contributed to her heightened awareness of workers' rights. She was much more assertive about workers' rights than virtually any other woman in the neighborhood, most of whom were homemakers, and more so than even most of the men. Her understanding of workers' rights was sometimes informed by, and conflated with, her commitment to Lebanese nationalism. She asserted that she, as a worker, had the right to strike in both her places of work, and she had participated in strikes at the bank, though not at the merchant's shop. In 1972 she had joined a one-day strike in sympathy with striking workers at the Ghandour factory. She felt it was important to support workers in other places who were striking for their rights. A year earlier, regular employees at the bank had struck for two days demanding higher wages. Marcel and her fellow cleaning workers did not join that strike, though. The strikers won wage and cost-of-living increases that covered the cleaning workers as well. However, workers for the merchant were afraid to strike, she pointed out. The merchant had not even closed his shop for national holidays until the government forced him to do so.

Marcel had not participated in any other work-related strikes, but she said she had struck in support of national causes. During the 1958 civil war, she did not go to work for one week in order to support the Kata'ib, the right-wing Maronite national party. After an assassination attempt on President Camille Chamoun, she participated in national strikes as well.

She strongly supported the Kata'ib. "They are nationalist and against evil," she claimed.

Asked in 1972 what the legal minimum work age was, Marcel responded eighteen. She thought that many, especially among the Armenians, worked as young as eight or nine. In fact, the legal minimum work age in 1973 was eight. Marcel thought the legal minimum wage was 173 LL ($53) a month. In 1973 it was in fact 225 LL ($69) a month. Marcel said there was a worker's union at the bank that was three years old. All of the workers were members, including supervisors. The union had a general membership meeting only once a year, at Christmas. As far as she was concerned, the union had benefited the regular workers but not the cleaners. She was not entirely sure how union leaders were elected. She thought that two to four lists of candidates were drawn up by the union directors and that workers voted on those lists.

There was no union for workers at the merchant's place, and there had been no attempt to form one. Marcel claimed that she would support unionization there if it was attempted. She had once won a pay increase at the merchant's place by threatening to quit. Wage increases at the bank were automatic. She had received wage increases from both employers in the previous two years (1971–73). She felt she could go directly to the bank director to ask for a wage increase, if she needed it. At the merchant's shop, she said, "You can only do it by force. I have to say give me an increase or I will leave in one month."

Marcel had not asked for a change in hours of work from either employer. When the bank director had asked her to switch to morning hours, she had explained that she could not finish her work before the bank's normal opening time. The director agreed with her. If she wanted to change her work schedule, the only choice at the bank would be to start work at 2:00 A.M., which she would not want. She liked her hours, but she said that if she should want a change in either place, she would just ask her boss directly.

She herself would not consider running for union office. "I am not educated and I know nothing of the process," she apologized. I asked her what she would have to do if she did want a union office. "Some people buy votes," she protested. "Some people make others love them. I will make good things and help workers and let them love me. I would defend workers." She understood that the union could offer protection if the employer unjustly fired a worker. "The union can force reemployment or get severance rights," she noted. If she were head of the workers' union at the bank, Marcel said that she would "defend all workers' rights. I would make work simple, like the big employers. I would give high cost-of-living benefits. The union leaders should be regular employees and poor workers because they feel more with their fellow workers." If she headed a union at the merchant's shop, Marcel said, "All overtime should be paid. All who exploit workers should be taken out of work. I would put only righteous and morally correct people as bosses. The union should protest for every right and for weak workers' rights. Everyone should be at the same level."

Co-worker Relations

Marcel did her cleaning when the businesses were closed, so she had little connection with fellow workers. She was nevertheless aware of the religious and ethnic composition at both places of work. She estimated that there were just under a hundred workers at the bank, about eighty of them Arab Christians, four Armenian Christians, seven Druze, five Sunnis, and one Shi'i. Ten people worked for the merchant—five Maronites, three Greek Orthodox, one Armenian Christian, and one Catholic. Ninety-three of the bank workers were Lebanese and seven were Bulgarians. The merchant's employees were eight Lebanese (one who had previously held Palestinian citizenship), one Syrian, and one Frenchman.

At the bank, roughly seventy-five of the workers were women and twenty-five were men. At the merchant's six were male and four were female. While Marcel did not know the age distribution at the bank, she knew that at the merchant's shop three were twenty to thirty years old, five others thirty to forty, and two up to fifty years old. She thought ninety-two of the bank workers were married and eight single, while six of the merchant's workers were married and four single.

Marcel figured that eleven of the bank workers were related to each other. None of the merchant's workers were related. Only one of Marcel's relatives, her sister's husband's daughter, worked in the bank with her. She had no friends or relatives at the merchant's shop.

Since the merchant's workers had little connection with each other, Marcel had no problems with peers there. At the bank, though, a guard had made sexual approaches toward her over a three-year period. Finally she told the bank director, who threatened to discharge the guard, and he stopped bothering Marcel. She had not had similar or other problems with her employers, she noted. Three of the bank co-workers had visited her at home about six times during the past year (1973), and one co-worker from the merchant's place had visited five times. The three from the bank were all Maronite. The one from the merchant's was a Shi'i. All were Lebanese.

Two of them lived in Beirut, one in nearby Sin el Fil and one in Zalqa, a few kilometers away. Marcel had not herself visited any of her co-workers in their homes, however.

She had borrowed money from co-workers in both workplaces, two Lebanese, Maronite men. She had also lent money to fellow workers at the bank and would have done so at the merchant's if asked. Her regard for fellow workers was such that Marcel would have been willing to let her daughter (if she had one) or son marry one of them. She also thought that if she were unjustly fired, all her fellow workers at both places would support her. In fact, when there was an attempt at the bank to replace her services with those of a cleaning firm, Marcel said all the workers had spoken to the director and the personnel officer on her behalf. Although they did not strike, they negotiated for her. She thought fellow workers at the merchant's would also negotiate on her behalf, and Marcel was willing to support a fellow worker if unjustly fired, by talking directly with the employer. If other workers struck on behalf of the aggrieved person, she would join the strike, but she would not initiate a strike.

Asked if fellow workers confided in each other about personal problems, Marcel said that they did at the bank but not at the merchant's. "I have more time at the bank," she explained. She felt she could seek her employers' help with a problem but would not discuss personal problems with them.

Household Finances

Marcel, with her son Rafik contributing, managed her household finances relatively well. Her expenses were modest, and she seemed relatively confident of keeping up with her needs. Rent for her apartment was 60 LL ($19) a month, down from the 65 LL ($20) rate that the landlord had originally charged her. While there was some family property that she stood to inherit, she said it had not been subdivided for many generations, so her share was probably worthless. She had neither income from nor expenses for that property. Maintenance on her apartment cost her an average of 20 LL ($6) a year; painting it in 1971 had cost 100 LL ($31).

She calculated that she spent about 400 LL ($123) a month on food, a large amount for two people, particularly given their total earnings of 765 LL ($235) a month. She and Rafik seemed to consume somewhat more than the average of meat, fresh fruits, sweets, and other specialty foods. Movies, eating out, and visits to coffeehouses took about 55 LL ($17) a month (mostly Rafik's expenditures). Rafik probably spent 15 LL ($5) in pinball machines and 130 LL ($40) a month on various personal expenses. Marcel's transportation costs for work were 90 LL ($28) a month.

The money she spent on clothing was quite high by neighborhood standards: about 525 LL ($162) in 1972 on herself and just under 700 LL ($215) on Rafik's clothes. No doubt her clothing expenses were related to job needs.

Local municipal taxes amounted to 23 LL ($7) a year. Marcel also contributed about 27 LL ($8) a year to her church, and she invested 20 LL ($6) a month in a family loan association that paid interest and guaranteed her principal. One hospitalization in 1972 had cost her 430 LL ($132) after coverage by the bank insurance. She had visited a doctor only twice in 1972, costing her 6 LL ($2) total, after insurance payments. The drugs prescribed totaled 15 LL ($5) after insurance. Marcel gave her mother 75 LL ($23) a year.

Marcel's finances compare favorably with those of many neighborhood households: She had more to spend, spent more, and was still able to lend money to a number of neighbors and work friends periodically. She managed to save as well. When I saw her in March 1993, Marcel complained that Rafik was not taking care of her or treating her well. Neighbors in 1993, 1994, and 1995 confirmed her reports. She was still working at a bank and still managing her finances adequately.

Conclusion

Marcel's story sheds light on the porousness of the boundaries between the visible and invisible sectors of the economy. People like Marcel straddle both sectors or spend parts of their lives in one, then the other. Marcel, like many other workers, was unaware of such categories as visible and invisible economies. She was quite aware, though, of the benefits of working in the bank as opposed to the merchant's shop. For Marcel, the experience of work concerned mostly the relationships with specific employers—those who were good to her and those who were not. While the difference between the bank and the merchant's shop were clear in this case, at times businesses in the visible economy treated workers such as Marcel much like shops of the invisible economy. The porousness of boundaries between visible and invisible sectors, therefore, results not only from the movement of workers between them but also from the frequent similarities of their business practices.

Marcel did not articulate an identity as a worker. Her identity, even prior to the 1975–92 Lebanese civil war, was primarily that of a Lebanese, a Maronite, a family member, and a mother. She certainly thought about her work and work conditions, was willing to discuss them, and had opinions on most questions related to her work. However, Marcel almost never initiated a conversation about the subject of work in the years I have known her since 1971.

She spontaneously talked about local and national politics, neighborhood events, family and personal relations, finances, and other topics. Whatever subject Marcel discussed, she seemed to have a definitive opinion. There were few conversations in which she seemed to be caught off guard, with nothing to say and no point of view. The clarity with which she organized her life, her worldview, and her relations with people belied the complex world in which she lived and the complexity she straddled. Gloria Anzaldua argued, "The new *mestiza* copes by developing a tolerance for contradictions, a tolerance for ambiguity. . . . Not only does she sustain contradictions, she turns ambivalence into something else."[3] Marcel lived ambiguities by turning them into certainties. She defined her work in terms that she could manage. While highly personal, her view of her work world included an implicit sociopolitical analysis of the relations between workers and employers, government and business, and government and citizens. Her movement between different sectors of the economy probably deepened her grasp of worker issues. On-the-ground analyses of people such as Marcel can only deepen our grasp of the complexities of marginal workers' structural positions in the economy and their own understandings of their relationships to society, economy, and government.

Notes

1. Samir Khalaf, "Changing Forms of Political Patronage in Lebanon," in Ernest Gellner and John Waterbury, eds., *Patrons and Clients in Mediterranean Societies* (London: Duckworth, 1977), 185–206.

2. Samir Khalaf, "Primordial Ties and Politics in Lebanon," *Middle Eastern Studies* 4, no. 3 (1968): 243–69; Suad Joseph, "The Family as Security and Bondage: A Political Strategy of the Lebanese Working Class," in Helen Safa, ed., *Toward a Political Economy of Urbanization in Third World Countries* (New Delhi: Oxford University Press, 1982), 151–71.

3. Gloria Anzaldua, *Borderlands: La Frontera—The New Mestiza* (San Francisco: Aunt Lute Books, 1987), 79.

13

Women in Cairo's (In)visible Economy

Linking Local and National Trends

Homa Hoodfar

Official figures indicate that Egyptian women's participation in blue-collar jobs has dropped since 1967, despite an overall increase in female labor market participation. Anthropological data on women's cash-earning activities in low-income neighborhoods of Cairo confirm this overall trend, indicating that less skilled and less formally educated women choose either to engage in informal-invisible cash-earning activities or to withdraw their labor from the cash market altogether.[1]

The term *informal* or *invisible* economy refers here to those small-scale (and in this case very small-capital) cash-earning activities that are outside state regulation. The most striking aspect of Cairo's invisible economy, however, is how visible in fact it is. Unlicensed crowded local markets (suqs) are a common sight in Cairo. Many women, and some men as well, sell goods on the street outside their homes. Others sell what they produce in operations within the home, trading chickens, pigeons, or rabbits raised on roofs and balconies. Without an official storefront, they find their customers through word of mouth. In short, the invisible economy is not "invisible" per se, but it has until recently largely escaped the eyes of official (male) economic data collectors. The decision of low-income Egyptian women to favor this invisible sector has given the officially recognized structure of the Egyptian female labor force a unique feature: The largest percentage of women in the labor market are concentrated in white-collar and skilled jobs, and only a small percentage are in jobs conventionally categorized as blue-collar.

This chapter uses anthropological data from several low-income neighborhoods of Cairo to draw links between the local and national labor market structures. Based on these data, I argue that the underlying cause of Egyptian women's lack of participation in blue-collar jobs is a rational economic calculation, as opposed to traditionalism, conservatism, or religiosity. In fact, women's invocation of religion and Islamic rights often has more to do with the protection of economic rights than with unquestioning submission to the traditional understanding of religion and customs. If development and social policy efforts are directed at improving the economic situation of less-privileged women in this poststructural adjustment era, then it is imperative to understand women's options and choices in the context of their day-to-day lives.

The central question is, why do the illiterate and less skilled, who by inference are among the poorer women, stay out of the labor market? Do the forces of patriarchy and male solidarity exclude them from more secure jobs? Is it Islamic ideology and conservatism that explain their absence from the labor market? Is the labor market too exploitative? In short, is there a material basis for low-income women's tendency to stay out of the formal labor market, or is it cultural and ideological factors that explain the phenomenon?

The literature dealing with the Middle East has tended to favor cultural explanations in this regard. It is assumed that Islamic ideology inhibits women from entering the labor market.[2] Since women's participation in the labor market continues to be viewed as congruent with women's liberation and with higher status, the literature has often explicitly or implicitly treated Islamic ideology as a major factor detrimental to the position of women in Muslim societies.[3] Nonetheless, recent research based on closer examination of women's views has thrown considerable doubt on these assumptions, paving the way for an alternative approach.[4]

My findings indicate that concrete external conditions influence the choices women make. It is their alert economic assessment of the terms of the labor market that keeps them out. Although at times they may justify their choices in terms of accepted ideology, generally the costs of this category of employment outweigh its benefits for women, whose opportunity costs are much higher than those of similarly qualified men. In contrast, the informal sector's flexible structure allows women to take full advantage of subsidized goods and free public services while combining their cash-earning activities with household responsibilities. In other words, despite the low monetary rewards of jobs in the informal economy, the net gains for women and their households are higher.

Moreover, women's decision to stay out of the labor market at this level is enhanced by their efforts to increase their power vis-à-vis their husbands. Contrary to conventional (particularly Western) assumptions, Muslim laws offer women certain privileges even while imposing restrictions. For instance, a man must provide food and housing for his wife and children, regardless of her financial status. Despite great interest in the topic of wo-men and Islam demonstrated within Western discourse, few studies have looked at Islamic rights and privileges of women. Even less attention has been paid to exploring the ways in which women exploit these rights in order to challenge the social order and advance their own interests.[5] In a context in which industrialization and development have almost universally discriminated against women, not the least by trivializing women's contributions to the household and the national economy, women are reluctant to overlook their Islamic rights. Women therefore adopt a wide range of strategies to protect their traditional rights even while profiting from the modern social system,[6] ranging from staying out of the labor market to taking up the veil.[7] They attempt to preserve the domestic division of labor by pressuring men to spend more time at their jobs, by asking other women (rather than their husbands) to help out with domestic tasks in emergencies, and by ridiculing men if they engage in housework.[8]

Such attempts to protect and further individual or group interests are an important part of everyday politics that, because of the limited conventional definition of politics, has traditionally been ignored.[9] Whether we adopt a cautious approach and categorize such forms of resistance as "bargaining with patriarchy"[10] or whether we employ a more receptive approach,[11] the process of contextualizing social behavior has presented social scientists— feminist scholars in particular—with an opportunity to understand what have appeared to them as "bizarre" and "backward" strategies.

The Setting: Local and National Employment Patterns

The study described in this chapter was conducted in three low-income neighborhoods of greater Cairo between 1983 and 1986, followed by several visits in 1988, 1990, and 1992. Although the wider sample (seventy-eight households) included some female-headed households, all sixty households included here encompassed at least one married couple, though some were extended households. The households of the few women who were in polygynous marriages were treated as nuclear, since each wife had her own unit of residence. Many women in the neighborhoods engaged in some kind of cash-earning activity at various times. Two-thirds of the households in the study included women who operated a business on their own or who regularly worked more than ten hours per week in the family business (see table 17).

Though some women were employed as blue-collar workers in the formal sector at the time of the study, only three married women were working in this sector. The low figure reflects the general trend in the neighborhoods, as well as within the country as a whole. Egyptian statistics indicate a substantial expansion of women's labor force participation since the 1960s (see table 18). Egyptian workforce data, like those of many other countries, are primarily collected in the formal sector, while a substantial number of women are engaged in the informal and subsistence sectors.[12] Moreover, even when attempts are made to include other sectors of the economy, the methodologies adopted are less sensitive to collecting information on women.[13] Despite their shortcomings, however, the official figures are the only macrolevel source available, and they provide some useful indication of the general trends in the country (see table 18).

Further breakdown of the data suggests a fundamental structural change in female labor market participation. The percentage of women in production has shrunk consistently since the 1960s.[14] As this trend is characteristic of many industrializing societies, some scholars attribute it to a process of

Table 17. Informants' Cash Earning Activities

Category	Number	Percentage
Formal Employment:		
White collar workers	7	11.6
Blue collar	3	5.0
Looking for employment	0	0.0
Informal Employment:		
Home produce for exchange	3	5.0
Working in family business*	7	11.6
Self-employed*	16	26.6
Maids and handy-women	4	6.6
Others: Not engaged in cash market	20	33.3
Totals	60	100.0

*Some women in these groups did not view themselves as cash earners, though they thought their labor was important for the family business.
Source: Field data.

Table 18. Economically Active Population of Egypt

Year	Total	Female	Females as Percentage of Economically Active
1960	7,781,957	618,196	7.94
1966	8,333,733	621,893	7.46
1980	11,037,093	983,546	8.94
1989	13,609,891	2,102,320	15.4*

*The increase is partly due to changes in the wording of the questionnaire. These figures do not include the 2.5 million Egyptians (mostly males) working abroad.
Source: International Labour Office, *Yearbook of Labour Statistics.*

female marginalization at a higher level of industrialization.[15] However, there is no evidence to support the marginalization theory in the case of Egypt.

The female labor force in Egypt differs structurally from that of other countries (see table 19). Far fewer female workers are engaged in occupations normally classified as pink-collar (that is, typically female) or in unskilled jobs.[16] Illiterate and less-educated women leave the formal labor market at a much faster rate than similarly educated males.[17] Particularly interesting is that the vertical distribution of the female labor force is weighted toward the top rather than the bottom. Scott has observed that "Egypt has a much higher proportion of women professional and white collar workers than Peru, or even the UK."[18]

Women's low participation in the labor force cannot be explained by the structure of labor demand, or by level and pattern of economic development, or by differential access to education.[19] Women in Egypt have lower levels of education than women in Latin America, but this should not have prevented them from entering unskilled occupations. On the other hand, while the gap between male and female education in Egypt narrows at the higher end, it still lags behind that of most Latin American countries and therefore cannot explain the greater proportion of Egyptian women in professional jobs.

Islamic ideology clearly is not a barrier for educated women who take advantage of jobs with higher status and greater rewards. In fact, in the neighborhoods all women with more than ten years of education whom I came to meet, or to know of, were employed in the formal labor market, mostly in the public sector. In the past, modern education and exposure to modernism was perceived as the antithesis of religious ideology. However, in the light of the recent re-veiling movement, which began in Egypt among

Table 19. Distribution of Female Wage and Salaried* Nonagricultural Employees by Occupational Class

Occupational class	UK (1971)	Peru (1987)	Egypt (1984)	Spain (1989)
Professional and technical	12.3	16.21	37.34	17.1
Administrative and managerial	1.0	2.65	3.92	0.48
Clerical	32.3	14.58	27.46	20.48
Sales workers	11.0	30.91	11.69	17.36
Service workers	23.3	20.17	5.77	28.37
Production workers	20.0	15.44	13.79	16.18
Total	99.9	99.96	99.97	99.97
Share total female employment	94.2	62.9	92.3	12.7

*Excludes agricultural and unclassified family labor and unclassified employment status.
Source: ILO, *Yearbook of Labour Statistics,* 1988, 1989, 1990; modified from Scott, 1986.

university women and was rapidly adopted by women in white-collar jobs, such an assumption is unwarranted.[20] The explanation for the absence of the women in lower-level jobs must lie elsewhere.

My findings indicate that the employment prospects of lower-income women were limited to work that was low in status, low in income, and physically demanding; consequently, they have resisted participating in the formal labor market and have found other ways to supplement family income. Two factors prominently influence this choice. The first is the relative stability of marriage in Egyptian society, contrasted, for instance, with the unstable *compromiso* union common in low-income Latin American urban communities. The second factor is women's Islamic right to material support from their husbands. Though the extent of husbands' financial responsibilities is open to interpretation, all agree that it includes food, shelter, and clothing appropriate to the husband's status; men are under great social and legal pressure to honor this obligation. Islamic ideology and practices play an important role in shaping women's social environment and worldviews, which in turn influence the choices they make within the confines of their possibilities.[21] Therefore, the valid question is whether Islamic ideology has prevented women from entering the labor market or whether it has allowed them the choice of staying out of it and resisting exploitation.

While unskilled men may benefit from this strategy, which limits the supply of labor and prevents wages from falling, the fact remains that most unskilled men have several jobs or work twelve- to fourteen-hour days to make ends meet.[22] Thus one may argue that if women entered the labor market, their husbands could work less. In that case however, women would have, in effect, two jobs: in the home and in the labor market.

Given the material conditions of low-income households, many women find temporary or long-term ways to contribute to their households, in cash or in services. These choices throw some light on women's absence from the labor market: low-income women prefer petty trading and cottage industries over blue-collar work. As the following case studies indicate, the real costs of blue-collar work outweigh its benefits for women. Job-related costs such as transportation, new clothing, and meals take up a good part of income earned. The net income does not compensate for the inconveniences and material losses to the household caused by the woman's absence for ten or eleven hours a day.

Zaynab, who sold soaked beans in the local market, complained that it was difficult to support her family on her small income. When I asked why she didn't go back to the factory job she had held before her marriage, she explained:

> Working in a factory is hardly the answer. They pay me around £E 30 per month. But I have to take a bus there every morning and I have to take my two children to my mother who lives far away. I also have to pay some money toward their food, as my parents are too poor to be able to feed my children every day. Even if I take my lunch like most women do, there are still occasional expenses. Worst of all, I cannot go to work in my old dress. I have to buy clothes. These expenses take up half my income. That leaves me with about the same money that I earn in the market. . . . But if I am here, the better-off households may pay me to help out and I can look after my children and my home.

She added that she would return to the factory if her salary were at least £E 50, but in that case she would not have given up the job in the first place.

The formal sector has other disadvantages besides low wages. While low-income households benefit from public services and subsidized goods, the long inflexible hours of factory work prevent women from taking advantage of these opportunities. For example, in 1988 a kilogram of meat cost £E 3.75 in government shops, while on the open market it was sold at

£E 8. However, subsidized goods were available infrequently, and shoppers had to wait in line for three or four hours. Since women who were not in close proximity could not take advantage of these savings, many women were reluctant to work away from the neighborhood in a formal job. Umm Sabah, who sells vegetables in the market, explained:

> I earn little by selling watercress and parsley but because I am here in the vicinity I learn when there is meat, chicken, or eggs in the government shop, and I can always leave my basket with my children or a friend and run to line up, or ask someone else to line up for me. This way I can buy items that otherwise we could never afford to eat. If I worked in the factory, I would perhaps earn £E 10 more, but I would have to spend more on clothes and transportation. And when I came home, I would have to buy everything from the open market at higher prices, and we would lose more than my extra wages.

To maximize their income, women often engaged simultaneously in quite diverse activities. A couple of women had managed to buy a sewing machine, and they made simple clothes such as pajama tops for the children and *gallabiyya*s for the neighbors. They also raised chickens and rabbits on their roofs. Others sold inexpensive clothes and bedding or worked as midwives or handywomen. Most women wanted to increase their income but were limited by their small capital (often not more than a few Egyptian pounds). Although selling fruit and more expensive vegetables was profitable, they were cautious about making large investments since the informal local markets were periodically raided by the police.

One woman sold vegetables and also cheese when she had enough capital. She took her portable kerosene stove with her to cook the family's main meal while waiting for customers. Other women sold items in, or just outside, their homes. When a crisis needed their attention, women put their business on hold for a day, or even for as long as a few months, while they attended to these concerns. The flexibility of the informal market is very attractive to women who have to cope with a double day.

Fatigue and loss of good health were other costs of blue-collar work. Mona gave up her factory job because, after deducting her expenses, her monthly income was only £E 5. After spending eleven hours each day at work and in commuting, when she arrived home she was too tired to take care of her basic domestic responsibilities. Few women were willing to work in the labor market if it did not yield a reasonable income and improve their material life. Factory jobs were difficult, women remarked, while white-collar employees often sat at their desks waiting for work. One woman said, "It is demanding. Working conditions are often terrible. The foreman treats you badly. Worst of all, the time schedule is very inflexible; it starts too early in the morning and it is often way out of town. By the time one returns home one has no energy to do housework. When there is a family crisis, women feel torn between home and the factory."

These ideas were echoed in a report on the working conditions of women in factories. A female interviewee said: "What woman in her right mind wants to be a factory worker? I am glad it is not encouraged in the text [the adult literacy textbook used in the factory]. We do it because we have to, not because we choose to."[23]

Since few informants had actually given up formal-sector jobs, I wondered if their preference for the informal market was a rationalization of their situation, guided by the awareness that access to these jobs was very limited. When asked whether it was difficult for women to find jobs in the formal sector, one out of forty informants said that it had become very difficult for educated women. Nineteen women said that there were plenty of jobs available. Thirteen said the problem was poor pay. Seven women said good contacts were necessary in order to find the better-paid jobs but that it was possible to find such contacts through neighborhood networks.

Jobs for unskilled women were probably not as plentiful as these women thought, but clearly their reason for not participating in the formal labor market was not the inaccessibility of these jobs. Many women didn't look for jobs beyond their neighborhood because the cost of working elsewhere would place too great a burden on the household. Some women who were employed in the formal sector had resigned after having children. Women used the same cost-benefit analysis as men, but because of the sexual division of labor their opportunity costs were much higher, particularly during the family-building cycle. However, despite the withdrawal of women from blue-collar jobs, the overall trend of Egyptian female labor market participation does not support the thesis that women in general leave the labor market during their family-building cycle.[24] Since 1960 the female participation rate has declined for women between the ages of fifteen and twenty and for women over the age of sixty. But participation among women between the ages of twenty and twenty-nine has risen consistently, even when the general rate of economic participation for the whole population decreased between 1966 and 1973. Two-thirds of Egyptian female workers are between twenty and forty-nine years of age.

Another factor was status. One of the peculiarities of Egyptian society at this period of economic transition from state control to free market is that wages do not necessarily correspond to status. Therefore, in choosing a job, people have to strike a balance between its economic possibilities and their status as perceived by others. Since most women rated blue-collar jobs at the same level or lower than petty trading and home production, formal employment did not offer a status incentive.

Since men had few domestic responsibilities beyond contributing cash, their opportunity cost was lower. Most female informants thought that unless men had specific skills, blue-collar work was their best option despite the low wages. Umm Halah explained:

> Working for the government is better for men though they are paid the same low salary as women. But they can always work overtime because they do not have to look after children. They are often asked to run errands for their superiors and are paid a little bit of money for that. Through their connections at work they often find a second job to supplement their income. It is important that they and their families know that in case of misfortune the government would pay the family a minimum salary so that they can survive.

According to Umm Halah and many others, low-level formal-sector jobs are worthwhile only if workers take advantage of the informal income-earning opportunities these jobs generate. However, married women cannot take advantage of these opportunities because of their already considerable domestic responsibilities.

Most women, including those who had decided to give up formal-sector jobs, regretted not having the security of a guaranteed income and an old-age pension. All women in my sample said that the major attraction of working in the formal sector was its pension and sick benefits.

Since there is no old-age pension in the informal sector, women have little incentive to continue working once the family's period of financial stress is over. Most women who earned cash in the informal sector said they hoped that when their children were grown up or their husbands found a higher-paying job, they would be able to give up work. This decision shows women's estimation that if cash was sufficient, they could contribute better to their households by investing their time in efficient shopping and better management of funds. This strategy was particularly valid at the lower end of the income scale, where most wives had full access to their husband's income and acted as their household's financial manager.[25]

In the real world, contrary to simple economic models, when men and women make decisions concerning their employment, they take into consideration not only wages but other possible benefits. Most informants said factory work was suitable for unmarried women if they were not qualified for white-collar jobs. It would offer the opportunities of getting out to meet people, gaining experience, and, more important, finding a suitor. Since daughters are not expected to contribute to the household, the money they earned could be put aside to buy items for their trousseau.

The reasons for unskilled women's preference for the informal market seem clear. But consider the situation of three blue-collar workers who kept their formal-sector jobs after marriage and having children. Karima, who had completed primary school, then worked in a pharmaceutical factory. In the mid-1970s, she said she had continued to do so because eighteen years previously her job had been considered well paid, and transportation was provided.

> At that time it never crossed my mind or my husband's that I should give up my job. Just before my first child was born, we moved into the same building as my mother so that she could look after my children. All along I had hoped to continue my education and get my high school diploma, which would qualify me for a white-collar job. But once the children were born, it became difficult to study, and after some years I gave up. Since I had more education than most other workers in my factory at that time, I was appointed to a better position. So I continued to work, but in the last ten years inflation has made a mockery of my earnings. However, since by now I have worked for eighteen years I feel it is a pity to give up my pension now. If I work a few more years, perhaps I can retire with a small pension.

She and other older informants explained that at the time they were looking for jobs, blue-collar jobs were considered well paying and there was much competition for them. No one would think of giving up such jobs after marriage. Mothers and relatives used to help with child care, since in those days housing problems had not begun to affect Cairo, and most people lived near their relatives.

Another woman, a cleaner and tea lady (a woman who earns cash by selling cups of tea to office workers), said that she continued to work because her husband was not reliable; he was lazy, incapable, and frequently unemployed. Her job provided some security, and to supplement her income she raised chickens and rabbits on the roof of the building. Moreover, as her office was only a half-hour walk from the neighborhood, she had no transportation expenses. As she put it, "I am lucky my mother lives in the same alley and looks after my two children so that I can go to work. I do not know what would happen to me and the children if my mother were not here." Her mother, who had raised three children single-handedly after the death of her husband, insisted that the daughter keep her job because it offered an old-age pension. Her advice was that "a husband you cannot count on in his youth would not be better in his old age."

All three women who had continued their blue-collar jobs lived near their mothers and other family, who helped with child care and shopping. This effectively reduced the opportunity cost of going to work. As Cairo grows in size and population, the opportunity for women to live near their kin becomes more remote, particularly for low-income households. For women, this means the loss of a support network that traditionally they could count on. In the absence of substantial wage increases or other improvements in working conditions, we might expect to see increasing female participation at lower levels of the job hierarchy in the informal rather than the formal labor market.

Attitude to Paid Employment

When asked whether women should "work" (engage in paid employment), all informants, whether employed or not, declared that according to Islam and custom, men as fathers and husbands should be the providers and that women should not have to be employed for pay. Their statements were almost always qualified by adding that if a woman chose to work, she had to do so without jeopardizing her domestic responsibilities, and that she should exercise complete control over her income and spend it in any way she wanted, without her husband's interference. All women, whether gainfully employed or not, felt there was no reason for a woman to "work" if she could not exert control over her income.

Umm Samir and her neighbor pooled their capital and started a business making and selling ice cream and bean sandwiches to neighborhood children. However, when her husband found out about it, he decided to cut her housekeeping allowance in half. Because she could not convince him to continue to pay the same amount, she quit her business. She told me, "I was doing extra work because I wanted to buy some household goods and improve our life, but he thought he might have opportunity to spend more money on himself. Why should I work harder for his pleasures? He married me. He wanted a wife and children so he has to work for them." She then jokingly added, "We do not spoil our men the way you do. We work at home and men should work outside and provide for us."

At a social gathering I attended, a few neighbors were giving advice to a newly married woman, a white-collar worker, whose husband had refused to pay her a housekeeping allowance or otherwise contribute to the day-today costs of the household. There was agreement among the women that the bride should first make sure of her husband's comfort at home and then find an excuse to take a leave without pay for a year or so. She could thus establish a routine in which he would pay the household expenses. Then she could return to work and retain control of her income.

One elderly woman at the gathering ran a fairly successful informal trade in clothes and bedding, and from the proceeds she had managed to buy a small piece of land where her husband and sons had built their house. She said, "I know, I have four married daughters. You have to watch these young men today. They want to have a family, but they do not want to pay for them. In our time, men would feel embarrassed even to ask about their wives' income. My husband discovered that I had money only when I announced that I was going to buy the land. . . . A real man would rather die than ask his wife to feed the household."

Although there were many examples of men who had not lived up to the ideal, there was great pressure on them not to deviate from their religious and conventional responsibilities. Nonetheless, while women insisted that men should pay all household expenses and that women should manage their own income, they agreed that women too have to invest, usually in household goods, to improve the family's lifestyle. It was generally accepted by male members of the community that women are more interested than men in improving the collective family life. In fact, many husbands considered it an asset to have a wife who found ways of demanding more money from her husband for purposes of saving or investing in durable goods. These women were not seen as grabbers or exploiters of men; rather they were viewed as more domestic and family oriented.[26] Some husbands criticized their wives for lacking these qualities.

As scholars have shown, households are not undifferentiated units where every member has equal access to resources.[27] Rather, a household is best described as a unit of "cooperative conflict."[28] Individual (but often concurrent) efforts to improve the household's collective gains are combined with individuals' efforts to strike a balance between their contributions and their actual or potential share of power and resources. However, contrary to some assumptions, the attempt to protect self-interest is not a male prerogative. Neither is it a right denied to Muslim women. Politics and strategies that people adopt as social actors are shaped by their social realities and the possibilities open to them. Had scholars working on women's issues accepted that, like their European and North American counterparts, women (and men) in other cultures are engaged in pursuing their interests, there would have been no need to employ problematic concepts such as "false consciousness" and "backwardness" in order to explain their choices. Nor there would be any place for presenting "other" women as exotic, non-rational pawns of their males, the patriarchs.[29] By reviving their traditional and Islamic rights, Muslim women have managed to improve their bargaining power vis-à-vis their husbands.

Acquiescence with the ideology of traditional gender roles did not prevent women from assessing fundamental economic changes and their impact on the household, and on marital relations in particular. Since women cannot easily change their own circumstances in the middle stages of their life cycle, their hopes for their daughters more aptly indicate their assessments of the way women should respond to socioeconomic change. Hence I asked my informants whether they would prefer that their daughters have a paid job or stay at home after marriage.

Of fifty-five women who were asked, the majority replied that they wanted their daughters to have paid jobs. All but five emphasized that they wanted their daughters to be educated and to hold prestigious white-collar jobs. It is noteworthy that the three women who said they preferred their daughter to stay at home were those whose daughters were adult and illiterate, for whom paid work would mean low-status jobs. Most women explained that, given rising prices and increasing needs for commercial products, it is not easy for a family to live on a single income; it is best, they said, if women earn money to help with their husbands' responsibilities. Others thought husbands respect a working wife because they acknowledge that she too is shouldering the cost of the household; the partnership was thought to be more equal when women, too, brought in an income. However, the question of financial security should a marriage fail was the informants' greatest concern, since among the poor, few parents or brothers can support divorced daughters or sisters and their children.

Conclusion

Women's low profile in the labor market results from the failure to recognize domestic contributions, which account for a substantial part of real national income, not to mention the national standard of living. Women's decision to participate in the labor market is influenced by domestic responsibilities, which they consider their most important contribution to the household. Domestic contributions, while freeing their husbands to engage in cash-earning activities, also legitimize women's claim to their husband's wages. The low wages of blue-collar jobs and their inflexibility, long hours, and physical strain discourage married women with less salable skills and less formal education from considering blue-collar work as an economically viable option. They choose to engage in the informal economy, which despite its low monetary reward offers them maximum flexibility, which in turn is translated into greater material benefit for the household.

A simple cost calculation shows the unprofitability of entering the low-wage blue-collar labor market. The lingering assumption of Arab-Muslim women's "unhealthy attitude" toward work and the acceptance of Islamic ideology, traditionalism, and conservatism as explanations of women's apparent lack of interest in employment distracts us from examining women's dual commitment and the contradictions they face.

The picture is further complicated by the dynamic within the household, as individual members strive to achieve a positive balance between their actual and potential power and access to resources, on the one hand, and their contributions on the other. This chapter argues that by invoking Islamic rights and traditional ideology, women try to ensure that additional contributions to the household on their part are not reflected in decreased contributions by their husbands.

Notes

A version of this paper was presented at the twenty-fourth annual meeting of the Middle East Studies Association, San Antonio, Texas, Panel on Informality in the Middle East (November 1990). I wish to thank Peter von Sivers for his valuable comments, which I have incorporated into this chapter. I also owe special thanks to Sherene Razack, Richard Lobban, and Patricia L. Kelly for their comments and suggestions.

1. See Nadia Khouri-Dagher, "Households and the Food Issue in Cairo: The Answers of Civil Society to a Defaulting State," in Diane Singerman and Homa Hoodfar, eds., *Development, Change and Gender in Cairo: A View from the Household* (Bloomington: Indiana University Press, 1997); Diane Singerman, *Avenues of Participation: Family, Politics and Networks in Urban Quarters of Cairo* (Princeton: Princeton University Press, 1995); and Diane Singerman, chap. 14 of this book.

2. Nadia Youssef, *Women and Work in Developing Societies* (Berkeley: Institute of International Studies, University of California, 1974); idem., "Women in Development: Urban Life and Labour," in Irene Tinker, Michelle Bo Bramsen, and Mayra Buvinic, eds., *Women and World Development* (London: Praeger, 1976); K. el-Korayem, "Women and the International Economic Order in the Arab World," *Cairo Papers in Social Science* 4, no. 4 (1981); Alison M. Scott, "Women and Industrialization: Examining the 'Female Marginality' Thesis," *Journal of Development Studies* 22, no. 4 (1986): 643–80.

3. Many studies have suggested that women's access to independent income may also mean more exploitation of women and more freedom for men to withhold a larger portion of their income for their own personal gratification. See, for example, Jan Pahl, *Money and Marriage* (London: Macmillan Press, 1988); and Homa Hoodfar, "Patterns of Household Budgeting and the Management of Financial Affairs in a Lower-Income Neighborhood in Cairo," in Daisy H. Dwyer and Judith Bruce, eds., *A Home Divided: Women and Income in the Third World* (Stanford: Stanford University Press, 1988).

4. Mona Hamman, "Egypt's Working Women: Textile Workers of Chubra el-Kheima," *Middle East Research and Information Project* 82 (1979): 3–7; Maria Mies, *The Lace-Makers of Narsapur: Indian Housewives Produce for the World Market* (London: Zed Press, 1982).

5. Homa Hoodfar, "Return to the Veil: Personal Strategy and Public Participation in Egypt," in Nanneke Redclift and M. Thea Sinclair, eds., *Working Women: International Perspectives on Labour and Gender Ideology* (London: Routledge, 1991); idem., "Survival Strategies in Low-Income Households in Cairo," *Journal of South Asian and Middle Eastern Studies* 13, no. 4 (1990): 22–41.

6. For a discussion of the concept of strategy, see Graham Crow, "The Use of the Concept of 'Strategy' in Recent Sociological Literature," *Sociology* 23, no. 1 (1989): 1–24.

7. Hoodfar, "Return to the Veil"; Arlene Elowe MacLeod, *Accommodating Protest: Working Women and the New Veiling in Cairo* (New York: Columbia University Press, 1991); Sherifa Zuhur, *Revealing Reveiling* (Albany: State University of New York Press, 1992).

8. Hoodfar, "Survival Strategies."

9. For a more comprehensive definition of politics, see Adrian Leftwich, *Redefining Politics: People, Resources and Power* (London: Methuen, 1983). For examples of unconventional studies of political struggle, see James C. Scott, *Weapons of the Weak: Everyday Forms of Peasant Resistance* (New Haven: Yale University Press, 1985), and Singerman, *Avenues of Participation.*

10. See Deniz Kandiyoti, "Bargaining with Patriarchy," *Gender and Society* 2, no. 3 (1988): 274–90.

11. Laura Nader, "The Subordination of Women in Comparative Perspective," *Urban Anthropology* 15, no. 3–4 (1986): 377–97.

12. R. Anker and M. Anker, "Measuring the Female Labour Force in Egypt," *International Labour Review* 26, no.4 (1989): 511–20; Lourdes Beneria, "Conceptualizing the Labour Force: The Under-estimation of Women's Economic Activities," *Journal of Developing Area Studies* 17, no. 3 (1981): 10–28; Barbara Ibrahim, "Strategies of Urban Labor Force Measurement," *Cairo Papers in Social Science* 6, no. 2 (1983).

13. Luci Saunders and Sohair Mehenna, "Unseen Hands: Women's Farm Work in an Egyptian Village," *Anthropological Quarterly* 59 (1986): 105–14.

14. Brent Hansen and Samir Radwan, *Employment Opportunities and Equality in Egypt* (Geneva: ILO, 1982); International Labour Office, *Yearbook of Labour Statistics* (Geneva: ILO, 1988, 1989).

15. Scott, "Women and Industrialization"; John Humphrey, *Gender and Work in the Third World: Sexual Divisions in Brazilian Industry* (London: Tavistock, 1987).

16. See Scott, "Women and Industrialization."

17. See B. C. Sanyal et al., *University Education and the Labour Market in the Arab Republic of Egypt* (Oxford: Pergamon Press, 1982), 59.

18. Scott, "Women and Industrialization."

19. Scott, "Women and Industrialization"; Youssef, *Women and Work,* 21–41.

20. Hoodfar, "Return to the Veil"; MacLeod, *Accommodating Protest;* Zuhur, *Revealing Reveiling;* and Fadwa el-Guindi, "Veiling Infitah with Muslim Ethic: Egypt's Contemporary Islamic Movement," *Social Problems* 28, no. 4 (1981): 465–87.

21. Islam and Islamic practices, though often justified by referring to the same Quranic text, vary widely among Muslims of different cultures. Like other religions, Islam is strongly influenced by local culture and beliefs.

22. Singerman, *Avenues of Participation;* Hoodfar, "Survival Strategies"; Nadia Khouri-Dagher, "La Survie Quotidienne au Caire," *Maghreb-Machrek* 10 (1985).

23. Hammam, "Egypt's Working Women," 7.

24. See V. K. Oppenheimer, *Work and the Family* (New York: Academic Press, 1982).

25. Hoodfar, "Patterns of Household Budgeting."

26. Hoodfar, "Survival Strategies"; and Unni Wikan, "Living Conditions among Cairo's Poor: A View from Below," *Middle East Journal* 39, no. 1 (1985): 7–26.

27. Nancy Folbre, "Cleaning House," *Journal of Development Economics* 22 (1986): 3–40.

28. For more discussion on the complexity, use, and abuse of the concept of "household," see Amartya Sen, "Gender and Cooperative Conflicts," in Irene Tinker, ed., *Persistent Inequalities: Women and World Development* (Oxford: Oxford University Press, 1990); and Folbre, "Cleaning House."

29. For a critical review of feminist approaches to the study of other women, see Marnia Lazreg, "Feminism and Difference: The Perils of Writing as Women on Women in Algeria," *Feminist Studies* 14, no. 1 (1988): 81–106; and Chandra Mohanty, "Under Western Eyes: Feminist Scholarship and Colonial Discourse," *Feminist Review* 30 (1988): 61–88.

14

Engaging Informality

Women, Work, and Politics in Cairo

Diane Singerman

Despite contentious debates surrounding the boundaries and nature of the informal sector, scholars and policy makers have largely investigated the informal sector from an economic perspective. Hidden and invisible sources of production and employment in the informal economic sector, recently "discovered" through new methodologies and conceptual frameworks, have been seen by some as possible antidotes to poverty and unemployment, and by others as the source of exploitation. Economists debated the extent of employment and production of the informal economy, its effect on wage levels, the structure of the sector, its relationships to the domestic formal economy, and its place within the increasingly globalized economy. Detailed fieldwork by anthropologists and economists, supplemented by macrolevel economic analysis, demonstrated the significant value of goods and services that women and men produced in the informal sector throughout the developing and developed worlds.[1]

We tend to think of the informal sector as a realm of exchange where the market or marketlike forces animate interaction. People associate, in other words, to buy and sell goods. Buying and selling, however, do not take place in a political vacuum. They are embedded in a wider sphere of social life in which people act together to build institutions and forge modes of activity that shape the boundaries, meaning, and character of exchange. Cultural and gendered understandings of work illuminate the behaviors and institutions that order communal life beyond the market. Clearly, market forces are influenced by other interests, values, and patterns of behavior. Too often, we distort analyses of the informal sector by isolating exchange from the larger social, cultural, and political context within which the informal sector functions.

In the study of women in the informal sector, the limits or distortions of conventional economic and quantitative approaches become apparent. A classic example is traditional economic frameworks that assume that unremunerated work, such as housekeeping, should not be included as national income because the lack of a paid exchange of goods and services makes it economically insignificant.[2] Yet when homemakers or home workers no longer perform the critical tasks of child rearing, cooking, cleaning, and day care, societies develop enterprises that pay people for such services. The treatment of unpaid domestic labor remains a contentious issue for economists and policy makers, as well as women around the globe.

Analytic categories often exclude groups of people who have been defined, for a variety of reasons, as marginal. The elusive nature of certain economic activities gave rise to the term *informal sector*, as microstudies of urban economies revealed labor that was not enumerated by macroeconomic instruments. The alternative term *invisible economy* has been adopted by scholars to emphasize previously unacknowledged economic activities that are not recorded and registered by government authorities for purposes of regulation. Castells and Portes argue that the informal economy is "not an individual condition but a process of income-generation characterized by one central feature: it is unregulated by the institutions of society, in a legal and social environment in which similar activities are regulated."[3]

Yet, if it is lack of regulation that defines the informal economy, then the informal sector is an inherently political phenomenon, since the decision not to regulate economic activities is as political as the decision in favor of regulation. Political elites who change regulatory behavior automatically change the parameters of the informal economy and its relationship to the formal economy.[4] Economic regulations are designed by elites to promote certain ends, and when informal economic activities manage to escape, avoid, or circumvent those regulations, there are political, as well as economic, ramifications. The fiscal capability of the state itself is at risk when its ability to collect taxes is weakened by informal economic activity. Massive sums circulating in informal economies may be responsible for changing class relations and the economic balance of power within a given polity.

Whether a man or woman engages in specific activities purposely to elude the reach of the state, there are political consequences of participation in an economy in which the organizational logic is to avoid the state. Regardless of individual intentions, the informal economy, in the aggregate, is political in nature. When economies are organized around evading the state, the institutions that spring up to facilitate that evasion can be used also to support opposition politics and to further the political preferences and norms of the community. Communal institutions in the informal sector serve to order and regulate its behavior, even if that regulation is not legally codified.

The economic resources that remain within communities rather than ending up in state coffers can be used to further community ends. One of the most important institutions in many informal sectors of the Middle East, specifically in Egypt, is informal networks that help organize financial interests. A microstudy of the popular sector in Cairo, the *sha'b*, reveals how networks serve as an institutional grid in lower-income communities. While this institutional grid is invisible and operates outside a juridical, formal order, it is by no means insignificant. Operating within an authoritarian political system that seeks to exclude men and women from formal political participation, informal networks in Egypt serve the collective interests of excluded groups. The informal economy and informal politics operate in tandem and are mutually reinforcing. It is crucial to see the informal economic sector within a larger institutional framework and a specific political context where the Egyptian state regulates both politics and the economy with a heavy hand.

In the 1970s, Egypt embarked on a move away from its socialist-oriented statist-led economic model and launched the *Infitah*, or Open Door Economic Policy, in 1974. President Sadat's government hoped this new economic regime would attract international and domestic private capital to jump-start Egypt's economy after the stagnation of the late 1960s and early 1970s. The consequences of the Infitah have been debated from a wide spectrum of ideological perspectives.[5] Both its critics and supporters would agree that significant economic and political changes have occurred in Egypt as a consequence of the Open Door Policy, including the growth of an informal economy.

Women and men depend upon informal networks which penetrate both formal and informal economic sectors. Women, who have less access to formal economic and political institutions, rely on networks to link them to other households, markets, bureaucracies, businesses, politicians, and public goods and services. Participation in the informal economy and in institutions that order the informal sector provides critical resources for women. If women's role in the informal sector is to be made visible, common accounts of the marginalized position of Egyptian women must be revised.

The Case Study

This chapter draws upon my study of one small community within the sha'bi, or popular sector, in Cairo. An examination of the economic participation of men and women in this community contributes to an understanding of the issues and frustrations confronting Egyptians today, particularly those who live with financial insecurity and have a lower social status. Conventional macroeconomics and elite political analysis has continually ignored not only the contributions of women but of the lower stratum of society as well.

In Egypt, the term *sha'b* refers to a collective people or folk. The adjective *sha'bi* refers to a wide range of indigenous practices, tastes, and patterns of behavior in everyday life. The indigenous nature of things *sha'bi* is key to its meaning among Egyptians. Wealthier, more Westernized Egyptians, in order to distinguish themselves and their way of life, use the term to describe the mainstream population.[6]

Although sha'bi behavior is more common to lower-income communities in Egypt, the word is not synonymous with lower class, since there is class heterogeneity within sha'bi neighborhoods. Skilled workers, owners of artisanal workshops and factories, lower-level professionals and civil servants, merchants, and traders live and work side by side. However, these men and women are disadvantaged in comparison with middle- and upper-class Egyptians. They tend to fall between the poor and the middle class, and they struggle continually with economic scarcity as they seek upward mobility. While millionaires and wealthy people live in sha'bi neighborhoods because they prefer the lifestyle or the proximity to their workplaces and kin, they are not numerous. More common residents are families that have prospered enough to purchase apartments in more middle-class Westernized neighborhoods yet do not want to cut themselves off from the social solidarities and lifestyle of sha'bi neighborhoods.

This study, conducted within households and workplaces in ten largely contiguous neighborhoods in Cairo, examined both women and men because such a methodology can uncover the ways in which gender impinges upon economic issues. A study of women exclusively is as distorting as a male-centric view of society or politics. In Egypt, men and women are in constant interaction, although prevailing gender ideologies serve to segregate men and women in certain activities.

The study was conducted during 1985–86, although residence in Egypt for several other years and subsequent trips also inform this research. There were nine independent introductions to the group of people I interacted with and interviewed, which eventually grew to 350 men, women, and children[7] (197 males and 153 females).[8] I have characterized these 350 people as a community because of their associations and networks. From the larger group, I constructed a subsample of the economically active population: 171 men and 121 women.[9] Living in households and visiting homes and workplaces brought to light many economic activities not usually captured by a national census because of methodological and administrative problems.[10]

Economic analyses that fail to go beyond visible activities and conventional methodologies severely underrepresent both the existence of the informal sector and the participation of women in both formal and informal economies. This study first examined the economically active population of the community through a fairly conventional occupational, industrial, and public/private sectoral analysis. The study divided the private sector further into self-employment and familial enterprises. This differentiation is particularly important when examining the participation of women in the economy since many of their activities involve the household as a site of production, in direct and indirect ways. Besides primary sources of income, there is an overwhelming number of secondary sources of income within this community, and many others like it throughout Egypt.[11] By examining secondary and tertiary sources of income, my study was able to capture the economic activity of this community more accurately and to uncover participation in the invisible economy.[12] Since many sources of secondary and tertiary income are technically illegal, people do not describe them to census enumerators, and national labor statistics severely underestimate secondary and tertiary employment. For example, it is technically illegal for public-sector employees to hold an additional job, although the practice is pervasive. Many self-employed people do not fully report primary or secondary income to the tax authorities. Even though noncash exchanges of goods and services are important to the household economy, they are rarely reported or recorded in census data.[13] This lack of reporting limits our understanding of the informal sector and of the Egyptian economy in general.[14]

I reexamined my economically active sample using Abdel-Fadil's occupationally based methodology of classifying informal economic activities, in addition to other criteria (discussed later).[15] This reexamination revealed the pervasiveness of the informal sector in this community: informal employment accounted for 38 percent of the primary sources of income of the economically active sample; it accounted for 87 percent of the secondary sources of income; and it totaled 71 percent of the tertiary sources of income. These figures refer to the economically active part of the population (the employed and unemployed) as opposed to the inactive part of the population (students, pension recipients, retired persons, housewives, and undefined economic activity). Most important, 62 percent of the community was engaged in informal economic activity in either the primary, secondary, or tertiary form.

Of the economically active sample (both men and women), 10 percent were women engaged in informal-sector activity as primary sources of income, and 21 percent were women engaged in informal activity as secondary sources. Among women in the economically active sample, 31 percent worked in the informal sector as a primary occupation, and an overwhelming 88 percent worked in the informal sector as a secondary occupation. Thirty-eight percent of all women in the sample (121) were economically dependent on the informal sector, where they gained income in cash or in kind. While more men than women were engaged in the informal sector, the sector provided a critical share of economic resources for women.

The employment of women in the informal sector is but one dimension of the informal economic sphere. Far more women are engaged in the informal sector than the previous figures suggest, through participation in its institutional and political aspects. Women create and maintain informal networks, participate in informal savings associations, and mold a communal ethos that regulates aspects of the informal economy.

The Informal Sector

While there has been a recent proliferation of studies on the informal sector, a great deal of interdisciplinary research is still needed. For many reasons, the number of employees, the production, and the extent of small-scale enterprises, microenterprises, and informal-sector enterprises remain difficult to estimate.[16] Yet, the proportion of informal-sector employment described in this chapter supports various estimates of the significant and growing size of this sector and its influence on the direction of the Egyptian economy and polity.

Research on the informal sector of the economy is plagued by debates about definitions, measurements, and enumerator training. There are challenges to the validity of national statistics, in which the measurement techniques do not capture a great deal of economic activity.[17] Handoussa has suggested that the informal sector accounted for 43 percent of all private nonagricultural employment in Egypt in 1986.[18] However, the definition of the informal sector used relies only on a size criterion; any establishment that employs fewer than ten workers is labeled informal. This understanding of the informal sector is quite imprecise, since many such establishments pay taxes, follow appropriate legislation for their industry and occupation, and are registered by various authorities. In a recent study of the informal sector that examines the corpus of macro and micro research in Egypt, Rizk presents the range of these estimates: "In 1986, estimates by Birks and Sinclair were 878,000; Abdel-Fadil 876,000;[19] Charmes, 2,281,000. For 1985, the number rises to about 3 million, according to CAPMAS."[20] Nader Fergany estimates that informal-sector employment, using the same "size per establishment" criterion, has grown from 2,434,000 in 1980 to 2,887,000 in 1985.[21] Rizk criticizes size of establishments as the definition for the informal sector adopted by these researchers and suggests the criterion of nonregistration. Although this criterion may be more appropriate, she too has to revert to the size criterion because the data on registration are not available, and her estimate of informal-sector employment based on 1976 figures (2,416,000) is just as imprecise.[22]

Microstudies, on the other hand, have offered new insights into the organization, management, and size of the informal sector, though their results are not generalizable. A 1985 study by the Central Agency for Planning, Mobilisation and Statistics (CAPMAS) of urban and rural settings defined the informal sector as "'those non-financial activities which break the laws regulating businesses and labor' and which deliberately sidestep the requirement to keep account books."[23] This study found that families were quite prominent in the management and financing of the informal sector, since "in 32 percent of the cases the business was inherited."[24] Another recent study by the National Center for Social and Criminological Research (NCSCR) of Ma'ruuf quarter in the 'Abdin district in downtown Cairo estimated that 35 percent of all economic activities were part of the informal sector. They defined the informal sector as small units, with limited capital and employees (less than £E10,000 and fewer than ten employees), whose operators do not keep accounts and pay a fee in lieu of a tax.[25] In an earlier study of the small-scale private industrial sector in Fayyum and Qalyubia governorates, which surveyed industrial establishments, handicrafts, and domestic production in small towns and rural areas in these two provinces, the authors found that 99 percent of the establishments, or 94,000 enterprises, employed fewer than ten workers. In the artisanal sector, the employed or self-employed totaled 140,000 men and women in these two provinces alone. But through a creative and painstaking analysis of various sources of data covering the entire nation, Abdel-

Fadil estimated that only 241,498 people comprised the artisanal sector throughout all of Egypt in 1977.[26] It seems highly unlikely that 58 percent of the entire artisanal sector was concentrated in two governorates. Rather the Fayyum and Qalyubia study probably captured a much higher percentage of very small-scale domestic and handicraft producers than did the Abdel-Fadil study.[27] Few of these studies focus upon the role of women in the informal economy or disaggregate their figures by sex.

Abdel-Fadil's pioneering study of the informal sector in Egypt used criteria for classification that were a compromise between standard definitions and particular features of the Egyptian economy.[28] To facilitate comparison with other studies, my analysis of informal-sector employment began with Abdel-Fadil's occupationally based classification, which include the artisanal segment, the informal services segment, and the odd-jobbers segment.[29] Based on these occupational categories and on my familiarity with most of the 292 people in the community studied, I defined the following sources of income as informal: (1) income that was unreported to tax officials (in cases such as public-sector employees with two jobs, self-employed people not registered with the proper authorities, or unregistered workers in family enterprises); (2) economic activity that was illegal (drug dealing, black market sales, or bribery); or (3) economic activity that was unregulated and thus outside the formal economy (such as child labor, home production of food products, or secondary production of industrial enterprises, such as trading in raw materials).

Among the economically active sample in my study, 38 percent were engaged in informal economic activity as a primary source of income. An even more significant segment of the active population, 87 percent, were engaged in informal-sector economic activity as a secondary source of income (table 20). Among those employed in a secondary occupation, a person was approximately six-and-a-half times more likely to be employed in the informal than in the formal sector. Among the total of 292 economically active persons in this sample, approximately 62 percent were engaged in informal-sector activities in at least one of their primary, secondary, or tertiary economic activities.

Table 20. Economic Activity among the Active Population of the Economically Active Sample (Percentages)

	Primary	Secondary	Tertiary
Informal	38	87	71
Formal	62	13	29

Tables 21 and 22 demonstrate that most informal-sector activity was concentrated in family enterprises and self-employment within this community. These two segments of the private sector comprised 68 percent of informal-sector activity among primary occupations and 65 percent among secondary occupations. Self-employment constituted almost half of all secondary employment in the informal sector. Family enterprises were largely semi-industrial enterprises or trading and commercial concerns in this community. It was somewhat uncommon for women to be employed in such firms unless they owned them. This difference can be partially explained by a preference among both men and women in the community that women obtain secure appointment in the public sector or a position in a private-sector firm or organization. For educated women, the public sector offered job security, a higher social status, government benefits such as generous maternity leave, a low but steady wage, and a relatively short and undemanding work day.[30] In contrast, the women who were self-employed as a primary income source were among the least educated members of the community. They largely provided services or were engaged in legal and illegal petty trade and commodity production.

There were only minor differences between primary and secondary categories in the distribution of informal sector activity by industry. Manufac-

Table 21. Informal Economic Activity in Private Sector, Primary Occupation (N = 83)

	Male	Female	Total	Percentage
Private enterprise	22	3	25	30
Family enterprise	30	10	40	48
Self-employed	10	7	17	21
Retired	1	0	1	1
Totals	63	20	83	100

Table 22. Informal Economic Activity in Private Sector, Secondary Occupation (N = 116)

	Male	Female	Total	Percentage
Private enterprise	23	8	31	27
Family enterprise	22	10	32	27
Self-employed	41	12	53	46
Totals	86	30	116	100

turing, trade, and community, social, and personal services remained the most heavily represented industries in secondary occupations, although the manufacturing sector decreased in secondary occupations and the trading sector increased slightly. This pattern can be explained by the common practice among proprietors of artisanal workshops who gained their primary source of income by investing their profits in the trade of raw materials and other commodities (legal and illegal). Many of these proprietors preferred to "work" surpluses in the market than to save them in the formal banking sector.

From data in the study I constructed ratios that suggest gendered preferences for formal and informal economic activity. In primary economic activity, the ratio of men in formal-sector employment to those in informal-sector employment equaled 1.44, while the ratio for women was 2.4. Women opted for formal-sector employment more than men for a variety of reasons. The public sector offers women secure employment, health care, retirement benefits, a generous maternity policy, and periodic promotions. While the wages of lower-level public-sector employees are not very high, the demands on employees are minimal. Women can leave their homes early in the morning and often return home by mid-afternoon. Working for the government is also a safe environment for women, and most men do not object if their wives or daughters work for the state, although they may not allow a daughter to work in a store or factory, where she might be vulnerable to harassment from her employer. Securing a government job typically means that a woman has met certain qualifications, and thus the position brings status, which employment in the informal or private sector does not elicit.

In secondary economic activity however, there was a striking, similarly high propensity for employment or income-generation opportunities in the informal sector among both men and women. Men were engaged in the informal sector over the formal sector by 6.14 to 1 and women by 6.77 to 1. Both men and women often chose informal-sector employment to earn additional, often irregular, income. Many women who were housewives sought employment in the informal sector because they lacked qualifications for the formal sector, and their domestic responsibilities did not allow them to work full-time (of the twenty-eight women who worked in the informal sector as a secondary occupation, ten were housewives as a primary occupation). Women who worked primarily in their homes had greater access to informal-sector activities located in their neighborhoods or perhaps within family enterprises. Among the group of ten housewives who worked in the informal sector as a secondary occupation were a textile worker, two participants in family enterprises in the lemon trade, a marriage broker, a peddler or *dallaala*, a black marketer who largely sold food obtained from government cooperatives, a barber's assistant, and a woman who prepared food for her husband to peddle on the street. (In their primary occupations, three were self-employed, one worked in the private sector, and six worked in family enterprises). These employment patterns do not reflect employment preferences as much as access to certain sources of income.

Despite the pressures of domestic responsibilities, the participation of women in the labor force was much higher in my sample than national rates indicate. During the years 1976–82, according to official national statistics (the decennial population census and annual labor force surveys), the overall female labor force participation rate was approximately 6 percent.[31] In 1986 the rate rose to 8.9 percent. The World Fertility Survey (1980) estimated that 75.3 percent of "ever-married women" between the ages of fifteen and forty-nine had never worked.[32]

According to preliminary results of the 1986 population census, female participation in overall urban employment is only 16 percent and in rural employment, 4 percent.[33] Efforts in the last decade to redesign census questionnaires and standard conceptions of employment and work have improved the precision of figures for the labor force participation of women in Egypt and throughout the world.[34] The higher rates of participation in the labor force in my sample can be explained by familiarity with the various economic activities of these women, repeated visits to many of their households, knowledge of their financial affairs, a full year as the reference period, and a much lower minimum work-time criterion. (Only activities performed regularly were counted, but no minimum hours/week criterion was possible.)

Many of the women in the sample who were seamstresses, leaders of savings associations, or involved in the black market would not describe their activity for classification as a profession (*mihna*), as a permanent, often government, position (*waziifa*) or as work (*shughl*), particularly to an unknown government official, such as a census enumerator. To administer

Table 23. Labor Force Participation among Women in the Economically Active Sample (*N* = 121)

Primary economic activity	56%
Secondary economic activity	27%
Either primary or secondary activity	71%

the Egyptian fertility survey, census enumerators were instructed to ask women whether they sold things, held jobs, worked on a family farm, or were self-employed.[35] From my experience in Cairo, many women (and perhaps men) who were economically active would respond negatively to these questions, even though their activities fell under the definition of work used in the survey.[36]

The higher percentage of economically active women in my sample is most likely not a reflection of an unrepresentative or particularly industrious community; rather, it reflects a methodology that captured primary, secondary, and tertiary economic activities and used a more generous reference period and work-time criterion. Men in my sample also participated far more extensively in the labor force than national indicators suggest (approximately 28 percent). Eighty-six percent of the men in the economically active population participated in the labor force in their primary economic activity, 61 percent in the secondary activity, and 98 percent of the men in either primary or secondary activity (meaning that only three men in the sample did not participate in the labor force.)

Table 24 suggests that both the informal and formal sectors of the economy are crucial to employment among the sha'b and that people survive, and at times prosper, by exploiting opportunities in both sectors. People kept their feet in both sectors to reap the particular benefits, status, and wages of each. Table 24 demonstrates that the most common arrangement for people in this community was to hold a permanent, legal, registered job in the formal economy and to earn additional income in the informal economy.

The informal sector is not marginal to the community nor a last resort for an unemployable or unskilled population. A majority of this community, 62 percent, depends on the informal sector for economic support. Thirty-eight percent of all women in the community were supported by the informal economy. This sha'bi community is as dependent on the informal sector as on the formal one and is thus sensitive and vulnerable to any changes in employment opportunities in either sector.

Table 24. Employment Combinations in Informal Sector

Combination	Number
1. Formal primary–informal secondary	57
2. Informal primary–formal secondary	1
3. Formal primary–formal secondary	14
4. Informal primary–informal secondary	27

The Institutional Dimension of Informality

The invisible economy is only one dimension of the informal sector in Egypt. The more political and institutional dimension of informality provides an institutional grid for women from the lower strata of society who have few other collective institutions to represent their interests. Women work with relatives, neighbors, colleagues, business contacts, bureaucrats, and local community figures to find employment for relatives, an apartment for an engaged couple, a source of inexpensive commodities, or a good teacher who can provide private tutoring for a child. Both women and men are constantly engaged with associates in their networks to achieve their ends. It is commonly understood that there is a formal and an informal face to any bureaucratic problem. Networks facilitate the complicated procedures in many realms of everyday life that would be routine in other societies.

Informal networks break down barriers between public and private worlds where gender ideologies and communal norms prescribe behavior. Networks begin in households and link households to each other before they weave in and out of local shops, markets, industries, schools, service establishments, and politicians' and bureaucrats' offices. By using networks, women can partially transcend socially constructed barriers to their mobility.

Reciprocity is an implicit and at times explicit aspect of informal networks; information, services, or favors are noted and repaid when the opportunity presents itself. Incorporating people with diverse characteristics into networks increases their utility. Being able to find subsidized goods in local markets may be as useful in an everyday sense as knowing a member of parliament who may be able to procure a subsidized apartment for his or her constituents. All types of contacts—wealthy or impoverished, professionals, artisans, police, and marriage brokers—can be useful to people who devote considerable time and resources to fulfilling their needs under conditions of scarcity. Some networks even lie beyond the national boundaries of Egypt as men and women migrate abroad, conduct business abroad, or arrange marriages while the groom or bride is abroad.

The Egyptian bureaucracy is felt by the sha'b on an almost daily basis. They take their ration books to buy chickens, detergent, or lentils from government cooperatives at subsidized prices, often waiting hours in the hot sun. In the following example, a young woman details her numerous visits to government offices to register as an employee with a private voluntary organization (PVO); the organization administered a day-care center where she had received a job offer (the result of informal networks, since her mother was an administrator at the PVO). During this exhausting process, the young woman realized the importance of informal networks.

First, in order to prepare the papers I had a *fiish w-tashbiih* [a declaration issued at a police station confirming residence in an area and the lack of an arrest record]. Then I went to get a copy of my birth certificate at the civil registry within the police station. The employee there said to come back tomorrow. I took the paper and returned the next day. He again said to come back tomorrow. When I went there the next day, he said my papers could not be processed because the date of birth was wrong. It was correct, but he was just lying to me, laughing at me. So I went the next day and told him the date was correct. He said to return tomorrow, at 1:00 P.M., because he was about to leave. When I returned the next day at that time he was turning out the lights and again told me to return the next day. When I returned, he told me that he couldn't find my name in the file and to come back the next day to see the person who specializes in birth certificates.

I went the next day and he said that my mother's name was in the dossier but that my name was torn off. "Is that my fault?" I asked. "It's the fault of those employees, not mine. After all this effort and work, you can't find the names?" He said that it wasn't his fault either and that he would prepare other papers that I had to purchase from the post office first. I stayed home for two days, realizing that he wanted money before he would process my papers. But I didn't know how to offer him money. Perhaps he would take the money, perhaps not. If he didn't and was insulted he could make my life difficult and send me to hell.

This young woman then sought the help of a friend's father, who knew a policeman in the local station, and arranged for the policeman to solve the problem of the missing birth certificate through several other costly visits to bureaucratic offices. Finally, she had the proper papers and returned to the civil registry.

At 8:00 A.M. I returned, and he stamped the paper to send it to the Ministry of Health for approval. Then he said that I should come back in twenty-five days. Nearly a month! I asked what I was supposed to do in the interim. He said that the law requires this. I said, "Is that my fault, those are your laws and your regulations." He said, "It's not in my hands, what do you want me to do?" I had made all that effort, all those visits, and tired myself out, and all of this was because he wanted money out of me. The paperwork could have taken an hour to finish but they want your money.

This young woman had visited these offices nine times over a period of eleven days. Despite her best efforts to exploit informal networks at the police station and registry, she was unsuccessful and still had to wait for some time for her papers to be processed, in order to receive payment in her new job. She had few expectations of government efficiency or due process, but still blamed herself for not mastering the art of informal politics.

Because the state regulates so many aspects of the economy, people create alternative institutions to "work" the bureaucracy in their favor or to circumvent it. It is in this dance with school officials, labor ministries, the police, and the courts that informal networks can be useful in accomplishing certain objectives, though they are not necessarily efficient. The informal economy thrives, on the one hand, as Egyptians try to avoid, circumvent, or manipulate the interventionary role of the Egyptian state in the economy. Yet, on the other hand, because of the growing economic pressures on the Egyptian state, it tacitly encourages, or at least allows, the informal economy to grow, since the informal economy provides goods and services and contributes to the gross national product.

In an analysis of the statist policies of the Egyptian government under President Nasser, Migdal argued that Egypt's strong society had been able to subvert or circumscribe critical state policies and initiatives despite its heavily interventionist economic policies and political repression.[37] I would argue that in the 1980s the invisible economy further neutralized many initiatives from the state. Informal networks, designed to remain invisible, out of sight of those with the power of coercion, gave the sha'b some access to economic and political resources and some power to achieve their ends. Networks are thus an informal arena of politics, albeit an intentionally invisible, amorphous, and flexible collective institution. Furthermore, since so many activities within the informal economy are illegal, extralegal, or irregular, it is the informal sphere of networks, not the formal, official sphere of the state, that organizes, facilitates, and orders the informal economy.

For example, without the level of trust necessary to ensure the reciprocity of informal networks, naked self-interest would mitigate against any collective activity on the part of the sha'b. Women and men rely on the familial ethos to ensure that individuals subscribe to communal morals and preferences. The familial ethos, fashioned by the sha'b, supports channels of arbitration, conflict resolution, economic assistance, and cooperation within the community, as well as the reproduction of the family (or marriage and children). Clifford Geertz describes an ethos as "the moral (and aesthetic) aspects of a given culture, the evaluative elements. . . . A people's ethos is the tone, character, and quality of their life, its moral and aesthetic style and mood; it is the underlying attitude toward themselves and their world that life reflects."[38] Geertz sets an ethos in a distinctly cultural context, and I would not diminish its cultural meaning, but an ethos is also a product of economic and political dynamics. This chapter's arguments about the significance of the familial ethos have to be placed within a context of financial insecurity, considerable government intervention in the economy, and a tradition of political exclusion in Egypt.

An ethos of cooperation, arbitration, and association with trusted individuals, which promotes a certain code of morality and propriety, is part of the realities of everyday life among the sha'b. The Egyptian government, through its legal system, ideology, executive power, and intervention in the economy, also promotes its own vision of justice, development, the good, and propriety. Its public relations vehicles attempt to influence values and norms in Egypt as well, so that a certain tension between communal norms and official norms and priorities pervades daily life within sha'bi communities. "Politics, power and control are not of necessity coterminous with the state," as Chazan argues, and communities that are oppressed both politically and economically struggle to control resources and to promote their authority and their vision of the good.[39]

A community's understanding of the good, of justice and fairness, based on a widely shared consensus of values and norms, can serve as the foundation of a wider-reaching political and philosophical outlook. There may be a convergence between the familial ethos at the local level and the way in which the sha'b judge national events and politics and envision a better Egypt. A communal philosophy can set the parameters for theory construction and praxis. Sheldon Wolin explains how creating alternative norms and visions has an implicit political dimension that sets the ground for challenges to the prevailing order.

> Theoretical founding has both a political dimension and politics. The former is the constitute activity of laying down basic and general principles, which, when legitimated, become the presuppositions of practices, the ethos of practitioners. The point of engaging in the politics of theory is to demonstrate the superiority of one set of constitutive principles over another so that in the future these will be recognized as the basis of theoretical inquiry. Thus the founder's action prepares the way for inquiry, that is, for activity which can proceed uninterruptedly because its presuppositions are not in dispute.

The familial ethos in sha'bi communities, then, is quite powerful. It orders individual lives, sets parameters of behavior in the community, and shapes the political vision of many Egyptian citizens. Like all other structures, the family is not wholly benevolent or harmless, and the familial ethos is deeply contested within the community. It is an ideal shaped by an ever-changing variety of new material, social, and political forces.[40]

Informal Savings Associations

It is the cooperative aspects of the familial ethos and the mutual trust among members of networks that have created informal savings associations, or *gam'iyyaat*. In a savings association, a small number of associates contribute a fixed sum to the leader at a regular interval; some associations are daily or weekly, particularly among merchants, but more commonly they are monthly. At each interval, the leader gives the collected money immediately to one participant, in a lump sum. The order of the lump sum payment to each member is agreed upon ahead of time. For example, if an association is organized among ten participants, each making a monthly contribution of £E 50 for a period of one year, each month one member of the association receives £E 500.

Such associations are not profit-making, the leader of the association does not claim a fee or salary, and participants are not charged any interest fees. While many members of the community have bank accounts in public- and private-sector banks, they are under no obligation to make regular deposits. (In addition, since formal interest rates hardly keep pace with inflation, there is little incentive to use the banking system.)[41] However, once a person is committed to participating in a gam'iyya, he or she must make regular payments for the duration of the association. These associations, therefore, promote a savings ethic in the community. The logic of the gam'iyya is similar to that of a Christmas club in the United States, a structured program offered by banks to customers to require saving for a specific goal under time constraints. In many societies throughout the world, similar associations, known as rotating savings and credit associations (ROSCAs), provide important financial services for women and men.[42]

The money saved in these associations circulates and is reinvested in the community, through purchases of jewelry, housing, furniture, or dowries for the critically important social goal of marriage. Gam'iyyaat lie completely outside the formal banking sector and outside government regulation or taxation. While such associations have existed for several decades, perhaps longer, they have recently acquired a new importance in this community as financial recession increasingly pressures households who aspire to a middle-class lifestyle. Yet informal savings associations, despite their importance to sha'bi communities, have remained hidden from national accounts, and deserve much greater attention from scholars, particularly economists and historians.[43] Standard analyses of the Egyptian economy rarely make reference to informal savings associations, either as a source of credit or as a vehicle for savings.

It can be argued that women are really the people's bankers of Egypt, since women, far more than men, organize and maintain gam'iyyat. Men, the traditional breadwinners, are more familiar with the formal banking system and other financial institutions in the business community. Women in sha'bi communities, often not wage earners, carefully save small sums from their household budget and participate in savings associations with close relatives, friends, or colleagues. As women join the labor force in greater numbers and become involved in their own business ventures, they are "working" their income in ROSCAs. People in sha'bi communities seek out women who have a reputation for honesty to organize savings associations. It is said that these women (and occasionally men) organize such associations for altruistic reasons, informed by a religious ethic that promotes cooperation and trust within the Muslim community and that forbids interest charges.[44]

Even men and women who have no immediate need to save money participate in savings associations so as to maintain a good credit rating. One woman participated in four gam'iyyaat, contributing only one-fifth of a £E 25 monthly share to each one, solely for the reason of maintaining a broad financial network. Clearly, ROSCAs have become institutionalized in Egypt and have grown more sophisticated as the leaders allow several people to finance a single membership. This behavior is similar to financiers who place their assets in several banks or securities to diversify their portfolio, enhance their financial networks, and minimize risk.

In a crisis, close friends or relatives form a new gam'iyya on behalf of someone unfortunate, who then receives the first lump sum payment. One of the women in the community who had been organizing gam'iyyaat for the previous thirty years first organized a savings association at the request of her landlord, who was adding an additional floor to his building for his son's marital apartment. After the gam'iyya ended, impressed with her skill, the landlord asked her to start another one, this time to finance his loan payments to a bank. Shortly thereafter a colleague's money was stolen, directly before one of the most important Muslim holidays, when the head of the household incurs considerable expense. The woman organized a gam'iyya on his behalf and gave him the first payment, and in the same way she helped another colleague to pay for her mother's costly funeral expenses.

Constant saving year after year by many families can build up considerable sums, even among people with low incomes. One woman who participated in three gam'iyyaat saved a total of £E 160 per month on an official salary of £E 50 a month, a pension of £E 55, and £E 70 from a temporary source of income, leaving her family £E 15 a month for their expenses. Other women routinely saved £E 50 per month when they received monthly salaries of the same amount. Their skill in saving money remains somewhat of a mystery, but their success is partially the result of shopping for the best-quality but lowest-priced goods and services. As structural adjustment pressures have increased in Egypt in the late 1980s and 1990s, and as the government has reduced its commitments to subsidized goods and services, Egyptians are less able to save in gam'iyyaat. The result may be downward mobility and increased social tensions (as prohibitive expenses delay marriage further).

Women and men who run informal savings associations are the source of occasional short-term loans as well, which they can usually afford because of the amount of capital circulating in their associations. Because they know the financial status of many people, they are also a vital source of sensitive economic information in the community. At times wives hide their participation in savings associations from their husbands, fearing that their husbands might decrease the size of the household budget (which is the source of their savings). Other men and women save in cooperation with neighbors instead of families because they do not want their families to realize the extent of their financial resources. Men may save money in groups of business associates so that their wives and relatives remain ignorant of their worth.

In summary, 'il-gam'iyya offers an alternate source of financing within the community, but the funds remain within the community and are neither taxed, reported, nor subject to seizure and confiscation. This capital is then used to buy land, housing, or goods or to invest in economic enterprises that improve the standard of living. Without the gam'iyya, people would be far more dependent for credit on the state-controlled banking sector, on moneylenders who demand high interest, and on relatives. It is a key financial institution that performs a vital public service for a constituency that has far less access to, and equity in, formal financial institutions.

Within densely populated sha'bi communities of Cairo, the invisible economy is vibrant and pervasive. Noting its capacity to provide employment and to organize production does not, however, imply a normative position on its relative merits. While a dynamic invisible sector may be seen by some as a harbinger of free-market capitalism, as an engine of growth and employment, others note its hidden costs to both individuals and society at large when workers lack health and pension benefits, corruption is institutionalized, unregulated zoning creates safety and environmental problems, or it is children who work. The economic and political ramifications of a growing invisible economy in Egypt, as well as the local, national, and global forces behind it, cannot be investigated here, but this chapter suggests that there are both economic *and* political ramifications of the invisible economy. Women and men are not only financially dependent on the informal sector, but they have also been engaged in building and sustaining informal political institutions that serve to structure and order this dynamic sector. Women, in particular, are deeply engaged in using informal networks and informal savings associations to further their interests. Such participation in the informal sector, particularly in its collective institutions, adds another dimension to the political activity of Egyptian women beyond the participation of elite and middle-class women in formal political institutions such as electoral politics, opposition politics, or interest groups. Buying and selling do not take place in a political vacuum. Buying and selling within the informal economy have produced informal political institutions that are useful to a wide constituency of voices within Egypt.

Notes

1. Cathy A. Rakowski, *Contrapunto: The Informal Sector Debate in Latin America* (Albany: State University of New York Press, 1994); Manuel Castells and Alejandro Portes, "World Underneath: The Origins, Dynamics, and Effects of the Informal Economy," in *The Informal Economy: Studies in Advanced and Less Developed Countries,* ed. Alejandro Portes, Manuel Castells, and Lauren A. Benton (Baltimore: Johns Hopkins University Press, 1989); A. Lawrence Chickering and Mohamed Salahdine, *The Silent Revolution: The Informal Sector in Five Asian and Near Eastern Countries* (San Francisco: ICS Press, 1991); Dipak Mazumdar, *The Urban Informal Sector,* Working Paper no. 211 (International Bank for Reconstruction and Development, 1975); Hernando de Soto, *The Other Path: The Invisible Revolution in the Third World,* trans. June Abbott (New York: Harper and Row, 1989); and Stuart Henry, ed., *Can I Have It in Cash?: A Study of Informal Institutions and Unorthodox Ways of Doing Things* (London: Astragal Books, 1981).

2. Lourdes Beneria, "Accounting for Women's Work: The Progress of Two Decades," *World Development* 20, no. 11 (1992): 1548.

3. Castells and Portes, "World Underneath," 12.

4. Ibid.

5. John Waterbury, *Egypt under Nasser and Sadat: The Political Economy of Two Regimes* (Princeton: Princeton University Press, 1986); Osama Hamed, "Egypt's Open Door Economic Policy," *International Journal of Middle East Studies* 13 (1981); Ali E. Hilal Dessouki, "Policy-making in Egypt: A Case Study of the Open Door Economic Policy," *Social Problems* 28 (1981): 410–16; Gouda Abd al-Khalek, "The Open Door Economic Policy in Egypt: A Search for Meaning, Interpretation and Implications," *Cairo Papers in Social Science* 2, no.3 (1979): 74–97; Alan Richards, "Ten Years of Infitah: Class, Rent, and Policy Stasis in Egypt," *Journal of Development Studies* 20 (July 1984): 323–38; Bent Hansen and Samir Radwan, *Employment Opportunities and Equity in a Changing Economy: Egypt in the 1980s* (Geneva: International Labour Office, 1982); Tim Mitchell, "America's Egypt: Discourse of the Development Industry," *Middle East Report* 169 (March–April 1991): 18–36.

6. A similar but distinct adjective, *baladi,* is associated somewhat more with one's place of origin and way of life. Egyptians use *al-balad*, the noun, to mean country and nation, but the same word also means village or town. An *Ibn al-balad* is a "son of the soil," a true, trusted, and sincere Egyptian "salt of the earth," with the best of connotations. Thus the term *baladi* has a more provincial connotation, since it is associated with the countryside and its peasantry, although it also describes the values and lifestyle of people who, perhaps generations ago, moved into urban areas in Egypt. See S. al-Messiri, *Ibn al-Baladi: A Concept of Egyptian Identity* (London: E. J. Brill, 1978).

7. Eleven of the sample who were under the age of fifteen were included in the sample either because they worked (seven of the eleven) or were otherwise central to an important event or problem in the community. The economically active population includes five boys and one girl under the age of fifteen, who worked as apprentices in local industries (the girl was unemployed but seeking employment as a seamstress in local establishments). In Egypt the Central Agency for Public Mobilisation and Statistics (CAPMAS) includes persons twelve to sixty-four years of age in its surveys of Egypt's economically active population. *Statistical Sources and Methods,* vol. 3: *Economically Active Population, Employment, Unemployment and Hours of Work Household Surveys* (Geneva: International Labour Office, 1986), 49.

8. The plurality of men in the sample can be partially explained by introductions made by several men to local merchants and manufacturers. I interviewed most of the employees in several workshops, thereby creating a slight gender imbalance, since few women were employed in these small, largely industrial workshops. For further methodological issues surrounding this research and discussion of the field sites, see Diane Singerman, *Avenues of Participation: Family, Politics, and Networks in Urban Quarters of Cairo* (Princeton: Princeton University Press, 1995).

9. According to the United Nations system of national accounts and balances, the economically active population "comprises all persons of either sex who furnish

the supply of labour for the production of economic goods and services . . . during a specified time-reference period"; *Statistical Sources and Methods,* 183. In my study the reference period was from September 1985 to August 1986. Fifty-eight people in the larger sample were excluded from the economically active sample because they were students who had no economic activity; or people whose occupational and employment status were unknown to me; or inhabitants of a village in the Delta that I had visited who were important to the larger sample but were excluded from the smaller sample since it had a Cairene focus.

10. In the sample the production of economic goods and services included "all production and processing of primary products, whether for the market, for barter or for own consumption, the production of all goods and services for the market and, in the case of households which produce such goods and services for the market, the corresponding production for own consumption"; ibid.

11. The primary source of income in this study was either the official position of employment (which was registered with various government agencies) or the occupation or income-generating activity by which workers in the informal economy described themselves. Secondary sources of income usually referred to part-time jobs, "moonlighting," and semiregular employment or income-generating activities. Tertiary sources of income were rarer and included in-kind exchange and self-employment that generated income for men and women. Primary sources of income were not always the most lucrative, although they tended to be more consistent and more secure than secondary or tertiary sources.

12. While the primary sources of income for the sample were known, I did not know the secondary occupations of ninety-three people, or roughly a third of the community, because of my inability to visit the homes and workplaces of everyone in the sample. Although I was unaware of other sources of income, they may have existed.

13. Homa Hoodfar, "Survival Strategies in Low Income Neighbourhoods of Cairo, Egypt" (Ph.D. dissertation, University of Kent, 1988).

14. National accounts data related to subsidiary occupations and the income received by the self-employed are "completely lacking"; Mohaya A. Zaytoun, "Earnings and the Cost of Living: An Analysis of Recent Developments in the Egyptian Economy," in *Employment and Structural Adjustment: Egypt in the 1990s,* ed. Heba Handoussa and Gillian Potter (Cairo: American University in Cairo Press, 1991), 220.

15. See Mahmoud Abdel-Fadil, *Informal Sector Employment in Egypt,* Series on Employment Opportunities and Equity in Egypt, no. 1 (Geneva: International Labour Office, 1980), 4.

16. For further discussion of these ambiguities, see Soad Kamel Rizk, "The Structure and Operation of the Informal Sector in Egypt," in *Employment and Structural Adjustment,* 167–88, and Mostafa Kharoufi, "The Informal Dimension of Urban Activity in Egypt: Some Recent Work," *Cairo Papers in Social Science* 14 (Winter 1991): 8–20.

17. See Kharoufi, "Informal Dimension of Urban Activity in Egypt," for a comprehensive review of micro and macro studies of the informal sector in Egypt and the methodological and definitional issues that researchers have been trying to overcome.

18. Handoussa, "Crisis and Challenge," 17.

19. In order to arrive at his estimates, Abdel-Fadil designated certain occupations and branches of economic activity, enumerated in national data collected by various ministries, as informal sector employment; Abdel-Fadil, "Informal Sector Employment in Egypt."

20. Rizk, "Structure and Operation," 171.

21. Nader Fergany, "A Characterisation of the Employment Problem in Egypt," in Employment and Structural Adjustment, 36, as cited by Rizk, "Structure and Operation," 173.

22. Rizk, "Structure and Operation," 171.

23. CAPMAS, "A Study on the Labor Market in Egypt: The Unorganized Sector" (Cairo: CAPMAS, June 1985), as cited by Kharoufi, "Informal Dimension," 12.

24. Ibid., 13.

25. Al-Mahdi and Mashhur, "The Informal Sector in Egypt," as cited by Kharoufi, "Informal Dimension," 13.

26. Abdel-Fadil, "Informal Sector Employment in Egypt," 12.

27. Mahmoud Badr et al., Small Scale Enterprises in Egypt: Fayoum and Kalyubiya Governorates, Phase 1 Survey Results, Rural Development Working Paper, no. 23 (Michigan State University, 1982).

28. Although I made partial use of this approach to define informal sector activities, many small workshops (one to nine workers) are not necessarily informal, but are licensed, pay taxes, and are properly registered with Ministry of Labor and the Department of Social Affairs. On the other hand, although I could distinguish which workplaces employed fewer than nine workers, I did not know the legal history of these workplaces. For this reason, I fell back upon the less precise method of classification.

29. See Abdel-Fadil, Informal Sector Employment in Egypt, 4.

30. For a more complete examination of working women in Egypt, see Arlene Macleod, Accommodating Protest: Working Women, the New Veiling, and Change in Cairo (New York: Columbia University Press, 1991); Hoodfar, "Survival Strategies"; and Barbara Ibrahim, "Family Strategies: A Perspective on Women's Entry to the Labour Force Participation in Egypt," International Journal of the Family 11 (1981).

31. Richard Anker and Martha Anker, "Measuring the Female Labour Force in Egypt," International Labour Review 128 (1989): 512.

32. CAPMAS, Egyptian Fertility Survey (1980), 4 vols. Fertility and Family Planning, vol. 2 (Cairo: CAPMAS, 1983), 9.

33. The rate of female participation in the public sector is somewhat higher, at

22 percent (30 percent of local government, 23 percent in government service authorities, and 11 percent in public enterprises). The overall rate of labor force participation in Egypt is only 28.4 percent; Handoussa, "Crisis and Challenge," 49–50, 79.

34. For a comprehensive analysis of definitional, methodological, and administrative questions about female participation in the labor force within the Middle East, see Hoda Zurayk, "Women's Economic Participation," in *Population Factors in Development Planning in the Middle East,* ed. Frederic C. Shorter and Huda Zurayk (New York: The Population Council, 1985), 3–58. A CAPMAS pilot study to improve collection of data on female labor force participation captured a greater participation rate by redesigning questions and training enumerators, particularly female enumerators, to direct questions specifically to women in the household. Traditionally, the male head of the household had responded to questions for his wife and other female members of the household, thus intentionally or unintentionally minimizing their labor force participation. These changes have since been adopted by CAPMAS in its annual labor force sample survey, and it has measured higher participation rates.

35. *Egyptian Fertility Survey (1980),* 4 vols. *Survey Design,* vol. 1 (Cairo: CAPMAS, 1983), 92–93.

36. The definition of work used in the *Egyptian Fertility Survey* was "Occupation apart from ordinary household duties, whether paid in cash or in kind or unpaid, whether own-account or family member or for someone else, whether done at home or away from home"; *Egyptian Fertility Survey 1980,* 4 vols. *Fertility and Family Planning,* vol. 2 (Cairo: CAPMAS, 1983), 10.

37. Joel S. Migdal, *Strong Societies and Weak States: State-Society Relations and State Capabilities in the Third World* (Princeton: Princeton University Press, 1988).

38. Clifford Geertz, *The Interpretation of Cultures* (New York: Basic Books, 1973), 126.

39. Naomi Chazan, "Patterns of State-Society Incorporation and Disengagement in Africa," in *The Precarious Balance: State and Society in Africa,* ed. Naomi Chazan and Donald Rothchild (Boulder, Colo.: Westview Press, 1988), 123.

40. Sheldon S. Wolin, "Max Weber: Legitimation, Method and the Politics of Theory," *Political Theory* 3 (August 1981): 402–3.

41. Khalid Ikram, *Egypt: Economic Management in a Period of Transition* (Baltimore: Johns Hopkins University Press, 1980), 60.

42. Shirley Ardener and Sandra Burman, eds., *Money-Go-Rounds: The Importance of Rotating Savings and Credit Associations for Women* (Washington, D.C.: Berg Publishers, 1995).

43. Nadim has emphasized the importance of informal savings associations in sha'bi communities, particularly among women, and suggests they are "prevalent on all levels of the Cairene culture, if not Egypt as a whole"; Nawal al-Messiri Nadim, "Family Relationships in a 'Harah' in Cairo," in *Arab Society: Social Science Perspectives,* ed. Nicholas Hopkins and Saad Eddin Ibrahim (Cairo: American

University in Cairo Press, 1985), 221. For a more recent study of ROSCAs in Egypt, see Mayada M. Baydas, Zakaria Bahloul, and Dale W. Adams, "Informal Finance in Egypt: 'Banks' within Banks," *World Development* 23 (1995): 651–61.

44. Men are more likely to organize gam'iyyaat along occupational solidarities in manufacturing or commercial areas and to use these associations to keep their wealth hidden from a variety of regulatory agencies that have access to formal banking records.

Appendixes

Appendix 1. Population of Selected Middle Eastern Nations

Population (in 1,000s)

Inhabitants/ Nation	1980	1985	1990	1992	Square Km.
Egypt	40,560	46,470	52,690	55,163	55
Jordan	2,920	3,410	4,010	4,291	44
Lebanon	2,670	2,670	2,740	2,838	273
Sudan	18,680	21,820	25,200	26,656	11
Tunisia	6,309	7,260	8,070	8,401	51
Turkey	44,470	50,230	56,070	58,775	75
Yemen (N&S)	7,960	9,180	11,230	11,952	23

Source: *UNESCO Statistical Yearbook,* Paris, 1994, pp. I/5–9. The density figures are given for 1992 data.

Appendix 2. Levels of Illiteracy of Selected Middle Eastern Nations (illiterate over 15 years of age)

Nation/Date	Numbers of Illiterate Total	Percentage Illiterate		
		Total	Male	Females
Egypt/1986	14,644,904	54.2	22.6	51.5 (1)
Jordan/1985			13.0	37.0 (2)
Lebanon/1985			14.0	31.0 (2)
Sudan/1983	6,551,501	67.6	55.5	79.0 (1)
Tunisia/1989	2,095,943	42.7	30.8	54.8 (1)
Turkey/1984			14.0	38.0 (2)
North Yemen/1985			73.0	97.0 (2)
South Yemen/1985			41.0	75.0 (2)

Sources: (1) *UNESCO Statistical Yearbook,* Paris, 1994, pp. I/14–18; (2) V. M. Moghadam, *Development and Patriarchy.* Helsinki: Wider Working Papers, 1992, table 9.

Appendix 3. Vital Statistics of Selected Middle Eastern Nations

Nation/Date	Birth Rate	Death Rate	Rate of Natural Increase	Infant Death Rate
Egypt/1992	30.3	7.7	22.6	(1989) 39.8
Jordan/1985–90	39.9	6.4	32.5	44.0
Lebanon/1985–90	27.9	7.8	20.1	40.0
Sudan/1985–90	44.6	15.8	28.8	108.0
Tunisia/1985–90	29.2	7.2	22.0	49.0
Turkey/1989	27.1	7.7	19.4	63.2
Yemen/1985–90	52.0	16.0	36.0	120.0

Source: *United Nations Demographic Yearbook*, New York, 1994, pp. 116–23.

Appendix 4. Labor Force Data of Selected Middle Eastern Nations
(data presented in thousands)

Nation/Date	Total Employed Males	Females	Agriculture Males	Females	Manufacturing Males	Females
Egypt/1990	1,095	3,410	3,824	1,773	1,609	258
Sudan/1992	244	—	11	—	10	—
Tunisia/1980	721	97	133	5	112	35(1)
Turkey/1992	13,461	6,067	4,421	4,364	2,375	799

Sources: *United Nations Statistical Yearbook*, New York, 1994, pp. 296–301, originally from the International Labor office, Geneva. (1) These data are from the Institut National de la Statistique, République Tunisienne, Enquête Population-Emploi, 1980, p. 288.

Appendix 5. Percentage of Women in Production and Manufacturing in Selected Middle Eastern Nations

	Percentage of Women Among:	
Nation/Date	Production Workers	Manufacturing Employees
Egypt/1984	5.8	12.3
Jordan/1979	1.0	(1980) 9.6
Lebanon/1970	10.0	?
Sudan/1973	5.4	16.5
Tunisia/1984	17.6	55.5
Turkey/1985	7.6	15.2
South Yemen/1973		13.5

Source: Extracted from V. M. Moghadam, *Modernizing Women,* Boulder, Colo.: Lynne Rienner Publishers, 1993, p. 40.

Appendix 6. Percent Distribution, in Major Sectors, of the Female Labor Force in Selected Middle Eastern Nations

Nation/Date	Agriculture/ Mining	Manufacturing/ Construction	Commerce/ Transport	Services
Egypt/1972	28.6	10.7	9.7	50.5
Lebanon/1970	23.6	20.0	—	56.4
Sudan/1956	82.1	13.1	0.6	4.2
Tunisia/1973	13.4	35.8	4.5	44.8
N. Yemen/1970	83.3	5.1	—	11.6
S. Yemen/1970	78.3	4.3	—	17.4

Source: These data are from the International Labor Office as presented in, and reconfigured from, E. L. Sulivan and K. Korayem, *Women and Work in the Arab World,* Cairo Papers in Social Science, 1981, vol. 4, no. 4, table 4, page 73.

Contributors

Nada Mustafa Ali worked as the Women's Program coordinator at the Cairo Institute for Human Rights Studies. Her research interests include gender, feminist epistemologies, Sudanese politics, and human rights. She is completing her Ph.D. in development studies at the University of Manchester in England.

Isabelle Berry-Chikhaoui is a geographer of Middle East urbanism. She is a researcher at the French Institute of Research on the Contemporary Maghreb (IRMC-Tunis) while she continues her associate researcher status at URBAMA, based at the University of Tours in France. Her research has focused on the informal economy and on urban communities' participation in planning for their own residences and in producing their own districts and public space.

Marie Butler is chair of the Department of Social Sciences at Oxnard College. She received her Ph.D. in sociology and demographic studies from the University of California at Davis. Recent research includes the political economy of Irish marriage practices during nineteenth-century colonialism and gender role socialization in public schools.

Evelyn A. Early is a symbolic anthropologist who has written about everyday life, medical anthropology, and popular culture in Lebanon, Egypt, and Syria. She is the author of *Baladi Women of Cairo: Playing with an Egg and Stone* and coeditor of *Everyday Life in the Muslim Middle East*. Her recent research has focused on political Islam and the media.

Sophie Ferchiou is a well-known Tunisian anthropologist and film-maker. She has been a research director for the National Center for Scientific Research and is credentialed at the Museé de l'Homme in Paris. Her work has included appointments at the Institute of Research on the Arab World in Aix-en-Provence and at various Tunisian research centers. Her work in Tunis has often focused on traditional arts, women in agriculture, religious cults, and gender in Islamic culture.

Elizabeth W. Fernea has done research with her anthropologist husband, Robert Fernea, in Iraq, Egypt, and Morocco. She has produced films and published books about women in the Middle East, including *Guests of the Sheik, A Street in Marrakech,* and most recently, *The Arab World: Forty Years of Change,* with Robert Fernea. She is professor of English and Middle Eastern studies at the University of Texas at Austin and a past president of the Middle East Studies Association.

Homa Hoodfar is associate professor in the Department of Sociology and Anthropology at Concordia University in Montreal. She has conducted extensive fieldwork in Cairo, Tehran, and Montreal. Her most recent publication is *Development, Change, and Gender in Cairo,* coedited with Diane Singerman.

Marcia Inhorn is associate professor of anthropology at Emory University in Atlanta. As a medical anthropologist, she specializes in gender and health and has written two books on the plight of infertile Egyptian women, both published by the University of Pennsylvania Press. She recently completed research on the introduction of medically assisted conception (artificial insemination, in vitro fertilization, and intracytoplasmic sperm injection) in Cairo. Her other areas of interest in medical anthropology include ethnomedicine, international health, epidemiology, and stigmatized health conditions. She is coeditor of the forthcoming *Anthropology of Infectious Disease: International Health Perspectives.*

Anne M. Jennings is an independent scholar and anthropological consultant in the fields of modern and ancient Nubia, African Islam, and women in the Muslim world. She has conducted three years of research in Egyptian Nubia and is currently engaged in a longitudinal study of the effects of tourism among Nubian women and their families.

Suad Joseph is director of women's studies and professor of anthropology and women's studies at the University of California, Davis. She has carried out fieldwork in her native Lebanon for more than twenty-five years on issues including the politicization of religion, state and community organization, education, youth, family systems, women's networks, and transformations in notions of rights and citizenship. Her edited book, *Intimate Selving: Self, Gender, and Identity in Arab Families* will soon go to press. Her recent journal articles include "Gender and Relationality among Arab Families in Lebanon" (*Feminist Studies*, Fall 1993) and "Problematizing Gender and Relational Rights: Experiences from Lebanon" (*Social Politics*, Fall 1994).

Barbara Larson is associate professor and chair of the anthropology program at the University of New Hampshire. She has done field research and rural development work in Egypt and Tunisia, and is the author of numerous articles on local markets, kinship and gender, and local-national integration. Currently she is working on a book entitled *Rural Markets in Egypt: Their Implications for Development, Gender, and Class.*

Richard A. Lobban, Jr., is professor of anthropology and African studies at Rhode Island College. For more than thirty years, he has researched and written about African ethnography and history in Cape Verde, Guinea-Bissau, Tunisia, and Nigeria, including six years of field studies in Egypt and the Sudan. Special interests include ethnicity, gender, and urban research theory and methodology. His recent works include three books on Guinean and Cape Verdean history. His works in progress focus on ancient Nubia and Islamic times in the Sudan.

Barbara J. Michael is an independent researcher and consultant, currently holding a Fulbright Fellowship at the Empirical Research and Women's Center, University of Sana'a, Yemen. Her anthropological research has focused on the Middle East, particularly the intersection of economics and gender among pastoral nomads. This work has resulted in both publications and a video. Her current research focuses on the sociocultural context of herbal medicine usage in Yemen.

Diane Singerman is associate professor in the Department of Government, School of Public Affairs, American University in Washington, D.C. She is the author of *Avenues of Participation: Families, Politics, and Networks in Urban Quarters of Cairo,* and she is coeditor with Homa Hoodfar of *Development, Change, and Gender in Cairo: A View from the Household.* Her research interests include social movements, political participation, gender and politics, and the informal economy.

Delores Walters is director of the ALANA (African, Latin, Asian, Native American) Cultural Center at Colgate University. As an educator-organizer, her anthropology courses involve students in community service. She has coordinated community programs on health, housing, and educational needs. Her doctoral research on African-identified Yemeni groups will culminate in a documentary video on diverse women's roles as agents of socioeconomic change.

Index